CHOO686999

A qualitative approach to the validation of oral language tests

STUDIES IN LANGUAGE TESTING 14

Series editors: Michael Milanovic and Cyril Weir

Also in this series:

A qualitative approach to the validation of oral language tests

Anne Lazaraton

University of Minnesota

CAMBRIDGE
UNIVERSITY PRESS

CAMBRIDGE UNIVERSITY PRESS
Cambridge, New York, Melbourne, Madrid, Cape Town, Singapore, São Paulo

Cambridge University Press
The Edinburgh Building, Cambridge CB2 8RU, UK

Published in the United States of America by Cambridge University Press, New York

www.cambridge.org
Information on this title: www.cambridge.org/9780521802277

© UCLES 2002

This publication is in copyright. Subject to statutory exception
and to the provisions of relevant collective licensing agreements,
no reproduction of any part may take place without the written
permission of Cambridge University Press.

First published 2002

A catalogue record for this publication is available from the British Library

ISBN 978-0-521-80227-7 hardback
ISBN 978-0-521-00267-7 paperback

Transferred to digital printing 2008

To Dad –

still my biggest fan

Contents

Series Editors' note

Qualitative approaches to language test validation are now making a significant impact on the field of language testing. We have tried to emphasise the important role such approaches can play in the Studies in Language Testing series, most specifically in this volume which focuses on the area of oral assessment, and in volume 5 authored by Alison Green entitled 'Verbal protocol analysis in language testing research: a handbook'.

We are pleased to be able to publish this volume by Anne Lazaraton, who has been working closely with staff at UCLES for the last ten years. Her contributions to the work of UCLES EFL have not only been stimulating in the academic sense but have also made a very valuable contribution in practical and extremely important ways. They have, for example, helped UCLES staff in the development and revision of speaking tests not only in relation to content but also in the procedures needed to monitor and evaluate how oral assessments are carried out.

Direct oral assessment is one of the cornerstones of the UCLES approach to language testing. However, it is well known that direct assessment is fraught with difficulties. At UCLES we believe it is important that we work towards a better understanding of these difficulties and seek to manage and control them in the most effective way. The Performance Testing Unit, part of the Research and Validation Group within the UCLES EFL Division is specifically charged with conducting research, and co-ordinating the research of others to further our capability to carry out direct assessment in speaking and writing most effectively. The task is on-going but we can see clearly how the quality of our assessments have improved over the years and continue to do so.

Professor Lazaraton's research, related to Cambridge EFL examinations, has engaged with a number of assessments and has built on work conducted by the UCLES EFL Division. Between 1990 and 1992 she worked closely with the UCLES team on the Cambridge Assessment of Spoken English (CASE). This assessment was developed largely as a research vehicle and Professor Lazaraton's work focused on using a qualitative discourse analytic approach to further understanding of the speaking test process with particular reference to the role of the examiner. The work subsequently contributed significantly to the development of monitoring procedures for a wide range of Cambridge examinations.

The work on CASE was followed by work on the Certificate in Advanced English (CAE), situated at level 4 in the Cambridge/ALTE level system. Specifically this research was intended to evaluate interlocutor adherence to the CAE *interlocutor frame* and analyze interlocutor speech behaviour, which led to the development of the CAE Examiner evaluation template. Professor Lazaraton then conducted similar work in relation to the Key English Test (KET) at level 1 in the Cambridge/ALTE level system and comparative research across the two levels.

Professor Lazaraton also carried out a number of studies that focus on *candidate* behaviour, as opposed to examiner behaviour, in speaking tests. This work focused on CAE, the First Certificate in English (FCE) and The International English Language Testing System (IELTS). The work on candidate behaviour started with a CAE study that was followed by one on FCE, the most widely taken UCLES EFL examination. Professor Lazaraton investigated the relationship between the task features in the four parts of the FCE Speaking test and candidate output in terms of speech production. The project has helped to provide data for the possible development of a task specific rating scheme for FCE. In 1997 Professor Lazaraton was asked to work on IELTS again with particular reference to candidate language. This work made a valuable contribution to the revision of the IELTS Speaking Test, which was introduced in 2001.

Anne Lazaraton has always understood the tensions that exist between researching issues in language testing and delivering reliable and valid language tests. While situated firmly on the research end of the language testing continuum, her energy, enthusiasm and openness have meant that she has been able to share much of enormous value with us. Her work emphasises the value of building research into the on-going validation and improvement of language testing tools and procedures leading to assessments of enhanced quality.

Preface

Language testers have generally come to recognize the limitations of traditional statistical methods for validating oral language tests and have begun to consider more innovative approaches to test validation, approaches that promise to illuminate the assessment process itself, rather than just assessment outcomes (i.e., ratings). One such approach is conversation analysis (or CA), a rigorous empirical methodology developed by sociologists, which employs inductive methods in order to discover and describe the recurrent, systematic properties of conversation, including sequential organization, turntaking, repair, preference structure, and topic management. CA offers a systematic approach for analyzing spoken interaction from a qualitative perspective, allowing one to make observations about a stretch of talk while at the same time interacting with it. One of its unique strengths as an analytic tool is its ability to validate intuitions about data; in terms of oral test validation, the results that emerge from such analyses make sense not just to researchers who undertake them, but to the test stakeholders, including those who develop, administer, and validate the tests, as well as the teachers who prepare the students who take the tests. In recent years, conversation analysts have turned their attention to various forms of 'institutional talk', including news interviews, job interviews, and standardized testing; CA has also been applied successfully to several EFL Speaking Tests by this author. Unfortunately, conversation analysis principles and techniques remain unfamiliar to many applied linguists, and this lacuna in understanding makes communication about such analyses and their applications to language testing difficult, if not impossible. This book aims to provide language testers with a background in the conversation analytic framework and a fuller understanding of what is entailed in using conversation analysis in the specific context of oral language test validation.

It is important to note that one cannot 'learn to do' conversation analysis by reading about it, although one may learn a great deal about its principles and methods from this book. Although not a 'how-to' text, practice analysis exercises are provided which enable the reader to become familiar with the conversation analytic data transcription system, and to have an opportunity to view and to analyze authentic oral test data and anecdotal accounts of them using the procedures described.

Chapter 1 overviews the recent accomplishments and current concerns of language testers, especially with respect to oral language assessment. It highlights some of the outcome-based work on speaking test validation, but suggests that this work has not, and in fact, cannot, shed light on the assessment process itself; qualitative research, especially discourse analysis, seems an especially well-suited approach for this task. The chapter concludes by reviewing a number of recent discourse-based studies on oral assessment.

Chapter 2 summarizes relevant literature on the conversation analytic framework, focusing on the organizing principles of interaction (turntaking, repair, sequence structure, preference structure, topic organization), the methodological considerations of the approach (including the analytic units 'turn', 'adjacency pair', and 'sequence'), its application to other forms of interaction (specifically, 'institutional talk'), and some potential shortcomings of the approach. Since one of the major goals of the text is to introduce readers to the historical roots, empirical findings, and current concerns of CA, numerous original sources are summarized and cited, so the reader can follow up on these topics.

The third chapter focuses on the initial stages of undertaking conversation analysis, including data collection, selection, and transcription. A number of points to consider when collecting data for a conversation analysis of speaking test data are made, including the type of equipment to use, camera/tape player set up, participant configuration, etc. This section also covers issues related to the potential intrusiveness of recording equipment and its effects on candidate and examiner performance. Additional suggestions are made about how much data to collect to ensure that a sufficient sample will be available for analysis. Also, criteria for selecting a sample for analysis are presented, if it is unfeasible, difficult, or impossible to transcribe and/or use all the data collected.

With respect to transcription, some philosophical issues in the representation of speech are noted: e.g., that any transcription system is selective in scope, and a 'perfect' transcript cannot be produced. Although there are numerous transcription schemes available to the researcher, the preferred conversation analytic system devised by Gail Jefferson (as in Atkinson and Heritage 1984; see Appendix 2) is presented. Tips for selecting transcribing equipment, setting up the page format, using the notation, and adapting the transcription system are put forward. Ideally, it is the researcher who produces the transcripts, since the analysis really begins in earnest with the emerging transcript at this point in the research cycle. It is also important to remember that the analyst should not rely on a reading of the transcript alone, since transcripts are always an imperfect reflection of how the actual interaction 'sounds'; they should always be used in conjunction with the tapes from which they were transcribed. Finally, it is at this stage that previously formulated research questions may take shape, may be discarded as uninteresting, or may suggest new avenues of inquiry to pursue. Because it may be necessary to hire a transcriber, training issues are discussed. This section also deals with transcribing and representing languages other than English as well as nonverbal behaviour.

Chapter 4 covers issues related to the analysis and presentation of speaking test data, once they have been collected and transcribed. The chapter begins by considering six methodological decisions the conversation analyst generally makes: using real, recorded data; segmenting the discourse into turns; looking at data in an unmotivated fashion; analyzing single cases, collections, and deviant cases; overlooking sociological variables; and refraining from coding and counting the data. CA insists on the use of real, recorded data, so that discourse produced in experiments or verbal protocols, and examples that are created or recalled from memory, have no place in this approach. Unlike some other discourse analytic approaches, conversation analysis operates at the unit of the turn, the adjacency pair, and the sequence, as discussed in Chapter 2. Conversation analysts normally eschew the explicit statement of research questions and/or hypotheses, although the researcher may have in mind some general areas of interest that the data may inform and some intuitions about potential outcomes of the analysis. One reason that formal questions are not normally posed before the data are collected is that preconceived ideas may cause the researcher to overlook other interesting or relevant features of the talk. Even if the analysis is intended to replicate a previous one, care must be taken not to be forced into a priori interpretations which were gleaned from another context. The conversation analyst engages in 'single case analysis' with an eye towards developing a collection of standard, marginal, and deviant case examples. Like other forms of qualitative research, CA can best be described in terms of a recursive analytic cycle rather than a linear approach. A solid analysis requires and is based on repeated, prolonged engagement with the conversational materials. Two related issues are covered in this section, the use of coding schemes and the quantification of data. As a rule, conversation analysts do not apply existing discourse analytic coding schemes to their data, although they do attempt to use knowledge gained from related studies (within the same analytic framework) to understand some new data. Secondly, conversation analysts do not quantify their data to determine frequencies, proportions, ratios, or other descriptive statistics that may seem useful or necessary. The justification for this stance is summarized from an important paper by Schegloff (1993) on this issue.

The second section of the chapter deals with actual analysis of speaking test data. First, five 'analytic tools' suggested by Pomerantz and Fehr (1997) are presented and exemplified with two data fragments. These tools include practice in identifying the boundaries of interesting sequences, characterizing the actions being accomplished by each turn in the sequence, determining how patterns of turntaking, packaging of actions, and timing of turns lead the participants (and the analyst) to certain understandings about what is 'going on' in the sequence, and relating these understandings to the particular roles, relationships, and identities that participants bring to the interaction. Then, several approaches to analyzing monologic data, where the speech of only one speaker is available or of importance, are illustrated. These approaches include rhetorical analysis of narratives and descriptions, functional analysis of a comparison–contrast task, and a structural analysis of linguistic features.

Once the researcher has undertaken an analysis, it is presented in the form of 'argument from example', a procedure which is defined and justified. Decisions need to be made about how to present the data to others who may or may not be familiar with transcribed spoken data, or with the particular form the transcribed data take. Sufficient sequential context for the feature of interest is necessary; it is unwise to shorten segments of talk to save space, if relevant analytic material is omitted. The sheer amount of data produced in conversation analysis (and in qualitative research in general) challenges the researcher to select data judiciously for presentation (unless, of course, the researcher has the luxury of being able to present all of them). Suggestions for selecting cases for presentation, formatting a research report, and evaluating other CA studies are made. The chapter concludes with five practice exercises based on actual data fragments that are either interactive or monologic. Appendix 3 contains guidance for approaching these problems.

Having laid the analytic foundation in previous chapters, Chapter 5 describes several EFL Speaking Test validation studies that employed conversation analytic techniques. After a brief review of Messick's theory of test validity, the Cambridge approach to EFL Speaking Tests is overviewed, followed by a series of validation studies that are summarized in terms of their goals, methods, results, and implications. The first set of studies analyses examiner behaviour in particular Cambridge EFL Speaking Tests (CASE, CAE, and KET), while the latter analyzed candidate behaviour on FCE and IELTS.

The final chapter reiterates the themes presented in the book, re-evaluates the potential contribution of conversation analysis to speaking test validation, and discusses other qualitative methods which are potentially appropriate for test validation tasks.

Acknowledgments

At UCLA, thanks to my dissertation committee, who expressed interest in this project from the very beginning: Lyle Bachman, who also put me in touch with Mike Milanovic and Nick Saville and was the impetus for the productive relationship we have; to Marianne Celce-Murcia; to Evelyn Hatch: words can't express my gratitude for her years of mentoring me; to Bob Kirsner; to Brian Lynch – who is also a good friend; and to Manny Schegloff, a true scholar of the highest caliber. I am still in awe of him to this day, and I believe his 1993 article on quantification in the study of conversation is the most seminal paper I have read in my academic career.

To Dennis Gouran at Penn State, I am grateful for the equipment and research assistantships he provided to undertake the work and for his encouragement during the early stages of the project.

Thanks also to my Penn State transcribers, who prepared most of the data that are described in this book: Amy Bargfrede, Erin Chervenak, Roger Frantz, Gina Fuller, Stacie Wagner, and Sharon Wilkinson.

The students in my discourse analysis seminars at Penn State and at George Mason allowed me to try out many ideas – some good and some terrible – on them, and Chapters 3 and 4 greatly benefited from their frank input.

I am very appreciative of Richard Young, who graciously provided me with a prepublication copy of Young and He (1998) so that I could cite much of the work therein. Richard has been a wonderful colleague and I have enjoyed presenting and interacting with him at conferences.

Thanks to Barry O'Sullivan, who made a number of insightful comments on an earlier draft of the manuscript.

At UCLES, many people provided me with information on or materials about various examinations: Angela ffrench, Ben Knight, and Dianne Wall. Lynda Taylor was most helpful in the preparation of Chapter 5. And last, but in no way least, Mike and Nick. You listened to me whine, moan, despair, you were always there with a helping hand and you said just the right thing to keep me going. Your consistent support and positive outlook were just what I needed at times. You guys are the greatest!

To my family, your endless support and good cheer have been lifesavers. Reading this book could probably relieve your collective insomnia! Dad: I wish you could have seen it in print!

1 An overview of oral language assessment

- Introduction

- Outcome-based research on oral language assessment
  - What are language assessment interviews?
  - Past research on oral language assessment
  - The ACTFL OPI
  - Empirical studies on the OPI
  - Research on other oral examinations
  - The need for process-based research

- Discourse-based studies on oral language assessment
  - Background
  - Lazaraton's research on ESL course placement interviews
  - Participant behaviour in oral interviews
  - Comparisons of interview behaviour with conversation
  - Comparisons of test format
  - Comparisons of test scores with produced discourse
  - Rating scale construction and validation

- Conclusion

Introduction

From its historical roots in the United Kingdom in 1913, and later in 1930 in the United States, the testing of English for speakers of other languages has become what we think of as modern language testing today (see Spolsky 1990, 1995 for a detailed examination of this topic). Bachman (1991), among others, has argued that language testing as a discipline has come of age within applied linguistics, as evidenced by its achievements – its attention to theoretical issues, including theories of language ability and the effects of test method and test taker characteristics, its methodological advances in psychometrics as well as statistical analyses (see Bachman and Eignor 1997), and its impact on test development, particularly communicative testing. The language testing community now has its own refereed international journal, *Language Testing*, several international conferences, such as The Language Testing Research Colloquium (LTRC), and has published numerous books on language testing written for the teacher (e.g., Bachman and Palmer 1996; Cohen 1994; Underhill 1987) and for other language testers (e.g., Bachman 1990; McNamara 1996; and the books in this series, *Studies in Language Testing*).

However, as Bachman (1991) points out, there are other areas in language testing in which further progress is needed. For example, the interface between second language acquisition (SLA) and language testing is not as strong as it could be (see for example, Bachman 1989; Shohamy 1994a; Swain 1993; Upshur and Turner 1999; and Valdman 1988). Additionally, we have only begun to see work on the role of technology in language testing, such as computers (see Brown 1997), and speech recognition technology (as in the PhonePass™ examination, www.ordinate.com). The ethics of language testing is also a topic of current interest (see, for example, the special issue of *Language Testing*, Ethics in Language Testing, Volume 14, 3, 1997). But as far as I am concerned, the most important development in language testing over the last ten or so years is the introduction of qualitative research methodologies to design, describe, and, most importantly, to validate language tests.

In general, qualitative research has a rather short history in the field of applied linguistics, which is still trying to grapple with its legitimacy (see Edge and Richards 1998 on this point). A comprehensive overview of the methodological features of interpretive qualitative research (especially ethnography) as it is conceptualized and carried out in applied linguistics can be found in Davis (1995). Briefly, Davis discusses the important role of personal perspective in qualitative research, as well as the central focus of 'grounded theory', which endeavours to connect 'a study by describing the relationships among the various parts, and it provides a theoretical model for subsequent studies' (p. 440). Davis also discusses the issue of obtaining contextualized information from multiple data sources (triangulation) in order to achieve research credibility. Davis points out that 'Data analysis generally involves a search for patterns of generalization across multiple sources of data … the analytic inductive method used in interpretive qualitative research allows for identification of frequently occurring events based on the data themselves. However, assertions should account for patterns found across both frequent and rare events. For assertions to hold any credibility, systematic evidence in the form of thick description must be presented in the research report' (p. 446). According to Davis, the use of narrative, quotation from notes and interviews, and transcribed discourse from tapes are all useful in presenting results. 'Particular description essentially serves the purpose of providing adequate evidence that the author has made a valid analysis of what the events mean from the perspectives of actors in the events' (p. 447). Davis also points out that the generalizability of data patterns can be described using frequency expressions such as 'all', 'most', 'a few', 'tended to', and 'generally', simple frequency counts, and inferential statistics.

But in a related article, Lazaraton (1995a) argues that the requirements of ethnography do not adequately account for the other ten or so qualitative research traditions in existence, traditions which have different disciplinary roots, analytic goals, and theoretical motivations. In fact, the guidelines discussed by Davis do not necessarily apply to other qualitative research approaches, particularly to qualitative discourse analysis in general, and to conversation analysis in particular.

The field of education, however, has a fairly long history of embracing qualitative research techniques, and this may account for the less skeptical reception of qualitative approaches to language testing in, for example, bilingual education. As far back as 1983, work was being done on the assessment of language minority children using ethnographic and discourse analytic techniques (see Rivera 1983). As Bennett and Slaughter (1983) note, 'The use of the analysis of discourse as a method of assessing language skills has very recently gained a high degree of respectability within the field of language proficiency assessment. The recent upsurge in interest in this area coincides with an increase in efforts to make basic research applicable to specific social problems' (p. 2). Furthermore, according to Philips (1983: 90), 'From a methodological point of view, an ethnographic perspective holds that experimental methodologies can never enable us to grasp the nature of children's communicative competence because such methods, by their very nature, alter that competence. Instead, observation, participant observation, and interviews are recommended as the research tools to be used in determining the nature of children's communicative competence.'

But it wasn't until 1984, when Cohen proposed using a specific qualitative technique, namely, introspection, to understand the testing process, that calls for a broader range of work in language testing became more frequent (e.g., Alderson, Clapham, and Wall 1995; Bachman 1990, 1991). Grotjahn (1986) warned that a reliance on statistical analyses alone will not give us a full understanding of what a test measures, that is, its construct validity; he proposed employing more introspective techniques for understanding language tests. Fulcher (1996a) observes that test designers are employing qualitative approaches more often, a positive development since 'many testing instruments do not contain a rigorous applied linguistics base, whether the underpinning be theoretical or empirical. The results of validation studies are, therefore, often trivial' (p. 228). A new respect for qualitative research as a legitimate endeavor in language testing can be seen even in unlikely places (e.g., Henning 1986 applauds the trend towards more quantitative research in applied linguistics research articles since quantitative methodology has 'certain profound advantages' over other research techniques, and yet, four years later, Dandonoli and Henning (1990: 21) remark on the 'fruitful data which can be obtained from ethnographic and qualitative research').

Specifically, more attention to and incorporation of discourse analysis in language test validation is needed (Fulcher 1987; Shohamy 1991). Fulcher remarks that 'a new approach to construct validation in which the construct can be empirically tested can be found in discourse analysis' (p. 291). Shohamy believes that tests need to elicit more discourse and to assess such language carefully, and she mentions conversation analysis specifically as one tool for examining the interaction that takes place in oral examinations. Douglas and Selinker (1992: 325) came to a similar conclusion empirically, in their study of ratings assigned to candidates taking three different oral examinations: 'This led us to a validation principle, namely that rhetorical/grammatical interlanguage analysis may be necessary to disambiguate subjective gross ratings on tests.'

McNamara (1997: 460) sees much the same need, as he states rather eloquently: 'Research in language testing cannot consist only of a further burnishing of the already shiny chrome-plated quantitative armour of the language tester with his (too often his) sophisticated statistical tools and impressive n-size'; what is needed is the 'inclusion of another kind of research on language testing of a more fundamental kind, whose aim is to make us fully aware of the nature and significance of assessment as a social act.'

The remainder of this chapter is devoted to describing the oral language assessment interview in more detail. First, a definition of an oral interview is given, followed by a summary of empirical outcome-based studies on oral assessment. The chapter concludes with a further summary of more recent discourse-based work on the interview, work which uses the actual talk produced as the basis for analysis.

Outcome-based research on oral language assessment

What are language assessment interviews?

There is some variation in terminology associated with language assessment interviews. Whereas such an encounter may be referred to as an 'oral proficiency interview', this usage can be misleading since the ACTFL OPI, the Oral Proficiency Interview, is an interview of a distinctive kind. Sometimes these assessment procedures are called 'oral interviews' or 'language interviews' as well. He and Young (1998: 10) prefer the term 'language proficiency interview' (LPI), which they define as follows:

'a face-to-face spoken interaction usually between two participants (although other combinations do occur), one of whom is an expert (usually a native or near-native speaker of the language in which the interview is conducted), and the other a nonnative speaker (NNS) or learner of the language as a second or foreign language. The purpose of the LPI is for the expert speaker – the interviewer – to assess the NNS's ability to speak the language in which the interview is conducted. The participants meet at a scheduled time, at a prearranged location such as a classroom or office in a school, and for a limited period. In the case of scripted interviews, an agenda specifying the topics for conversation and the activities to take place during the LPI is prepared in advance. The agenda is always known to the interviewer but not necessarily to the NNS. In addition to the agenda, the interviewer (but usually not the NNS) has access to one or more scales for rating the NNS's ability in the language of the interview.'

The Cambridge examinations (on which much of the empirical work reported in this book is based) are referred to as Speaking Tests which employ two Examiners who rate the candidate, one an Interlocutor who conducts the assessment, and the other a passive Assessor who observes, but does not take part in the testing encounter. This terminology will be used in reference to the Cambridge examinations.

Past research on oral language assessment

The assessment of second language speaking proficiency, particularly as measured by the Foreign Service Institute–Interagency Language Roundtable (FSI/ILR) interview (Lowe 1982; Fulcher 1997: 78) considers it 'the generic ancestor of today's generation of oral tests'), the ACTFL/ETS Oral Proficiency Interview (OPI) (ACTFL 1986), and the Speaking Tests in the University of Cambridge Local Examinations Syndicate examinations (UCLES 1998c), has been a topic of considerable interest to the language testing community in the latter half of the 20th century (see Fulcher 1997 for a historical overview). There is now an extensive body of research on issues such as construct validity (e.g., Bachman and Palmer 1981, 1982; Dandonoli and Henning 1990; Henning 1992; Magnan 1988; Reed 1992), reliability and rating procedures (e.g., Bachman, Lynch and Mason 1995; Barnwell 1989; Brown 1995; Conlan, Bardsley and Martinson 1994; McNamara and Lumley 1997; Shohamy 1983; Styles 1993; Thompson 1995; Wigglesworth 1993; Wylie 1993), comparisons with other oral testing methods (e.g., Clark 1979, 1988; Clark and Hooshmand 1992; Douglas and Selinker 1992; Henning 1983; Stansfield and Kenyon 1992), aspects of the communicative competence construct (e.g., Henning and Cascallar 1992), and other aspects of oral testing (e.g., Chalhoub-Deville 1995; Clark and Lett 1988; Hill 1998; Merrylees and McDowell 1998; Raffaldini 1988; Shohamy 1988; Upshur and Turner 1999).

The ACTFL OPI

The ACTFL OPI is the most widely used face-to-face oral proficiency examination in North America, which has put it in a position to receive (perhaps more than) its fair share of criticism. For example, Lantolf and Frawley (1985, 1988) object that the ACTFL definitions of proficiency are based on intuitions rather than empirical facts about natural communication (see also Clark and Lett 1988 on this point), and on a native speaker norm which is indefensible. Bachman and Savignon (1986) and Bachman (1988) believe, first, that the OPI does not distinguish language ability from test method in its current form, thus limiting our capability to make inferences about language ability in other untested contexts, and second, that it is based on a view of unitary language ability, namely 'proficiency,' a stance which is supported by neither theory nor research. Lantolf and Frawley (1988: 10) make a similar point: 'Proficiency is derived from policy and not from science or empirical inquiry.' Kramsch (1986) takes issue with the construct of proficiency itself, pointing out that it is *not* synonymous with interactional competence. Finally, Savignon (1985) criticizes ACTFL's 'obsession with accuracy'. In response to this last point, Magnan (1988) suggests that Savignon and others have defined 'grammar' too narrowly, if not erroneously, since the skill as rated also includes appropriateness. (See also Hadley (1993) for additional responses to these criticisms of the OPI.)

But the basic objection to the OPI procedure is that is incapable of measuring what it should, namely, oral proficiency. One criticism is that the oral interview cannot provide a valid sample of other speech events because it samples a limited domain of interaction (Byrnes 1987; Clark and Lett 1988; Raffaldini 1988; Shohamy 1988). Raffaldini claims that the oral interview format, which is basically conversational, is the main reason why it fails to tap some important aspects of communication: a limited number of speech functions is sampled and so interviewees have little opportunity to display either discourse or sociolinguistic competence. Byrnes (1987: 167) admits that the ratings of the oral interview underrepresent pragmatic and sociolinguistic ability, while overemphasizing linguistic ability. But this is due to the fact that L2 studies 'rarely look at global performance features such as hesitations, false starts, repairs, and corrections', and, as a result, their meaning for aspects of communicative competence is unknown. Without this information, a description of sociointeractional, sociocultural, and sociocognitive ability cannot be included in oral proficiency rating scales.

Byrnes also makes an important point about the role of the tester in the interview. It is incumbent upon the interviewer, she maintains, to be 'keenly aware' of natural conversational behaviour, and to attempt to engage the interviewee in a 'genuine conversational exchange (the archetype occurrence of spoken language) to offset the constraints of the testing procedure' (1987: 174). This implies not only that the interview is not in itself conducive to interactional, negotiated speech, but that the achievement of a negotiated form of interaction in an interview is a collaborative accomplishment between interviewer and interviewee. To remedy this situation, Shohamy (1988) proposes a framework for testing oral language that includes a variety of interactions, each including a variety of contextual factors, that approximate 'the vernacular', which is what the oral interview fails to do. Another possibility that Clark and Lett (1988) suggest is that we check if candidates can do what the scales imply they can in the real world, perhaps by gathering self-ratings or second party ratings.

Empirical studies on the OPI

In response to these criticisms of the OPI, a number of studies have been undertaken to provide empirical evidence for the reliability and validity of this assessment procedure and the underlying ACTFL Proficiency Guidelines. For example, Dandonoli and Henning (1990; see also Henning 1992) conducted a multitrait-multimethod validation of these guidelines by considering OPI data from 60 French as a Second Language and 59 English as a Second Language students at American universities. They conclude that 'the analyses provide considerable support for the use of the Guidelines as a foundation for the development of proficiency tests and for the reliability and validity of the OPI' (p. 20).

Another validation study, focusing specifically on the role of grammar in the OPI guidelines, is Magnan's (1988) research on 40 novice-mid through advanced-plus speakers studying French. She looked at the frequency of incorrect grammatical usage of seven syntactic categories (verb conjugation, tense, determiners, adjectives, prepositions, object pronouns, and relative pronouns) to determine how they were distributed by proficiency level. She found there was a significant relationship between accuracy and level, but it was not linear and was highly dependent on the particular grammatical structure in question.

Reed (1992) looked at 70 OPIs given to ESL students at an American university in order to determine if the OPI gives 'unique' information when compared with the TOEFL. He concluded that the OPI does measure distinct skills and is thus construct valid.

Henning and Cascallar (1992) sought to determine how the four components of communicative competence (grammatical, discourse, sociolinguistic, and strategic, as per Canale and Swain (1980)), are related to each other and what their construct validity is. They tested 79 American university students on 18 performance variables, 6 pragmatic functions, 2 social registers, and 2 modalities; raters assessed 5-minute intervals of performance on a variety of communication activities. Subjects also took the TOEFL, TWE, and TSE. Among the many results were the presence of a strong interaction between performance variables and pragmatic/situational (register) functions; the importance of strategic variables in language assessment; and the continuing need to assess language structure directly, even in 'communicative' tests.

Other research has compared the face-to-face OPI with a corresponding semi-direct assessment instrument, the SOPI (Semi-Direct Oral Proficiency Interview). J. L. D. Clark has conducted several studies comparing direct and semi-direct tests. His 1979 paper discusses the methods in terms of their reliability, validity, and practicality, and concludes that semi-direct tests are 'second-order substitutes' for more direct tests (p. 48). In an empirical study, Clark (1988) compared the live and SOPI formats of an ACTFL/ILR-scale based test of Chinese speaking proficiency taken by 32 American students studying Chinese. The statistical analyses indicated that there was a consistent relationship between the ratings of the two test forms when there was only one rater; results with multiple raters were more problematic. However, the candidates overwhelmingly self-reported a preference for the live format (89%), describing the semi-direct version as more difficult and 'unfair' (cf. Hill 1998 mentioned below).

In another empirical study of the live OPI and the SOPI format, Clark and Hooshmand (1992) tested Arabic and Russian learners at the Defense Language Institute in both a face-to-face interview and one conducted via teleconferencing. Quantitative and questionnaire results suggested that the live format can be simulated in a teleconference and is acceptable to examinees as a substitute if necessary.

Stansfield and Kenyon's (1992) study also lends support to the equivalence of the OPI and a SOPI version. Their analyses showed that both measures are equally reliable and valid as measures of the same construct: 'they may be viewed as parallel tests delivered in two different formats' (p. 359). However, the SOPI may allow for a more accurate assessment of strategic competence, while the OPI is clearly preferable for tapping face-to-face interaction. And, as is now known, and has been demonstrated empirically, the same score on an OPI can represent different performances, and different scores can represent similar performances, due to the fact that a live interlocutor is present in the face-to-face interview.

At least two studies have investigated rater behaviour on the OPI. An early study by Shohamy (1983) examined the stability of oral assessment across

4 oral examination formats which differed by interviewer, speech style, and topic. Eighty-five Hebrew as a foreign language students in the U.S. were rated on these 4 methods by 2 independent raters; her analyses detected the main difference to be in the fourth test, where candidates reported information instead of being interviewed; she concludes that 'speech style and topic are significant factors influencing students' scores on oral proficiency' (p. 537). She suggests (somewhat contrary to her later opinion (Shohamy 1988)) that the OPI is well suited to testing other sorts of communicative behaviour.

Thompson (1995) also investigated interrater reliability on the OPI given to 795 candidates in 5 languages: English, French, German, Russian, and Spanish. A total of 175 raters assessed the interviews. Her results showed 'significant' overall interrater reliability with some variation due to proficiency level and language tested. Furthermore, she found that second ratings, done after the fact from audiotapes, were likely to be lower than original ratings.

Finally, Barnwell (1989) analyzed 4 OPIs in Spanish taken by American students and evaluated by 14 'naive' raters, all native speakers of Spanish, who were given OPI rating scales translated into Spanish. Barnwell found first, that the naive raters ranked the subjects in the same order, but the actual ratings for each of the 4 individual candidates varied, and second, that the naive raters were generally harsher than ACTFL trained raters.

Research on other oral examinations

There have also been many studies that have delved into these issues – validity, reliability, test method comparisons, and rating scale construction – with other oral examinations. Two early construct validation studies on the FSI (The Foreign Service Interview, the precursor to the ACTFL OPI) were conducted by Bachman and Palmer (1981, 1982). The first study (1981) examined the performance of 75 ESL students at an American university on 6 measures, comprised of 2 traits (speaking and reading) and 3 methods (interview, translation, and self-rating). Their results, based on correlations and factor analysis, showed respectable convergent and divergent validity for the FSI. In the second study, Bachman and Palmer (1982) used an adapted FSI oral interview procedure as one measure of communicative competence to assess the language ability of 116 ESL students at an American university. Factor analysis was employed to test three proposed traits (grammatical, pragmatic, and sociolinguistic competence) using the interview, a self-rating, a writing sample, and a multiple choice test. Their results suggested the existence of a general factor and two specific traits, grammatical/pragmatic competence and sociolinguistic competence.

The issue of rater reliability on other oral exams has been fruitfully explored as well. Several studies have explored the role of raters in the IELTS

Speaking Test (International English Language Testing System; UCLES 1999a). For example, Wylie (1993) probed the ability of raters to provide the same ratings, on two different occasions, of a single candidate performance on IELTS. Her examination of 18 Australian interviews showed high overall correlations (.906) for the ratings of all candidates. Styles (1993) also looked at rater behaviour on IELTS, specifically the reliability of ratings done in live assessments, from audiotapes, and from videotapes. He considered the assessments of 30 European candidates and concluded that the reliability of audiotaped assessments is as good as or better than videotaped assessments, both between and within raters, although the quality of the videorecordings was criticized by the raters and might have led to lower estimates of reliability. A somewhat contrary result was found by Conlan, Bardsley, and Martinson (1994), who compared live and audiotaped interviews of 27 IELTS candidates rated by 3 examiners. In 10 out of 27 cases, the audio recording was scored a full band lower than the live interview; they conclude that some examiners are more sensitive to extralinguistic, paralinguistic, and nonlinguistic information than others.

Bachman, Lynch, and Mason (1995) investigated the performance of 218 American Education Abroad students on a tape-mediated Spanish speaking test involving a summary of a lecture and an extended response. Both G-theory and FACETS were used to estimate rater reliability; they conclude that these two measurement models provide useful, complementary information: relative effects of facets are identified by G-theory while Rasch measurement allows the researcher to determine rater or task specific effects.

Brown (1995) examined a face-to-face oral test for Japanese tour guides for possible rater bias. Fifty-one subjects were assessed by 33 raters, including native and near-native speakers of Japanese who were either teachers of Japanese as a Foreign Language or actual tour guides. Her multifaceted Rasch results found no significant rating bias for either linguistic skill or task fulfillment, but the application of and perceptions about the specific rating criteria did differ among rater groups.

An interesting study of rater perceptions is McNamara and Lumley (1997). Using Rasch analysis to analyze the questionnaire responses from 7 Occupational English Test raters assessing the audiotapes of 70 candidates, they concluded that perceptions of poor audiotape quality led to harsher candidate ratings. Additionally, three salient factors emerged with respect to perceived competence of the interlocutor. First, there was a significant and consistent effect for candidates who were paired with less competent raters (they were rated higher, and thus compensated for poor interlocutor performance). And, a similar but stronger effect was detected for candidates who were paired with interlocutors who failed to achieve good rapport (again, they received higher ratings). They propose that rater perceptions of tape audibility should be included as a facet in analyses in order to neutralize its effect in resulting measures. More worrisome, though, for McNamara and Lumley, is the issue of fairness raised by the results on perceived interlocutor competence: 'the greater richness of face-to-face interaction in the assessment of speaking brings with it its own difficulties: the candidate's score is clearly the outcome of an interaction of variables, only one of which is the candidate's ability. It is important that the extent of the influence of these other variables be understood, both for the theoretical reasons as part of our ongoing attempt to conceptualize the nature of performance assessment adequately, and for practical reasons in ensuring fairness to candidates' (p. 154).

An early study on the relative usefulness of various test methods was Henning's (1983) research on the performance of 143 EFL learners in Egypt on an FSI-like interview, an imitation test (where subjects repeated declarative sentences and interrogative questions of various lengths), and a completion test (where subjects completed introductory incomplete sentences ranging from 1–3 words). He found the imitation test, the interview, and the completion test to rank in that order for the validity measures that he considered. Additionally, he found a strong relationship between the FSI-like interview and grammar skill.

More recently, a study of test format was undertaken by Douglas and Selinker (1992), who gave 3 tests to 31 chemistry graduate students at an American university: a field-specific test, the CHEMSPEAK; a general SPEAK test, and a teaching performance test, the TEACH. They determined that the field-specific test was better than the general test for predicting teaching performance, and that these subjects had difficulty with the CHEMSPEAK test, possibly attributable to rater inconsistency.

Other recent research has focused on understanding participant reactions to the tests and on constructing rating scales. For example, Hill (1998) analyzed test taker reactions to both live and tape-based versions of the **access:** test (the Australian Assessment of Communicative Skills in English). Questionnaires were completed by 83 subjects who took both versions of the test; Hill examined her results by gender, employment status (student vs. professional) and language background. Her FACETS results demonstrated a clear preference for the interview format, although she found that both versions appear to be face valid for the subjects she tested. Additionally, females reported finding the live version more difficult than the taped version, while the Asian subjects reported feeling more nervous during the live test. From the interviewer perspective, Merrylees and McDowell (1998) surveyed 113 IELTS examiners using a questionnaire to determined their attitudes to the format, sections, and rating criteria of the test. Results showed general satisfaction with the current test format and generated suggestions for fine-tuning the test.

With respect to rating scale construction, Chalhoub-Deville (1995) examined data from 6 Arabic as a Foreign Language learners on three tasks: an oral interview, a narration, and a read-aloud. The speech samples were rated by 3 groups of native speakers: Arabic as a Foreign Language teachers, Arabic speakers living in the U.S., and Arabic speakers living in Lebanon. Holistic scores were analyzed using Multidimensional Scaling techniques, which generated 3 rating dimensions: 'grammar–pronunciation', 'creativity in presenting information', and 'amount of detail provided'. She concluded that 'generic component scales' should be used, since there was variability in the dimensions across the three tasks and the ratings of the speech produced on them.

Finally, Upshur and Turner (1999) described a test development project where they attempted to analyze the systematic effects of test method and discourse produced on ratings in order to address concerns of both language testers (test method effects on ratings) and second language acquisition theorists (data elicitation method on produced discourse). FACETS was used to analyze 805 ratings from 12 raters of 255 Grade 6 ESL students retelling a story and composing an audiotaped letter. As expected, they found that task and rater influenced ratings, and discourse was affected by task. They concluded that rating scale construction requires an analysis of discourse produced on specific tasks, and that rating scales should be task-specific.

The need for process-based research

All of these studies share a common shortcoming – they do not look much beyond the outcomes of these interviews – in most cases, the actual ratings of proficiency assigned to candidates – to the interview process itself, an undertaking that would allow us to 'identify and describe performance features that determine the quality of conversational interaction' in an oral interview (van Lier 1989: 497). Van Lier's seminal paper was to change all that, by stimulating an interest in undertaking empirical research into the nature of the discourse and the interaction that arises in face-to-face oral assessment. Specifically, van Lier called for studies that would even go beyond detailing the oral assessment process, to inform us about the turn-by-turn sequential interaction in the interview and whether the resulting discourse is like, or unlike, 'conversation'. That is, a more microanalytic focus on the actual construction of oral test discourse by the participants would enable us to determine whether these same conversational processes are at work in the oral interview, and thus, how test interaction resembles non-test discourse (and see Turner's (1998) reflections on a more fundamental question, whether it should). He concludes his article by urging us to '... understand the OPI, find out how to allow a truly conversational expression of oral proficiency to take place, and reassess our entire ideology and practice regarding the design of rating scales and procedures' (p. 505).

And it is in the context of conversation that an oral proficiency interview can and should be examined, because much of the literature written on it refers to its 'conversational' nature. It should be pointed out that what is said about the Oral Proficiency Interview (in either its FSI or ACTFL guise) applies generically to other language interviews as well. Also, it is not the case that the problem of linking of conversations and interviews in the literature is solely a matter of semantic usage; what is important is that there may be a difference between what goes on in oral testing situations and in other settings of everyday life, and these differences bear on the assessments which those engaged in oral testing want to make.

To get a feeling for the extent of the confusion on this very issue, here are some descriptions of the oral interview. Interviews are 'special cases of conversation that are examiner-directed' writes Oller (1979: 305), who goes on to say that 'it is fairly obvious why conversational techniques such as the interview constitute a pragmatic speaking task ...' (p. 306). Others refer to the 'conversational phase of the interview' (Clark and Lett 1988; Raffaldini 1988). In particular, the FSI Oral Interview, as described by Bachman and Palmer (1981: 70) 'consists of a 15- to 30-minute structured conversation during which one or two examiners try to elicit from the examinee a rich sample of speech by using a variety of question types and covering a wide range of topics and situations.' Madsen and Jones (1981: 23) undertook a survey of 60 tests of speaking ability, which indicated that the most frequently used approach is 'a direct test through conversation' with the most common technique being 'question and answer'. For Clark (1980: 17), the ideal method for testing oral proficiency is a 'face-to-face conversation ... the interviewing process is a reasonably close, if not an absolutely realistic reflection of real life conversation.' Jones (1978: 91) goes even further: 'the oral proficiency test is not an interview, but a conversation.'

Other researchers, while still casting the interview in a 'conversational' light, have noted some of the differences between oral interviews and conversation. While the oral interview has been characterized as a 'relaxed, natural conversation,' this notion is mistaken because the interaction is actually a test conducted under time constraints (Lowe 1981: 71). Lowe believes that 'conversational interview' better captures the essence of control over the encounter by the interviewer, control which is realized in a pre-arranged, deliberate structure. Yet, 'conversation is still basic to the oral interview' (p. 73). In a similar vein, Clark (1979: 38) notes that even though direct speaking tests rely on a highly realistic format – 'a face-to-face conversation with a native speaker' – they are not truly realistic, because the interviewee is talking with an examiner (as opposed to a friend). Another problem is that the interview makes it difficult to elicit several common language patterns 'typical of real-life conversation', such as control of interrogative patterns, because the interviewer dominates the conversation in the role of question asker.

Lest one construes these statements as some sort of historical misunderstanding that has since been corrected, here are two recent quotes. He and Young write (1998: 1), 'Although there are certain practical problems associated with setting up an *interview* with a learner – there has to be a native or very proficient speaker available, and there has to be enough time available for a reasonable *conversation* to develop between the interviewer and each learner....' [emphasis added]. And finally, 'The goal of language proficiency *interviews* (LPIs) is to evaluate how well a language learner might function in *conversation* with native speakers of the target language' [emphasis added] (Egbert 1998: 149).

Discourse-based studies on oral language assessment

Background

In the last decade, there has been a proliferation of applied linguistics studies that analyze aspects of the discourse and interaction in oral interview situations; this section reviews some prominent discourse-based studies on oral tests (see also Young and He 1998). Celce-Murcia (1998) contends that two features unite this work. First, actual recorded data which have been carefully transcribed are used for analysis; she sees this as particularly notable because '... although there exists a literature on using interviews for the assessment of language proficiency, until very recently, studies of LPIs [language proficiency interviews] ignored the central validity issue of oral proficiency assessment: namely, the ways in which the LPI is accomplished through discourse' (p. vii). Secondly, discourse-based studies on oral assessment are multidisciplinary in nature. In fact, the studies summarized below take a number of interesting perspectives on oral test discourse, including conversation analysis, accommodation theory, and interactional sociolinguistics.

This section begins with a summary of Lazaraton's (1991) dissertation, which is taken by some (e.g., McNamara 1996) to be the starting point of empirical, discourse-based research on oral assessment. The studies which follow have all been conducted in the last ten years and are grouped thematically. First, research which investigates how the participants behave in the interview context (as candidates, as interviewers, and as compared to and influenced by each other) is reviewed. Next, studies which compare the behaviour in the oral interview context with what is known about behaviour in natural conversation are detailed. Then, studies which compare test formats, especially direct vs. semi-direct tests, are mentioned. The section concludes with one study which looks at the relationship between interview ratings and produced discourse and two final studies that show how discourse analysis can be used to construct or validate oral proficiency test rating scales.

Lazaraton's research on ESL course placement interviews

As a direct result of van Lier's (1989) call for research on the structure of and interaction in the oral interview, Lazaraton's (1991) dissertation was designed to address the question of how the interactional features of the interview bear on oral assessment by employing conversation analysis techniques to describe a corpus of language interview data. Twenty oral interviews conducted to place students in ESL oral communication skills courses were audio- and videotaped on four occasions at the University of California at Los Angeles in 1990–1991. Both audiotapes and videotapes were transcribed using conversation analysis conventions and were examined microanalytically for several structural and interactional features. Three main findings were salient.

First, the overall structural organization of the interviews was clearly identifiable. The interviews proceeded through distinct phases which correspond to the structural boundaries of the interview agenda used by the interviewers. The interviews opened with greeting and introduction sequences in which the candidate's name was elicited and written on an evaluation form. The transition to the 'body' of the encounter was accomplished by the interviewer both verbally ('okay') and nonverbally (looking at the agenda); it opened with an agenda-based, neutral, nondirected question 'tell me about yourself.' Candidates routinely provided relevant information about themselves, a course preference, and a rationale for that preference, all of which was negotiated sequentially in the interaction. At the point where sufficient information had been given to satisfy the interview agenda requirements, the interviewer produced an agenda-based preclosing from 'I don't have any more questions … Do you have any questions for me?' The structural position this creates for a new sequence was invariably taken to discuss business matters, such as where to get test results, and to report 'bad news', such as problematic enrollment circumstances. When the pre-closing matters had been collaboratively accomplished, the closings occurred, accompanied by major postural shifts by both participants. Both the candidate and the interviewer could initiate the closings, which contained the conversational 'bye'–'bye' sequence, or something more institutional, such as 'thanks'–'you're welcome.' Lazaraton concludes that while these 'encounters share features with conversations … they are still characteristically instances of interviews, and interviews of a distinctive kind, for the participants' (Lazaraton 1992: 383).

A second finding was the modification of the preference organization system in conversation in these interviews as it applied to a certain type of assessment sequence, self-assessments of language ability. The preferred structure in conversation – where agreement with assessments is preferred and disagreement is dispreferred, except in the case of self-deprecations, where the reverse is true – was modified in these encounters as a result of and to accomplish certain interactional goals. So, when candidates disparaged their language ability with negative self-assessments, the interviewer, instead of disagreeing with the assessment, as one would expect in conversation, in some cases gave noncommittal responses that allowed judgements to be deferred until a later time; this lack of response seemed to be preferred here as a mark of objectivity. In other cases, the self-deprecation was countered with a compliment, a dispreferred response in this context, which candidates read as an unfavorable prognosis for their being admitted to the courses for which they were applying. They were then faced with the task of decisively rejecting the compliments in order to ensure course admission. Lazaraton (1997a) concluded that these patterns of preference structure are evidence of a social practice by which the institutionality of the encounters is instantiated on a turn-by-turn basis; it is these practices that define the encounters as interviews, and interviews of a distinctive kind, for the participants.

Finally, three forms of interviewer question modification in the face of perceived 'trouble', whether or not any 'trouble' – broadly construed as linguistic, cognitive, and/or social-interactional difficulty – actually exists for the participants, were found. Question recompletion was the primary form of modification, where some problematic element in the question turn was explained or clarified at a point past possible completion of the initial turn. These recompletions appear to be undertaken to make questions 'answerable' after the clarification was accomplished. In some cases, the recompletion was 'intercepted' by the student, who responded just at the point where the interviewer attempted some remedy; in this way 'trouble' was deflected. Lazaraton hypothesized that there may be a preference for this interception/ deflection, because interactional trouble is avoided and candidates can show their competence in responding to questions, even those that are less than totally clear. On the other hand, other recompletions were produced with no attempt by the students to cut them off; the result was almost always some form of disagreement, a social-interactional form of trouble. Two kinds of 'or' choice questions also showed features of turn modification. In contrast to 'from the outset 'or' choice questions', where two choices were meant to be produced from the outset and where no trouble was projected or perceived, 'add-on alternative 'or' questions' had a second 'choice' added after possible completion where some first 'choice' was not responded to 'on time'. 'Trail off 'or' questions' were produced when an initial question was asked, an 'or' was appended, and then the question trailed off. A third type of question modification was turn reformulation, where a question turn was redesigned rather than added to. Lexical or syntactic simplifications tended to be intercepted and shown as unnecessary, while follow-up and related question reformulations responded to potential disagreement.

As a result of these findings, Lazaraton (1991) concluded first, that the interviews import their fundamental structural and interactional features from conversation, but are characteristically and identifiably instances of 'interviews' for the participants, and, second, that her study illustrates a promising approach to the analysis of oral interaction in both testing and non-testing contexts.

Participant behaviour in oral interviews

A. Candidate behaviour

A number of recent studies have considered the role of proficiency level in candidate performance. For example, Young's (1995a) quantitative study compared First Certificate in English (FCE)-level candidates on their conversational styles. He found that the 12 advanced-level candidates differed significantly from the 11 intermediate-level speakers in that they talked more and faster, they elaborated more in their answers, and they were better able to construct stories. In addition, he noted that interviewers did not vary their own style for each group. While this last result suggests that the test administration is somewhat standardized, Young concludes that '... if the discourse dimensions of conversation between NNSs and native speakers are to be part of oral proficiency assessment, then scripted interview formats such as the FCE are an inappropriate means of assessment' (p. 37), since rigid interviewer behaviour may disadvantage higher-level speakers.

In addition to ascertaining the effect of proficiency level, Wigglesworth (1997) investigated the effects of planning time (one minute or no time) on oral test discourse. Twenty-eight recorded semi-direct **access:** oral tests in which planning time was manipulated were transcribed and coded for features of complexity (measured by subordination), fluency (measured by repetitions and self-repairs) and accuracy (of plurals, verb morphology, and articles) and then subjected to quantitative analyses. She claims that while planning time was beneficial for high-proficiency candidates in terms of accuracy, low-proficiency candidates did not benefit from increased planning time.

Yoshida-Morise (1998) also reports results on the effect of proficiency level on the use of communication strategies by 12 native Japanese speakers, representing four such levels, taking the OPI in English. She ascertained that six of the eleven strategies investigated were used differentially by level of proficiency. Despite some methodological difficulties in her study, she believes the results point to the importance of considering strategic behaviors in oral interviews.

Three recent studies have examined other factors that may affect candidate test discourse: the consequences of interlocutor familiarity, the effect of native-speaker nonnative-speaker status, and the role of the L1. With respect to interlocutor familiarity with examinees, Katona (1998) looked at the types of meaning negotiation that took place in the Hungarian English Oral Proficiency Examination between three Hungarian interviewers and 12 Hungarian interviewees. She found that the variety of negotiation sequences and exchanges present accounted for a more natural interaction when the interlocutor was known to the candidate, while with an unfamiliar interlocutor, misunderstandings resulted that made for a more formal, stilted interaction.

Viewing the oral interview from the perspective of native-speaker nonnative-speaker status, Moder and Halleck (1998) investigated how 10 native English speakers and 10 nonnative English speakers behaved in an OPI format interview, specifically, how they went about asking questions and taking turns. Their statistical results indicated that the nonnative speaker candidates took fewer turns that were longer and that the interviewers themselves took fewer turns with this group. Additionally, both groups of candidates asked information-seeking and clarification questions about equally; however, the nonnative speakers asked significantly fewer information-checking questions than the native speakers did. OPIs, they conclude, are authentic speech events which sample numerous forms of communicative behaviour, even if these behaviors are not exactly those that might be displayed in more informal conversation.

In order to highlight the crucial role that response elaboration, and more generally L1 'conversational style', plays in the oral interview, Young and Halleck (1998) compared the 'talkativeness' of 3 Mexican Spanish and 3 Japanese speakers representing different proficiency levels on the OPI. A topical structure analysis (Young 1995a) revealed that the Mexican candidates and the higher proficiency candidates contributed more to the interaction, spoke faster, and shifted topics more frequently than did the other two groups. They argue that the transfer of 'conversation style' can negatively impact a candidate's ratings if that style requires or prefers under-elaboration of answers in a setting where elaboration is valued.

B. Interviewer behaviour

In a series of studies, Ross and Berwick have investigated interviewer behaviour in the OPI. Ross and Berwick (1992) were among the first researchers to examine whether or not and the degree to which ten speech modification features occurred in the OPI and what the impact of such accommodation on ratings might be. Their quantitative analysis regarded the talk produced in the OPIs as a product of native–nonnative discourse, described in terms of features of control (e.g., topic nomination and abandonment, reformulations) as well as features of accommodation (e.g., clarification requests, display questions, and simplifications). Ross and Berwick came to the conclusion that the OPI shares features of both interviews and conversations: features of control primarily support the interview process while accommodation features can be varied to define and gauge language proficiency. In fact, they propose that candidate ratings may be predictable from the amount and type of accommodation that interviewers use.

In another study, Ross (1992) questioned the product orientation (i.e., reliability of judgements) that oral testing research has traditionally taken, and suggests that a focus on process (i.e., the validity of the interview, as was also suggested by van Lier) might be more enlightening. He believes that interview discourse can be better understood by looking to second language acquisition theory, specifically accommodation theory, to understand how interviewers make language comprehensible to interviewees. In an empirical study of 16 OPIs conducted in Japan, transcribed interviews were coded for 7 types of accommodation and 5 types of antecedent triggers for such accommodation. The statistical results identified the most salient triggers of accommodation to include candidate response to the previous question, the structure of that response, the level of the candidate, and whether the interviewer had used accommodation in the previous question; transcripts of actual OPIs are used to support these characterizations. Ross suggests that in assigning final ratings, the amount of accommodation that occurred should be taken into account so that the role of the interviewer in the interaction is included. He also claims that in interviewer training it would be useful to look at how responses are influenced by simplification and what necessary versus superfluous accommodations are.

Ross (no date) analyzed the 'procedural script' and formulaic speech that interviewers use in OPIs. By engaging in a contrastive analysis of the behaviour of two experienced OPI interviewers, Ross postulated that one interviewer's approach to questioning (asking short questions and accepting short answers) may have led to lower ratings for candidates since they were not encouraged to provide more language; the approach of the second interviewer, who asked long and involved questions, required a great deal of listening ability and may have led to confounded ratings. Both of these approaches to questioning can be viewed as deviations from a 'procedural script' which add unwanted variance to the testing process and which have an impact on test validity.

Berwick and Ross (1996) considered the OPI from a cross-cultural perspective. Their thesis was that the OPI is a rule-governed cross-cultural encounter which has effects on discourse that can be linked to systematic cultural variation in interviewer approaches to the examination. Using statistical and discourse analyses, they demonstrated that the Japanese interviewer was form-focused and engaged in 'instructional care-taking', while the American interviewer seemed to focus on content and expected the interviewee to be willing to 'engage the issues' (p. 47). They believe that test developers will have to come to terms with the tension between the effect of local norms on discourse and the need to keep oral assessment procedures standardized.

Lastly, Morton, Wigglesworth, and Williams (1997) looked at interviewer performance on **access:** by having raters grade the interviewers on their behaviour using a questionnaire. Their dataset consisted of 370 candidate performances conducted by 66 examiners which were graded by 51 raters. FACETS analysis was used to rank the examiners from 'best' to 'worst'. The results from the questionnaires indicated that the raters considered interviewers 'good' if they established rapport with candidates (especially those at lower levels), modified interview prompts, and asked additional, nonscripted questions. By analyzing transcripts of the ten 'best' and ten 'worst' interviewers, they concluded that the former used significantly more markers of politeness and more backchannels and were more actively involved in the interview.

C. Comparisons of interviewer and candidate behaviour

The seminal study which undertook to compare the behaviour of candidates with behaviour of interviewers in the oral examination is Young and Milanovic (1992). Their quantitative study of the interview section of the Cambridge First Certificate in English (FCE) examinations explored the features of dominance, contingency, and goal orientation (i.e., quantity of talk, topic initiations, reactiveness, and topic persistence) as well as contextual factors (interview theme and task, and examiner gender) in both interviewer and interviewee speech. Their findings indicate that the resulting discourse was highly asymmetrical, with both examiners and candidates constrained in terms of what they could contribute to the interaction.

Another study of participant behaviour in an interview is Fiksdal's (1990) research, in which she collected 'natural conversation data' in 16 academic advising sessions between native speaker advisors and foreign (both native-speaking Canadians and nonnative-speaking Taiwanese) students at a large American university. The encounters were videotaped and then played back to the participants to determine the saliency of various interactive features and to obtain comments on the interaction from their point of view. Her results indicated that speakers pay close attention to what they believe to be the expectations of their listeners, and they use conventionalized methods of demonstrating this attention. The most important of these methods is what she terms 'listener responses', such as 'yeah', 'mmhmm', and related nonverbal behaviour like nods. In her time-based model she found that speakers provide 'listener cues' to signal a listener response is warranted; these include falling intonation, postural shifts, and gaze. Sometimes, though, inappropriate listener responses (e.g., responses not signaled by a listener cue, such as 'uh huh' at an inappropriate place without an accompanying head nod) occurred. These were the greatest problem for the Taiwanese students she studied, responses which resulted in 'uncomfortable moments' and threatened rapport. Fiksdal hypothesized that spoken interaction is organized on two interdependent levels: a level of turntaking and a level of rapport, both of which adhere to the underlying tempo in the interaction.

D. Effect of interviewer behaviour on candidate performance

At least one empirical study has attempted to determine how interlocutor behaviour affects candidate performance on the IELTS Speaking Test. Brown and Hill (1998) used FACETS to analyze interviews from 32 IELTS candidates, each of whom was interviewed twice by 2 of 6 different interlocutors in order to identify, first, when a candidate's ability was judged at two different ability levels, and second, which interlocutors were 'easy' or 'difficult'. Then, transcripts of 10 interviews where candidates were rated differently (and were interviewed by the two easiest and two most difficult interlocutors) were analyzed for number of turns, turn length, question form and focus, and number of topics. 'Easy' interlocutors used more frequent topic shifts, asked simpler questions, and engaged in more question–answer exchanges, while the 'difficult' interlocutors challenged candidates more and acted more like a conversational participant. They suggest that the test developers take steps to ensure that candidates receive equal treatment from the interlocutors.

Comparisons of interview behaviour with conversation

A growing number of studies endeavor to compare the behaviour in interviews with what is known about natural conversation. For example, Johnson and Tyler (1998) analyzed a transcript from a training video Level 2 OPI between a Korean female and two trained interviewers. They investigated a number of conversational features in the transcript, including turntaking, sequence structure, and topic nomination. They conclude '... that in terms of prototypical aspects of everyday conversation, ... the face-to-face exchange that occurs in this OPI interview cannot be considered a valid example of a typical, real life conversation' (p. 28).

In a case study of one potential international teaching assistant who had failed his oral interview, He (1998) analyzed the candidate's answers to interviewer questions, using a conversation analytic framework, in order to understand why he might have failed. Her results suggest that he used 'yeah' in strange ways (for example, to show non-understanding) and was not competent at eliciting repair. He argues that discourse competence deserves more attention in oral assessment.

Also using a conversation analytic framework, Egbert (1998) compared the organization of repair in a dataset of modified OPIs evaluating the proficiency of American college students learning German with the repair features present in conversations between native German speakers. Three notable results were reported. First, in the interviews, the organization of repair was explained metalinguistically to the candidates while it remained unstated in conversation. Secondly, the interviewees used more types of repair initiation than did the native German speakers. Finally, interviewers used a more elaborate turn structure in repair with these interviewees than was found in the conversational data. Egbert reasons that '[w]hile it is necessary to examine LPIs by means of multiple methods, conversation analysis seems particularly apt for the analysis of interactional structures displayed in the talk, especially since LPIs constitute social encounters that are quite complex at the microanalytic level' (p. 169).

Finally, Kim and Suh (1998) used conversation analysis to investigate confirmation sequences (where an interviewer-question candidate-answer sequence is followed by an explicit confirmation request by the interviewer, to which the candidate responds) in nine Korean language course placement interviews. They determined that such confirmation sequences allowed the candidates to ratify the higher status of the Korean interviewers, to avoid or to lessen any potential threats to face, and to respond favorably to a topic nomination by the interviewer. Although Kim and Suh believe that baseline data obtained from Korean conversation are needed to interpret and to bolster the significance of these results, future work can and should apply these findings to the construction of assessment instruments which measure interactional and sociolinguistic competence.

Comparisons of test format

Another fruitful avenue of discourse-based research is the effect of test format on produced discourse. In support of her thesis that test validation can benefit from considering data generated from multiple data sources, Shohamy (1994b) compared the candidate output on two tests of spoken Hebrew, one a tape-mediated SOPI and the other a face-to-face OPI. First, she conducted a content analysis of the elicitation tasks as set out in the test specifications; the results indicated that the SOPI format samples more widely for low-level candidates while the OPI seems to be better suited to high-level candidates. In the second phase of the analysis, 10 tapes from each test format were statistically compared on numerous language features, such as syntax, communication strategies, speech functions, and the like. She found that candidates self-corrected and paraphrased significantly more on the SOPI and switched to their first language significantly more on the OPI. Shohamy claims that the long process of test validation can be enhanced by analyzing test data from multiple perspectives.

In a related study, Koike (1998) compared transcripts from 10 Spanish SOPI and OPI performances on accuracy, various management strategies, and several structural components. Her quantitative analysis revealed that the SOPI generated significantly more fillers, and fewer turns, quotes, speech acts, and switches to the L1 than the OPI did; however, Koike cautions that task type and specific topic influenced language production more than test modality did (results which in fact contradict those reported by Shohamy). However, the test format did seem to have a role in other areas – OPIs produced language that was more interactive and SOPIs generated more formal language that was better organized. Koike recommends employing assessment procedures which elicit a wider range of speech functions and rating scales which include management strategies and propositional organization.

In another comparative study of the OPI and SOPI format, O'Loughlin (1995) looked at the lexical density of the discourse generated by twenty candidates taking the **access:** oral interaction subtest using these two test formats each employing four different tasks (description, narration, discussion, and role play). The forty interview transcripts were coded for three features of lexical density: grammatical items, high-frequency lexical items, and low-frequency lexical items, and then tabulated. His quantitative results indicated that the effect of test format, task, and their interaction were all statistically significant, but the differences did not appear to be large. He concludes that the SOPI format generates a more literate (that is, lexically dense) kind of language; however, 'the degree of interactiveness, rather than test format, emerges as perhaps the single most important determinant of candidate output in the study' (p. 236). He suggests that altering the interactivity of test tasks could generate language that is even more different (in terms of lexical density) than the language data with which he worked.

Kormos (1999) compared performance on non-scripted interviews with role plays in an oral examination taken by 30 EFL learners in Hungary. Her analysis was based on counts of many features; she found that the interaction in the role play was more symmetric; candidates introduced and ratified more topics and were able to interrupt, open, and close the interactions. She notes that role play is one way to get at conversational competence in an oral interview situation.

Finally, Hoekje and Linnell (1994) evaluated three tests used to assess the ability of international teaching assistants: the SPEAK, the OPI, and an institution-specific performance test. Using Bachman's (1990, 1991) definitions of authenticity, they looked at method facets, the actual discourse elicited, and its similarity to language use in the target context. Their qualitative analyses led them to conclude that the three tests show substantial differences with respect to the language produced, and that the performance test was best for their intended purposes.

Comparisons of test scores with produced discourse

In one of the more intriguing discourse-based studies of the oral assessment process, Douglas (1994) undertook a quantitative and qualitative analysis of oral test scores and oral test discourse to see how they were related. Six American university students took the AGSPEAK test and were rated for pronunciation, grammar, fluency, and comprehensibility. The ratings were used to identify 'similar' candidates, whose discourse was then transcribed and compared on a number of variables, such as grammar, vocabulary, content, and rhetorical organization. His results indicated very little relationship between score given and discourse produced; he attributed this somewhat perplexing conclusion to inconsistent rating, or rating of factors which were not part of the rating scale. Douglas strongly urges more studies on the rating process to follow up on these results.

Rating scale construction and validation

Finally, at least two studies have used discourse analytic techniques to construct or validate oral assessment rating scales. To construct an oral examination rating scale for fluency, Fulcher (1996a) used 'grounded theory methodology', a qualitative analytic technique, to produce a 'thick description' of language use. These data were then operationalized into a fluency rating scale, which Fulcher evaluated for both reliability and validity, using more traditional test evaluation techniques. He recommends that test developers must take validity seriously in the development process and not wait to deal with it as some sort of after the fact endeavor.

Young (1995b) critically analyzed the rating scales used in two oral assessment procedures, the ACTFL OPI Guidelines (ACTFL 1989) and the Cambridge Assessment of Spoken English (CASE; UCLES 1992) from the perspective of second language acquisition theory, specifically discontinuous language development. His analysis indicates that both scales fall short in portraying, and measuring, language ability as both modular and context-dependent.

Summary

These studies, and surely others which are underway, have begun to analyze interview discourse as an inherently fundamental aspect of language testing, although asking different questions and using different analytic frameworks. Hopefully, findings such as these will help us better understand the nature of interaction in language assessment situations and in other institutional contexts where native and nonnative speakers interact.

Conclusion

What we see, then, is a discipline in the midst of exciting changes in perspective. It has become increasingly clear that the established psychometric methods for validating oral language tests are effective, but limited, and other validation methods are required, not just for empirical validation but, based on the many misperceptions about conversations and interviews noted above, for us to understand the basic nature of the oral assessment process. As Jacobs (1990) comments, 'Qualitative methods have been sufficiently successful that at this point the task is not to decide whether or not to admit them into the methodological arsenal of practicing researchers; the task is to articulate their rationale so that they can be used in an informed and self-conscious fashion' (p. 248). This book represents one such avenue towards this end, that of using qualitative discourse analysis, and conversation analysis in particular, as a uniquely suited solution for these validation tasks.

2 Conversation analysis, institutional talk, and oral language assessment

- Approaches to discourse analysis

- Conversation analysis

  - Background
  - What is conversation analysis?
  - What is conversation?
  - Nonverbal behaviour in conversation
  - An evaluation of conversation analysis

- Institutional talk

  - What is an interview?
  - The organization of the interview

- Conclusion

This chapter treats two important topics. First, conversation analysis is situated within the study of discourse analysis, an endeavor which encompasses a number of different strands of interest. After describing conversation analysis and some of its major findings, an extension of its methods to another form of interaction, institutional talk, is detailed. This background sets the stage for an introduction to the methods of conversation analysis that are presented in Chapter 3.

Approaches to discourse analysis

The sort of approach being advocated in this book falls under the heading of discourse analysis. Discourse, in the broadest sense, is a multi-disciplinary interest of scholars in linguistics, applied linguistics, philosophy, psychology, sociology, anthropology, computer and cognitive science, and rhetoric. In fact, the analysis of discourse covers such a vast range of interests, one might wonder if there are any conceptual or methodological threads which link them. According to Schiffrin (1994), current approaches to discourse share a number of principles, although any one approach will emphasize some features while de-emphasizing, or even overlooking, others:

1. *Analysis of discourse is empirical: actual data rather than intuitions are used; analyses are accountable to the data and are meant to be predictive of other as yet unencountered data.*

2. *Discourse is more than a sequence of linguistic units; its coherence cannot be understood if attention is limited just to linguistic form and/or meaning.*

3. *Resources for coherence jointly contribute to participant achievement and understanding of what is said, meant, and done through everyday talk. In other words, linguistic forms and meanings work together with social and cultural meanings, and interpretive frameworks, to create discourse.*

4. *The structures, meanings, and actions of everyday spoken discourse are interactively achieved.*

5. *What is said, meant, and done is sequentially situated; that is, utterances are produced and interpreted in the local contexts of other utterances.*

6. *How something is said, meant, and done – that is, how speakers select among different linguistic devices as alternative ways of speaking – is guided by relationships among the following:*
   a) speaker intentions,
   b) conventionalized strategies for making intentions recognizable,
   c) the meanings and functions of linguistic forms within their emerging contexts,
   d) the sequential context of other utterances,
   e) properties of the discourse mode – narration, description, exposition,
   f) the social context, e.g., participant identities and relationships, structure of the situation, the setting,
   g) a cultural framework of beliefs and actions.

(Adapted/taken from Schiffrin 1994: 416)

Schiffrin employs a useful typology to discuss six approaches to discourse; brief descriptions of these approaches follow. The last approach, conversation analysis, will be discussed in greater detail, but the interested reader is urged to consult Schiffrin (1994) or the cited sources for a more complete description of the other discourse analytic approaches. He and Young (1998) also note some useful links between these approaches and discourse-based studies of oral testing.

1. *Interactional sociolinguistics* (e.g., Gumperz 1982a, 1982b)
   'Discourse as social, cultural, and linguistic meaning'
   A linguistic/anthropological approach that examines interpretations of speaker intent based on social and linguistic meanings which are encoded in verbal (especially prosodic) and nonverbal cues and which are part of one's cultural repertoire.

2. Speech acts (e.g., Austin 1962, Searle 1969)
   'Discourse as action'
   A philosophical approach which details performative acts such as promising and asserting; it differentiates between an utterance's locutionary force (e.g., 'It's hot in here'), its illocutionary force (e.g., 'Open the window'), and its perlocutionary force: (the window gets opened).

3. *Pragmatics* (e.g., Grice 1975, Levinson 1983)
   'Discourse as individual, intention-based meaning'
   A philosophical approach that proposes four 'maxims of cooperation' (relevance, truthfulness, quantity, and clarity) which provide the inferential apparatus necessary to determine a speaker's intentions.

4. *Ethnography of communication* (e.g., Hymes 1974, 1982)
   'Discourse as a reflection of cultural and social reality'
   A reaction to Chomsky's narrow focus on linguistic competence, this anthropological approach seeks to find holistic explanations for cultural conceptions and constructions of meaning and behaviour, such as prayer, weeping, and silence.

5. *Variation analysis* (e.g., Labov 1972, Labov and Fanshel 1977)
   'Discourse as a reflection of one's speech community'
   A linguistic approach which looks to social and linguistic factors to understand patterns of language variation and change.

6. *Conversation analysis* (e.g., Sacks, Schegloff, and Jefferson 1974; Schegloff and Sacks 1973)
   'Discourse as a local construction of social order'
   A sociological approach that attempts to uncover the systematic properties of sequential organization of talk and the social practices that are displayed by and embodied in talk-in-interaction.

It is to this last approach that we now turn.

Conversation analysis

Background

Conversation analysis (also referred to as CA) is sociological in origin, tracing its roots to Garfinkel's ethnomethodology and Goffman's interaction analysis (Clayman 1995; Goodwin and Heritage 1990; Heritage 1995; Psathas 1995; Schiffrin 1994). Garfinkel (1967) was strongly influenced by phenomenology, but rejected mentalistic claims about social activities in favor of a process-based approach for discovering how such activities are constituted and made understandable by those who take part in them (Clayman 1995). Specifically, Garfinkel wanted to uncover the methods of reasoning, which are procedural, social, and shared, that are used to both produce and understand social interaction (Heritage 1995), and how such knowledge and actions are linked (Schiffrin 1994). These ethnomethodological influences can be seen in conversation analysis's emphasis on actual events (rather than idealizations, constructions, or reconstructions of events) and on the role of context for understanding social action. However, ethnomethodology differs from CA in its focus on context; all the particulars of the actual social context, its 'situated practice', come into play in ethnomethodology, whereas for CA, the sequential turn-by-turn context is most important. (See Clayman 1995 on this and other differences between the two enterprises.)

Goffman, on the other hand, as a social anthropologist, was interested in the ritual, moral, and normative aspects of face-to-face social interaction rather than the actual procedures for its construction (Heritage 1995; Psathas 1995). Goffman's work focused on the 'interaction order' (e.g., 1981; see also Drew and Wootton 1988), some of which is summarized here (from Kendon 1988). Goffman observed that when individuals are copresent at a 'gathering' and they share 'a sustained focus of attention', they engage in communicative 'interchanges', where A does something, and then B does something in response. Some of these 'doings' are 'explicit acts' that require a response (others are 'inexplicit acts', which don't); participants know which acts are 'explicit' (and should thus be responded to) via 'frame attunement'. From these facts Goffman hypothesized that both 'system requirements', the components that are necessary for any system of communication, and 'ritual requirements, the 'social constraints which smooth social interaction' (Hatch 1992) are necessary for communicative interchanges to take place. However, Goffman realized that the system requirements alone could not explain some observable aspects of interchanges. This led to his proposal of ritual requirements that could account for such facts as participants' willingness to abide by the system requirements, their level of attention and response, and their agreement on how to shut down an encounter. That is, system requirements are necessary for communication to take place, but are insufficient to explain how and why it does take place. (See Hatch 1992 for an applied linguistics view of system and ritual requirements.)

This is one point at which the conversation analyst and Goffman part ways: for Goffman, ritual requirements and 'face' (both highly individualistic, and perhaps culture-specific concepts) are the rules governing, and the motivating basis for, interaction. For the conversation analyst, the domain of interest is the system organization itself, irrespective of whatever individual characteristics the participants bring to the interaction (Schegloff 1988). A second notable difference is that while Goffman would use naturally occurring data, he was also comfortable working with data obtained from observations and notes, or even created data (Psathas 1995); in contrast, the conversation analyst insists on naturally occurring data which are recorded: data gathered from memory, role plays, and experiments are also eschewed in CA.

Since the work of both Garfinkel and Goffman underlies the tradition of conversation analysis, it is a useful introduction to the research on talk-in-interaction, in which social organization is viewed through an analysis of direct, face-to-face communication. It is to the analysis of conversation, the interaction prototype, that we now direct our attention.

What is conversation analysis?[1]

Conversation analysis (henceforth, CA) is an area of study which emerged in the 1960s when Harvey Sacks studied under Garfinkel, and later, with Schegloff, under Goffman. Now, more than thirty years later, one can find literally hundreds of published CA papers which not only explore the traditional areas of interest (i.e., the organizational systems of English conversation; see below) but also a broad range of new topics, such as institutional interaction, conversation in languages other than English, and the like (Heritage 1995). Heritage (1999) notes that the field of CA 'has begun to show certain signs of maturity: different practitioners have developed distinctive styles of working and a variety of analytical preoccupations, major domains and subdomains of study have crystallized, and there are developing relations with researchers from other fields with distinctive disciplinary commitments ... we now know a great deal about the core practices through which actions are designed, sequences are organized, and activities are accomplished in interaction' (p. 69).

The primary goal of conversation analysis is to identify and describe recurrent patterns of organization, present in a variety of materials, produced by a range of speakers, and to do the same for deviant cases, in which some regularly produced form or procedure is not used or realized. In both cases, the analyst tries to relate these conversational procedures to interactional activities. The basic question facing the analyst is, 'Why this now?' instead of 'that' or instead of 'later'. The analyst attempts to model the procedures and expectations employed by the participants by proceeding as the talk does: on a turn-by-turn basis. Unlike other approaches to discourse, the conversation analyst avoids appeal to 'speaker intent', since knowledge of the internal states of the participants is as inaccessible to the analyst as it is to the participants: all that is there is the talk, and the talk that has gone before. In theory, no feature or observation based on it is too small, too random, or too irrelevant or insignificant. What 'counts' can only be determined through a systematic examination of naturally occurring materials. This is one reason why the conversation analysis transcription process is so lengthy and detailed: there is no way to know beforehand which features of talk might be important in later analyses. Just as important is the fact that there is no way to know who might be interested in using the data at a later time, and what their research agenda might be. Conversation analysis, then, is really a process more than a product, because it grows out of the transcription and repeated and prolonged examination of materials.

It is also worth noting that although conversation analysis has its roots in the discipline of sociology, it differs from most sociological research in two important ways: it focuses on descriptive analyses of single cases instead of statistical analyses of large data aggregates, and it eschews giving any a priori importance to demographic variables such as gender, class, and the like. Nor is CA like linguistics, which focuses on isolated sounds or words, or sentences which are often created. And it is unlike other forms of discourse analysis in applied linguistics: while a number of these approaches view language as a form of social action, use recorded interactions as the basis for analysis, consider context as important, and attempt to model the expectations and perspectives of the interactional participants, CA differs in several important ways. As Pomerantz and Fehr (1997) point out, CA 'rejects the use of investigator-stipulated theoretical and conceptual definitions of research questions' (p. 66). Rather, the conversation analyst attempts to replicate the important interactional contingencies that the participants are oriented to. This means that classifying participants by their gender, position of power, and the like cannot be taken as 'omnirelevant' for analysis; 'persons who occupy different positions in some status or power hierarchy do not necessarily make that difference the basis for all and every interaction between them' (p. 66). Secondly, the conversation analyst is first and foremost concerned with the temporal organization of talk and the interactional contingencies therein. Actions must be located within an ongoing series of actions. Finally, 'rules' of talk in CA are not meant to explicate human conduct by means of a theoretically derived formula; rather, they are seen as 'situationally invoked standards that are part of the activity they seek to explain' (p. 67).

What is conversation?

From the conversation-analytic perspective, conversation is but one form of talk-in-interaction, although it has a 'bedrock status' in relation to other forms of talk (Heritage 1995; Sacks, Schegloff, and Jefferson 1974); in other words, it is the archetypal form of talk-in-interaction. But simply labeling any kind of interaction as one type or another does not make it so; that conclusion can only come from an analysis of how the participants orient themselves to the encounter (Gumperz and Berentz 1993; Schegloff 1988, 1989). In other words, it is only through an examination of their joint contribution to the interaction that we can characterize any encounter as a conversation, an interview, or something else.

Conversation can be characterized by a small set of generic forms of organization (see Levinson 1983, and Psathas 1995, for a complete discussion of this topic, and Richards and Schmidt 1983, and Markee 2000, for a second language acquisition perspective). The turntaking system of English is perhaps the most obvious aspect of conversational organization (Sacks, Schegloff, and Jefferson 1974; but see Oreström 1983, and Duncan 1972, for different accounts of the turntaking system in English). Turntaking can be described by a set of rules with ordered options that operate on a turn-by-turn basis; this is why turntaking is characterized as a 'locally managed' system. It can explain why only one speaker speaks at a time, how next speakers are selected, where and how overlaps (points where two or more speakers talk simultaneously) are placed, and how periods of silence occur within the talk of one speaker (a pause) or between the talk or two or more speakers (a gap). A turn is made up of *turn-constructional-units* (TCUs) which have syntactic, intonational, semantic and/or pragmatic status as potentially 'complete'. Because a TCU may be a sentence, a clause, a phrase, or a word, syntax matters a great deal for determining completeness. Speakers will initially be allotted one TCU (although most turns are more than one unit) and the turntaking apparatus applies at the end of each such unit, which is known as a *transition relevance place*, or TRP. In fact, we find that the ends of TCUs and turns are highly predictable using the four 'completeness' criteria listed above; this accounts for 'the recurrent marvels of split-second speaker transition' (Levinson 1983: 297). This is not to say that overlaps don't occur, but that when they occur at TRPs, they are quickly resolved by the turntaking machinery. An interesting hypothesis proposed by Good (1979) is that casualness in conversation depends for its realization, in a fundamental way, on turntaking. Stated in another way, casualness is intimately related to the permitted length of utterances by participants in a conversation. This line of thought has implications for a characterization of the oral interviews which are of interest to us, in which the system of turntaking, as well as turn length, is hypothesized to differ systematically from what occurs in conversation.

A second domain (and for some, the most fundamental one: see Zimmerman 1988) of conversational organization is concerned with the sequencing rules which apply to such talk. The basic structural unit is the *adjacency pair* (Schegloff 1990; Schegloff and Sacks 1973), consisting of a first-pair-part (FPP) and an adjacent, conditionally relevant second-pair-part (SPP), produced by different speakers. Examples of adjacency pairs include Question–Answer, Request–Acceptance/Denial, Summons–Response, and so on. These basic adjacency pairs can be expanded in various positions which can be described as *insert sequences* (Schegloff 1972), in which one sequence is embedded within another, (where turns 2) and 3) in the following example form the insert sequence: 1) A: Can I have a coffee? 2) B: Large or small? 3) A: Small. 4) B: Coming up.) and *pre-sequences* (Schegloff 1968, 1980) in which one sequence regularly occurs before another sequence (for example, a pre-invitation which checks potential acceptance of the invitation before it is asked in order to avoid rejection: 1) A: What are you doing tonight? 2) B: Nothing. 3) A: Wanna go out? 4) B: Sure.). There are also *side sequences* (Jefferson 1972) which are not 'adjacency pairs' in the same sense. In such sequences there is a temporary termination of an ongoing sequence to deal with some other matter, after which the original sequence is resumed.

The system of repair is a third organizational system which operates to remedy trouble situations in conversation (Schegloff, Jefferson, and Sacks 1977), specifically problems in speaking, hearing, and understanding. We can differentiate *repair initiation*, where the existence of a problem is acknowledged, from *actual correction*, which is where the trouble is remedied. Repair can be initiated in four different positional 'slots': same turn, transition space to possible next turn, next turn, and third turn. In all cases but next turn, there is a preference for self-initiation of repair and for self-correction. Self-repair has been examined by Schegloff (1979a), but other-initiation and other-correction have been studied in more detail (e.g., Schegloff 1992. See also two notable applied linguistics studies using conversation analysis to study repair, Gaskill 1980, and Egbert 1997).

Preference organization, a fourth organizational system of conversation, is an important aspect of the sequential organization of talk-in-interaction (Sacks 1987 [1973], Pomerantz 1984). Not all potential second-pair-parts to the first-pair-part of an adjacency pair are of equal 'rank': some are 'preferred' while others are 'dispreferred'. Preference does not refer to psychological or individual preferences of the speakers who produce the talk, but to the structural notion that there are junctures at which participants have alternate but unequal courses of action available to them – at the level of lexical choice, turn type, sequence selection, and so on (Lazaraton 1997a). In other words, dispreferred responses are 'marked' and as such are shown as dispreferred by various means, such as delays in response and prefaces like 'yeah' or 'well'. Granting a request and accepting an invitation are examples of preferred responses; refusing and declining the invitation are examples of dispreferred actions.

The overall structural organization of an occasion of talk can be identified by the openings, pre-closings, and closings sections of conversation (Schegloff 1979b; Schegloff and Sacks 1973). An examination of conversation shows that participants orient to these sections in and by their talk and to the work that is accomplished in them. For example, openings in telephone conversations are characterized by summons-answer and identification-recognition sequences as well as greetings and 'how are yous'. The openings in face-to-face talk are characterized by greeting sequences, and in some cases, introduction sequences. Preclosings provide a structural position in which to bring up some as yet unspoken talk on a speaker's agenda. Closings are recognizable by closing implicative talk (such as making arrangements), passing turns ('okay'–'okay'), and a terminal exchange ('bye'–'bye'). (Fuller 1993 and Bargfrede 1996 are two applied linguistics studies on nonnative speaker competence with telephone openings and closings.)

A final organizational system that has received some, but not much, attention is topic organization. The simple reason for this lack of focus is that 'topical maintenance and shift are extremely complex and subtle matter[s]' (Atkinson and Heritage 1984: 165). In fact, it may be easier to identify places where topic changes than to say what it is at any one point in an interaction (Ross and Berwick 1992). In addition, topic is negotiated throughout an interaction; it is not static (Dorval 1990). We can distinguish between 'stepwise topical movement', where one topic flows into another, and 'boundaried topical movement,' where one topic is closed and then another is initiated. Two conversation analysis studies have looked at topic: Button and Casey (1984) on how topics are generated via 'topic initial elicitors' (expressions like 'what's new?'); and Jefferson (1984) on how topics are closed. Hobbs (1990) and Reichman (1990) have taken a more cognitively-oriented, yet data-based view on topic; in applied linguistics, Wilkinson (1994) looked at topic nomination strategies in a conversation between two nonnative speakers of English and found that the students strongly preferred strategies with overt linguistic markers of topic change, such as 'first' and 'what else'.

Nonverbal behaviour in conversation

Essentially all of the CA work cited so far has been derived from an analysis of audiotaped conversation data. It is probably safe to say that nonverbal behaviour is the least well understood aspect of spoken interaction, but acknowledged as just as important as the words which are spoken; in fact, it may be crucial for truly understanding face-to-face interaction. We all know the difference between listening to something on the radio and seeing it on television. Why, then, don't more conversation analytic studies highlight nonvocal activities? One important reason is that much early CA work was done on telephone conversation where speakers are not co-present to begin with. Another reason is that researchers may not have access to videotaping equipment, or be reluctant to use it because it adds another element of unpredictability and influence into the encounter. Equally problematic is the fact that transcribing even small segments of nonverbal behaviour is frustrating, time consuming, and unwieldy. Finally, videotaping has its own consequences, as Goodwin (1994: 607) points out: 'like transcription, any camera position constitutes a theory about what is relevant within a scene – one that will have enormous consequences for what can be seen in it later – and what forms of subsequent analysis are possible.' As a result, researchers (including myself) tend to rely on audiotaped data up to the point where questions cannot be answered without consulting the visual record of the interaction, if it is available. Even then, the videotaped data are usually supplemental to the audiotaped data and are given a thorough (but not systematic) examination.

This is not to say that nonverbal behaviour has not been analyzed in its own right. Researchers interested in language and social interaction have looked at the role of gaze in interaction, for example, Goodwin (1981), who presents an extremely detailed analysis of the role of gaze in turn construction and self-repair (see also Goodwin 1984; Maynard and Marlaire 1992); the role of gesture, for example, Kendon (1985), who proposes that gestures are related to speech production when a speaker is concerned about transmission conditions, such as when communicative circumstances make speech reception difficult, or about interpretative adequacy, when a speaker wants to enhance a spoken utterance or express things that are not easily represented in speech (see also Kendon 1994; Schegloff 1984a); the role of other bodily movements, for example, Heath (1986), who reports on a multilevel analysis of verbal and nonverbal behaviour in medical interaction (see also Maynard and Marlaire 1992; Tannen 1990); and combinations of these three (e.g., Dore and Dorval 1990; Heath 1984; McIlvenny 1995; Ochs, Gonzales, and Jacoby 1996; Streeck 1994).

At least one published applied linguistics study has explored the role of nonverbal behaviour in native–nonnative interaction in a language assessment interview. Neu (1990) undertook an interactional analysis of two oral interviews used for ESL course placement purposes and found that second language learners can 'stretch' their linguistic competence by effectively using nonverbal behaviour. She concluded that nonverbal communication plays a critical role in conversational performance, because such behaviour aids in the discourse management of topic initiation, topic maintenance, and turntaking. While this conclusion may seem intuitively obvious, what is important is the empirical evidence she found in support of these commonsense notions.

These studies should remind us of the importance of considering all of communication in the study of interaction. As Birdwhistell (1972: 404) remarks, 'Any ... analysis which would attend to one modality – lexical, linguistic or kinesic – must suffer from (or, at least be responsible for) the assumption that other modalities maintain a steady or non-influential state.'

An evaluation of conversation analysis

This brief overview of conversation analysis should acquaint the reader with some of the major findings about conversation; the data collection, transcription, and analytic methodology of CA will be introduced in subsequent chapters. However, it is worth noting that conversation analysis has not received universal acceptance from all discourse analysts. One criticism is that the analytic methodology itself and the descriptive categories employed are too poorly defined to be usable, teachable, or learnable (Brown and Yule 1983; Cortazzi 1993; Eggins and Slade 1997; Wolfson 1989). A second criticism is that conversation analysis pays insufficient attention to the relationship between form and function (Schiffrin 1994; see also Levinson 1983). Furthermore, the CA transcription system does not account for intonation or paralanguage (Cortazzi 1993) and is therefore useless for those working with the suprasegmental aspects of language. There are also questions as to the universality of the turntaking system proposed by Sacks, Schegloff, and Jefferson (1974) (Cortazzi 1993; Wolfson 1989; see also Levinson 1983 for response to this criticism), the 'bedrock status' of conversation as the basic form of speech exchange (Cortazzi 1993), and the reducibility of all sequences to adjacency pairs (Wolfson 1989). Two additional problems noted by Hopper, Koch, and Mandelbaum (1986) are first, that CA methods are very difficult to learn except in a group with a trained leader, and second, that some researchers will find it difficult to refrain from coding and counting data, as CA suggests (see also Eggins and Slade 1997 on this point). Finally, on a more conceptual level, Wetherell (1998) argues that the technical analyses of CA based on participants' orientations are too narrow; 'complete or scholarly analyses' must also be responsive to and take into account the social and political consequences of these particular orientations (but see Schegloff 1998 for a response). Or, as Eggins and Slade

(1997) argue: 'Rather than just seeing conversation merely as good data for studying social life, analysis needs to view conversation as good data for studying language as it is used to enact social life' (p. 32).

On the positive side, it is clear that CA has made invaluable contributions to our understanding of spoken interaction. Heritage (1995: 410) notes that 'in this dynamic interplay between findings, theory, and methodology lies the real strength of CA as a growing and diversifying empirical initiative in the study of oral communication.' Furthermore, Goodwin and Heritage (1990: 301) believe that CA has much to offer other disciplines, such as linguistics, anthropology, and applied linguistics because it 'transcends ... traditional disciplinary boundaries ... by providing a perspective within which language, culture, and social organization can be analyzed not as separate subfields but as integrated elements of coherent courses of action.' The recent book *Interaction and Grammar* (Ochs, Schegloff, and Thompson 1996) is an excellent example of work that derives from but synthesizes the three perspectives of anthropology, sociology, and functional linguistics. In addition, CA is 'an approach and a method for studying social interaction, utilizable for a wide, unspecified range of social phenomena ... it is a method that can be taught and learned, that can be demonstrated and that has achieved reproducible results' (Psathas 1995: 67).

Most importantly, the empirical findings on conversational structure have been used in the last 15 years by conversation analysts who have turned their attention to other forms of talk-in-interaction, specifically talk that occurs in institutional settings. And the prototype of institutional talk is the interview, the topic which we now consider.

Institutional talk

Interviews are one form of 'institutional talk', interactions in which 'more or less official or formal task- or role-based activities are undertaken' (Heritage and Greatbatch 1989: 47). According to Drew and Heritage (1992), there are three salient features of institutional talk. First, it shows an orientation to a set of institutional goals which are relevant to the encounter (e.g., obtaining a medical diagnosis, courtroom testimony, or a language sample). How and whether these goals are met is a matter that is negotiated by the participants in the course of the interaction. Secondly, it is quite clear that there are constraints on the quantity and quality of contributions that participants make in institutional encounters. Whether these constraints are of a legal sort (as in courtroom testimony) or more informal, as in an oral interview, conduct is shaped according to these constraints. Finally, the interactional inferences that are operative in conversation may be modified, or even suspended, in institutional talk. For example, a range of behaviour common in conversation (expressions of surprise, anger, and the like), if withheld, may indicate rudeness or boredom, whereas in institutional contexts, participants seem to reinterpret these behaviors with the particular institutional goals in mind (for example, being objective). Since this book is concerned with a specific form of institutional talk, the interview, we will now look at this form of talk in more detail.

What is an interview?

Interviews are ubiquitous in the social sciences: it is estimated that 90% of social science investigations use interview data (Briggs 1986). The instrumental purpose of the interview is not to be overlooked: an interview is, above all else, a measurement device whose purpose is to collect valid and reliable data (Halberstam 1978).

From a sociological perspective, the structure of interview discourse, which cannot be divorced from the structure of social participation in an interview, is a worthwhile object of study in itself. To begin with the same caveat with which conversation was discussed, one instance of talk-in-interaction cannot be arbitrarily labeled 'an interview' while another is designated 'a conversation', because one must look at the way the participants orient themselves in and to the interaction in order to say that 'this is an interview' and 'this is a conversation' (Schegloff 1988, 1989).[2]

Traditionally, the analysis of institutional talk has been done contrastively, in terms of features of conversation, describing how participants construct the interaction using such features. For example, Button (1987) proposes that an instance of talk-in-interaction is realized as an interview by the participants through their orientation to its organizational and sequential structure. And the most fundamental way in which participants orient themselves to a particular instance of talk-in-interaction as an interview is through a special speech exchange system of turn pre-allocation in which one party asks questions and the other answers (Button 1987; Frankel 1990; Greatbatch 1988; Schegloff 1989; West 1983). Examples of this type of talk-in-interaction include classroom talk (McHoul 1978, 1990); course admission interviews (Gumperz 1992a; Lazaraton 1991); courtroom questions and answers (J. M. Atkinson 1992; Atkinson and Drew 1979; Drew 1992); doctor–patient discourse (Frankel 1983, 1990; Heath 1986, 1989, 1992; Maynard 1992); employment interviews (Button 1987, 1992); health visitor encounters (Heritage and Sefi 1992; Heritage and Sorjonen 1994); news interviews (Clayman 1988, 1989, 1992; Greatbatch 1988, 1992; Heritage 1985; Heritage and Greatbatch 1989); school counseling interviews (Erickson and Schultz 1982); survey interviews (Suchman and Jordan 1990); and standardized oral testing situations (Marlaire 1990; Marlaire and Maynard 1990; Maynard and Marlaire 1992; Roth 1974).

Quite a bit of the early work on institutional talk, some of which is cited above, was based on the premise that the conversation turntaking system is modified in institutional talk, but Heritage and Greatbatch (1989; see also Drew and Heritage 1992a; Heritage 1995) warn that no *single* interactional feature will be able to account for the resultant interaction in these institutional contexts. Heritage (1995) suggests that conduct in institutional talk is a 'narrowing' of conversational behaviour in socially imposed ways. Although conversation is often used as a reference point for comparison with other forms of talk (or 'formal talk' (see J. M. Atkinson 1982 on this point), there is now a call for those engaged in this comparative work to show how participants undertake and develop the interaction 'so as to progressively constitute and hence jointly and collaboratively realize' ... their talk and ... social roles in it as having some distinctly institutional character' (Schegloff 1989 cited in Heritage and Greatbatch 1989: 49). That is, we must look at how the talk is actually constructed for evidence of the participants' orientation to such institutional role-based identities. In other words, whatever variations we find in interactional practice in an interview must lead the *participants*, first and foremost, and us as analysts only secondarily, to see the encounter as an interview (Heritage 1995). And, as Heritage says, finding ways in which interviews are 'done differently' is one thing; specifying how they differ is quite another matter.

However, it is still the case that interviews (and other forms of non-archetypal talk-in-interaction) *are*, in observable ways transformations of ordinary conversation (Sacks, Schegloff, and Jefferson 1974). Greatbatch (1988), in his study of news interviews, found that the pre-allocated nature of turntaking in institutional interview contexts is a transformation of the locally allocated system present in ordinary conversation. West's (1983) findings from medical interviews are similar: conversations and interviews fall along a continuum regarding predetermination of the degree to which they allow the use of alternative utterance types by speakers with different identities. For West, it is not only the order of the turns which is pre-allocated, but their length and content as well (see also Button 1987 on this point). In fact, multiple continua may exist for interviews and conversations: in the range of questions that are asked, in their interactional thrust and import, in the formats used to construct them, and in the type of answers permitted to them (Sacks, Schegloff, and Jefferson 1974; Schegloff 1988).

A second point that can be made is that the interview participants may orient themselves to the encounter as an interview at one point, but this does not guarantee that the interaction will continue to be realized as such later on in the talk. An example of this is Schegloff's (1989) analysis of the Bush–Rather encounter. At some point in the interview, the interviewee (Bush) began to talk before the interviewer (Rather) had finished his question; there was also the emergence of competitive overlap. Both of these phenomena indicate that the interview 'as an interview' had broken down, because in an interview the participants display their understanding of the fact that it is an interview by observing the practice that interviewee does not talk before the interviewer has finished the question. One possible result of such a breakdown is that the interaction will become a conversation, or a confrontation (as Schegloff shows that it did for Bush and Rather), or some other kind of talk.

The organization of the interview

The basic characterization of an interview as a speech exchange system with pre-allocated Question–Answer turns is now examined in greater detail. To highlight some of the findings about the organizational systems mentioned earlier (especially turntaking, sequence structure, and repair) with respect to institutional talk, we first take up the system of turntaking. The features of turntaking present in the news interview data which Greatbatch analyzed (1988), and which apply more generally to most interviews, include:

1. *Interviewers and interviewees systematically attempt to produce turns which are (at least minimally) recognizable as questions and answers, respectively.*

2. *Interviewers systematically withhold a range of responses that are routinely produced by questioners in ordinary conversation.*

3a. *Although interviewers might produce statement turn components, these are normally done prior to the production of questioning turn components.*

3b. *Interviewees routinely treat interviewers' statement turn components as preliminaries to questioning turn components.*

4. *Interviews are overwhelmingly opened by interviewers.*

5. *Interviews are customarily closed by interviewers.*

6. *Departures from the standard question-and-answer format are frequently attended to as accountable and are characteristically repaired.*

(Greatbatch 1988: 404)

These facts imply that there is a system of turn-preallocation at work in news interviews, but it is not just the allocation of turns which is remarkable: it is also the content of the turns which is modified in this form of institutional talk. Several of these observations regarding the Question–Answer format of news interviews (specifically, 1, 2, 3, and 6) were made in a general way quite early on in the history of conversation analysis by Sacks, Schegloff, and Jefferson (1974: 729–31); they have been reiterated more recently by other researchers looking at a variety of different institutional contexts. For example, the survey interviews investigated by Suchman and Jordan (1990) showed a preponderance of question–answer sequences, and they claim that these sequences differ in systematic ways from question–answer sequences in conversation, specifically in what is accepted as an answer. That is, what is recognizable as an answer is negotiated in the interaction. At times, elaboration of an answer is disallowed, while at other times an answer that would be 'good enough' in conversation requires more elaboration in the survey interviews; it is an orientation to these practices which contributes to the unfolding reality of this experience as an 'interview' for the participants.

West (1983), in an examination of question types found in medical interviews, classified questions as either 'forward looking' or 'backward looking'. A forward-looking question focuses on the next object in a sequence whereas backward-looking questions look back to previous talk for an answer to the question that they present. Repair initiators (like 'Huh?'), understanding checks ('You mean John?') and surprise markers ('Oh really?') all look backwards in time and are 'conditionally relevant' questions. Her results showed a marked dispreference for patient-initiated (forward-looking) questions and a behavioral orientation to this dispreference by doctors and patients. These findings were confirmed by Frankel (1990).

Heritage and Sorjonen (1994) looked at the structure of the questions themselves in home health care visits and found that 'and-prefaced' questions supply a way to achieve 'agenda-based nextness' in question design. 'And-prefaced' questions treat prior answers as unproblematic and move the talk forward within or across topic/sequence boundaries as part of a larger 'agenda' of questions. (It is interesting to note that this feature of question design has been found in oral assessment interaction as well; cf. Lazaraton 1994a.)

As for the answers that occur in institutional contexts, Heath (1992) found that in medical consultations, patients withhold substantive responses to doctor diagnoses, even when invited to do so; Heath sees this behaviour as a way in which institutional role asymmetries are preserved. In another study of answers, Greatbatch (1992) looked at the way interviewees in panel discussions were able to push the question–answer format to escalate disagreements with others on the panel by framing their answers to interviewer questions in certain ways. Unlike conversation, where disagreements need to be resolved by the participants, in the news interview this is the job of the interviewer, so panel participants did not need to worry about finding a way to 'exit' the disagreement.

Answers were problematic for Gumperz's (1992a) subjects, speakers of North Indian languages, who were interviewed by native British English speakers for job training placement. Gumperz found a pattern of 'minoritization', a process by which stereotypes were formed or confirmed for these speakers who used stigmatized 'contextualization clues', which are culturally based communication patterns. The nonnative speakers in the study seemed to be disadvantaged by the sorts of downgraded, minimal, or irrelevant responses they gave to interviewer questions (see also He 1998 on this point).

With respect to sequence structure, researchers looking at other specific institutional contexts have found that the basic structural unit organizing the talk is not the two-part sequence of Question–Answer (with no third position receipt markers), but a three-part sequence of Initiation–Reply–Evaluation. This 'instructional sequence' (Mehan 1979, 1985) has been found in classroom discourse; a similar pattern has been observed in medical encounters (Todd 1983) as a reflection of the sociopolitical context of talk, and as a means by which the doctor can control topic by ending a segment. 'Okay' and 'alright' are two common evaluation tokens that both mark and manage the closure of one sequence or activity and the transition to another. They also indicate acceptance and recipiency of a proposed answer (Marlaire and Maynard 1990).

The work of Marlaire (1990), Marlaire and Maynard (1990), Maynard and Marlaire (1992), and Roth (1974) deserves special attention because its focus on standardized testing situations is closely related to the language assessment situations which are of interest here; their work will be mentioned again below. To the point at hand, Marlaire (1990) has labeled three-part sequences of Prompt–Answer–Acknowledgment 'elicitation sequences' (or 'testing sequences' in Maynard and Marlaire 1992) and has found them similar to Mehan's instructional sequences. By taking a closer look at these third-position acknowledgments, Marlaire and Maynard (1990) note that a problem may arise if the intent of the acknowledgment is confused because it may supply inappropriate feedback to the student. Does 'good' or 'okay' in third-position mean that an answer itself is correct (an evaluation) or that the supply of an answer is adequate (an acknowledgment)? This is one reason why testers are urged to withhold all such replies (see also Lazaraton 1996b, on this point).

On the other hand, Greatbatch observed that news interviewers seem to systematically *withhold* a range of responses normally produced by questioners in conversation. These include the full range of third-position receipt markers, including 'oh' (Heritage 1984), continuers ('mmhmm'), third-position assessments ('great!') and pro-repeat newsmarks ('He did?'). These responses are withheld in order to avoid expressing personal reactions to the veracity or adequacy of a given answer; thus, the neutrality of the interviewer is maintained because s/he declines the role of 'report recipient' in favor of the neutral role of 'report elicitor' where 'expressive caution' is achieved. (See J. M. Atkinson 1992 and Clayman 1988, 1992 on these points.)

Another organizational feature of conversation studied in interviews is the withholding of repair by interviewers (Button 1987; Suchman and Jordan 1990). Button's study of answers in employment interviews indicates that interviewers do not undertake correction of problems in understanding on the part of the interviewee. Understanding, or the lack thereof, is an interactional accomplishment that occurs as a result of the way participants organize their speech. He also found that an interviewee was systematically precluded from returning to an answer that was just given, by the interviewer ending the questioning altogether, asking a second, topically relevant but sequentially disjunctive question, or assessing the relevant answer but talking past a 'transition relevance place' (a place in a speaker's turn where it is possible for another speaker to begin speaking). It is this second phenomenon (disallowing a return to a given answer) that, in part, gives the interviewer the appearance of objectivity by distancing him or herself from the answers given by the interviewee. More generally, Button's (1992) study of repair initiation and accomplishment in these job interviews showed how the speech exchange itself is organized and structured by the participants, and how such practices embody the social setting of the interview. By comparing the practices in ordinary conversation with these interview data, Button demonstrated how participants orient to the interview context as a relevant locus for these practices.

Button found that third-position repair initiation by job interviewers was withheld. Suchman and Jordan (1990) also found a lack of repair in the survey interviews they examined, but of a different type. The withholding of correction in the face of interviewee repair initiation, along with a set of prescribed questions, is thought to contribute to the standardization of the interview, a crucial prerequisite for it being considered a scientific procedure. Standardization, in the sense of not varying the wording of questions in the face of repair initiation by the interviewee, is aimed at preserving the meaning of the original question. Yet, what may result is differing interpretations of question meaning by interviewees, which can be a troubling source of uncontrolled variation. Theoretically, the negotiation of meaning can be suppressed by the interviewer by not responding to clarification requests, but this attempt shows a deep misunderstanding of the encounter as a fundamentally interactional event.

Marlaire and Maynard (1990) show how, in standardized testing situations, candidates can use 'tentativeness' in their replies to initiate repair. Unmitigated answers present no problems for the participants, although the student is still sensitive to any evaluative follow-up by the interviewer. But tentativeness (as in a partial utterance) is actually an interactional resource which they hypothesize students may use to elicit repair initiation by the interviewer, the outcome of which is an answer that is the product of interviewer–interviewee collaboration.

In other words, the results of standardized testing are, in fact, *a collaborative achievement.* Over twenty-five years ago, Roth (1974) questioned the assumption that intelligence, as measured by IQ tests, is really an individual phenomenon, based on his study of black and white children who were administered the Peabody Picture Vocabulary Test by a white assessor. The taped and transcribed interactions showed that children understood and responded to test items in ways that were not, and, in fact, could not, be recorded by the test. Roth claims that while the testing process may be 'standardized' against population norms (a psychometric issue), the 'normatively organized interaction' (a sociological issue) on which such psychometric standardization is based cannot be taken for granted, since there is no guarantee that all testers will uniformly administer the test to subjects. The sociological 'rules' for testing interactions are always embedded in a particular context, and the processes of interaction in these contexts will vary from subject to subject, even if the outcomes (i.e., scores) are equal.

In two related studies, Marlaire (1990) and Marlaire and Maynard (1990) looked at a specific standardized testing situation, special education assessments of children with developmental disabilities. Like Roth, they found that test results are really collaborative productions: testing prompts are not preformulated and given as simple stimulus items; in fact, they can be elaborated, reformulated, or reduced. That is, the tester is more than just a conduit for questions, and test 'performance' is really a collaborative achievement. While they do not claim that interactional processes distort the test scores, they see the interviewer as more or less implicated in student performance, because the assessment process is by nature co-produced.

Maynard and Marlaire (1992) also studied a 'blending' test, where a clinician breaks up words into parts and the child reconstitutes the word by saying it correctly. Videotaped data of three clinicians testing 10 children, 3–8 years old, were analyzed. Their major finding was the existence of what they term the 'interactional substrate' of such testing, defined as the skills of both the clinician and the child that are employed in the encounter to arrive at an 'accountable' test score; these skills include questioning, answering, initiating repair, correcting, evaluating via feedback, and the like. Although these actions aren't being tested, Maynard and Marlaire posit that the abilities which are fundamentally depend on them. One result of this substrate is that children can be socialized in the test situation to produce an incorrect response, which shows not incompetence *per se* but rather the (unintended) effects that the structure of the interaction has on testing outcomes. They see this substrate as an uncontrolled environmental condition that impacts on the validity of resulting test scores: 'Ultimately interviews as real-worldly accomplishments are inseparable from the substrate or scaffolding of skills through which participants make both the process and its products observable in their specificity' (p. 196).

Summary

To conclude this section, an important point made by Suchman and Jordan (1990) is that it is not the case that interviews are 'structured' and conversations are not; rather, conversations and interviews fall along a continuum and the difference between the two lies in where the structure resides – 'inside' the interaction, as in a conversation, or primarily, but not exclusively, external to the interaction, as in an interview. And as Heritage (1995: 410) points out, there is no single 'royal road' to analyzing institutional talk since it varies so widely by task and setting; however, we are lucky to have a wealth of empirical findings, some of which have been summarized here, from which to start.

Conclusion

This chapter has overviewed the analytic approach of conversation analysis and its relationship to institutional talk. The empirical findings of CA in relation to both conversation and interviews are fundamentally relevant to our work in applied linguistics, as they supply a means by which we can understand oral interaction. More specifically, CA offers us a method with which we can analyze the interaction that takes place in face-to-face oral assessment, which, until very recently, was overlooked in the test validation process. Subsequent chapters will detail the steps in the CA process, which will ultimately allow us to examine specific oral test validation questions that have been, and can be, answered using this research methodology.

Notes

1. Since entire books have been written on this topic, the whole of CA cannot be covered adequately here, or even in this book; suffice it to say that this section is a very abbreviated version of what can be found in Atkinson and Heritage (1984), Levinson (1983), and Psathas (1995). The interested reader is urged to consult these original sources. A glossary of some important CA terms can be found in Appendix 1.

2. And it is not just researchers studying oral interviews who seem to be confused by this issue. Duncan, in his 1972 paper on turntaking, uses 'conversation' in the title, 'face-to-face interaction' in the abstract, but switches to 'interview' in the paper itself. Schiffrin (1987) admits that her data come from interviews but then goes on to report the results as if they originated in a truly 'conversational' context. Several times Fiksdal (1990) mentions the goal of collecting 'natural conversation' in her study but continually refers to the encounters as 'interview' sessions. The point is

not to disparage the work of these researchers or that of the language testers cited earlier, but to demonstrate that the confusion over the terms 'conversation' and 'interview' is both deep and widespread.

3 Data collection and transcription

Since it is only possible to undertake the type of qualitative discourse analysis that this book describes if one has access to audiorecorded and/or videorecorded data that can be represented visually via a transcript, decisions about the technical issues of data collection and transcription are important aspects of the research process.

There are a number of issues to consider before, during, and after collecting oral assessment data, such as integrating data collection into the assessment process, reducing the potential intrusiveness of recording equipment and its possible effects on candidate and examiner performance, collecting enough data to ensure that a sufficient sample will be available for analysis, setting criteria for selecting a sample if it is unfeasible, difficult, or impossible to transcribe and/or use all the data collected, and deciding whether to collect only audiotaped data, only videotaped data, or both. The second section of this chapter explores issues related to data transcription, including becoming familiar with the actual notational conventions, learning the system and training others to use it, transcribing languages other than English, and transcribing nonverbal behaviour. Although transcription is, without a doubt, a tedious task, detailed, accurate transcriptions of taped interactions are critical for doing quality conversation analysis, since the transcripts along with the tapes become the data for the project. It may be tempting to produce a 'quick and dirty' transcript, but such a plan often backfires when later on a feature transcribed superficially, or not transcribed at all, emerges as an important factor in the analysis. Additionally, since a theory of interaction and of the world may be unconsciously implied by the way one designs and produces a transcript (Ochs 1979), care at this stage is crucial.

Data collection and selection

Introduction

It is axiomatic to say that a conversation analysis of interactional data cannot take place in the absence of carefully prepared transcripts, and reliable transcripts can only be produced if one has a quality record of the interaction from which to work. Up until very recently, tapes of oral examinations were collected for rating purposes only, so that such tapes could be rated at a later time, or compromises could be reached in the case of rater discrepancies. For these reasons, little attention was paid to audiotape *quality*: interactions may not have been completely recorded, with the beginnings and/or endings cut off; one might be able to make out the candidate's words, but not more than that. In other words, issues of completeness and hearability were not a primary concern.

With a new interest in collecting oral examination data for research and training purposes, in addition to the rating uses they may have, concerns about tape quality have emerged as important issues. A number of researchers working with oral test data have found that poor audiotape quality not only limited their analyses, but may have had a negative influence on raters themselves (see McNamara and Lumley 1997 on this last point). Fortunately, if one goes to the trouble of recording oral data at all (in terms of obtaining equipment, setting it up, and training examiners to use it), it requires only a modest additional effort to get the equipment and the recordings up to standard for the type of analysis this book advocates. However, we can anticipate some resistance to any changes in examination procedures, some of which are worth considering. Let's look at these in turn.

First, examiners may see no need to audiotape data at all if rating is done on the spot. However, it is unlikely that there are many large-scale examinations that do not tape data for later rating or other purposes.

A second more problematic objection might be that it is one thing to record examinations for later rating, but to record them for analysis is another matter. What if the examiners themselves fear that a more careful recording of the tapes will make it easier to put the spotlight on them and their actions? Actually, tape quality makes little difference here for noting gross violations of proper interview protocol.

Perhaps the examiners themselves will claim they have too much to worry about without the additional burden of having to collect taped data, much less quality taped data. However, if the test administrators make quality data collection part and parcel of the examination process, it will become a standard procedure. At a recent UCLES Senior Team Leader Conference, the UCLES staff informed the leaders that careful recording of tapes is now a *routine* part of the assessment process, that test validation is ongoing, and that recording is one aspect of that validation process.

A quite legitimate concern is that the candidates and the examiners will be negatively impacted by the presence of any recording equipment, whatever the purpose of having it might be. This issue applies to essentially any social science research that depends on some sort of observation of behaviour, and is a classic example of the 'observer's paradox' to which Labov (1972) refers. The problem comes down to the conflict between, on the one hand, needing data on how people behave when they are not conscious of being observed, and on the other, needing to use potentially intrusive means to gain access to such data. Fulcher (1996b) and Wylie (1993) both noted that their subjects reported feeling nervous in the presence of a video camera. However, because many oral examinations do videotape the assessments for a variety of purposes, Fulcher suggests that 'if recording equipment is to be used during the test, its position and proximity to the students must be considered carefully' (p. 32). And even though we can detail precisely how any recording was accomplished, we cannot, unfortunately, calculate the effects of recording on that interaction.

Yet, there is research which indicates that while the presence of recording equipment is a potential concern for its effect on interaction, the equipment invariably becomes a routinized element of the scene and does not interfere with the willingness to interview or be interviewed (Kendon 1979). Furthermore, participants in an interaction (except perhaps on the telephone) routinely orient their behaviour to observation by others, so it is really a question of whether the communicative behaviour in front of camera differs from behaviour without it (Goodwin 1981). It is commonly thought that after about five minutes, participants get used to the camera or tape recorder being there and forget about it. Also, if recording is a normal aspect of the assessment process, while perhaps distracting, it is, in fact, part of the interactive context.

Collecting audiotaped data

Now let's look at some suggestions for collecting quality audiotaped data.

The first suggestion is to consider carefully the location of recording equipment. The fact is, to get really high quality tapes, recording in a studio will always be superior to a regular classroom (Alderson, Clapham, and Wall 1995). Additionally, the use of external, lavaliere microphones is a way to guarantee quality recordings. While these are perhaps valid suggestions for recording tapes for training and standardization purposes, they are probably unfeasible for regular test administrations. The technical expertise and financial investment required, and the potential for intrusiveness of this artificial setting may make such a decision undesirable, if not impossible. So, assuming that studio recording is not possible, here are some other suggestions:

- Use a quiet room, one where the assessment will not be interrupted by other people, and where distracting noises such as airplane noise, street traffic, sirens, telephones, and the like will be minimized. It is a good idea to make test recordings beforehand to detect unwanted sources of noise.
- Arrange the candidates and equipment in ways that maximize hearability (for audiorecording) and visibility (for videotaping). Some examinations now dictate how candidates should be arranged. A face-to-face arrangement encourages interaction; a side-by-side configuration encourages attention to a third party or object (Goodwin 1981). The important point is to make sure the candidates are closest to the microphone, and equally so, since distance from the microphone seems to be a more important factor in tape quality than microphone quality (Goodwin 1981). Here are the directions for room set up for the Key English Test (UCLES 1997a, p. 6–7):

Before starting any speaking tests, examiners should try and arrange the furniture in the room in the most suitable way.
*A **non-intimidating atmosphere should be created.***

An ideal situation is a room containing a round table so that candidates and examiners can position themselves as in Diagram 1. The assessor should sit at a suitable distance from the table so that he/she can clearly hear the candidates and interlocutor, but far enough away so that it is obvious to the candidates that he/she will take no part in the interaction. The assessor should be able to see the candidates and be visible to them.

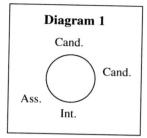

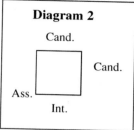

Sometimes, examiners will have to put long tables together or use a square one. Then, seating should be organised as in Diagram 2.

Candidates should be facing the interlocutor in Part 1, and facing each other in Part 2.

- Use a high quality tape recorder with prominent external microphones, or use multiple recorders, if necessary.
- Test all equipment before the assessments start and after any breaks.
- Don't put papers on top of or near the microphones; they muffle and interfere with the sound.
- Use high quality, longlasting audiotapes that will withstand repeated playing.
- Alert candidates in pre-materials that they may (or will) be taped as part of the assessment process. This lets candidates know beforehand that this will happen and why – they will not be surprised by the presence of audiotaping (and/or videotaping) equipment when they arrive at the examination.
- Be sure the tape recorder is turned on prior to the candidates coming in to the room and is not turned off until *after* they have left. This takes practice! Remember, the beginnings and endings of an interaction may be important, if not for rating, then for other analytic purposes.
- Remind candidates to speak up so they can be heard. Probably 25% of the oral assessment tapes I have listened to over the years have been unusable because candidates, particularly soft-spoken females, did not speak loudly enough to be recorded. This reminder to candidates has been made a regular part of a number of UCLES Speaking Tests.
- Record only one assessment per side of an audiotape. Not only does this make it easier to keep track of how many tapes and interactions there are (1 per side = 2 per tape), it is a frustrating waste of time to have to play through a side of a tape to find the beginning or some other part of another interaction.
- Label each tape clearly according to instructions. There is nothing more annoying than having tapes mismarked, or not marked at all. When one is dealing with large datasets that are taped and include score sheets and

other printed materials, the better the labeling system, the easier it will be to locate the appropriate material. Test administrators should come up with an easily understood and efficient system beforehand and make sure that examiners know how to follow the system.

- Once the assessments are complete, make copies of all tapes before doing anything else. This is crucial! Tapes have a way of getting misplaced, recorded over, etc. And using a high quality tape duplicator will ensure that copies are as good as the originals, which can be put away for safekeeping.

Collecting videotaped data

The earlier discussion of nonverbal behaviour in Chapter 2 reminds us of the additional philosophical (is videotaping more intrusive than audiotaping?), methodological (how will I deal with the data that I collect?), and technical issues (what kinds of things can go wrong with a videocamera?) that arise with videotaping. Nevertheless, there is widespread agreement that videotape is inherently superior to audiotape for analyzing face-to-face interaction. Interactions 'come alive' in a way that one cannot imagine if one has not been exposed to the audiotape of an interaction and then the videotape. Having access to the visual channel means that the nonverbal behaviour which occurs can heighten or contradict what is heard on the oral channel. It is easy to see who is saying what when there is more than one examiner and/or candidate; this is especially useful if there is more than one speaker of the same gender, and particularly if they are of the same L1. Finally, videotape provides a nice backup if the audiotaped data are unusable.

In addition to the suggestions made above about audiotaping, here are some additional considerations with videotaping:

- Generally, videocameras with built-in microphones will not pick up sound to the degree necessary for a microanalysis of the data – it will still probably be necessary to audiorecord the data as well.
- Consider the tape format used for recording, and be sure that it will be compatible with other videotape players that may be used (VHS, NTSC, PAL, Super 8, etc.).
- Be sure to instruct any camera operator about how to record the data. Since camera position itself has theoretical implications in terms of what is considered important in a scene (Goodwin 1981), decide beforehand where the cameras should be. The cameras should be turned on and run until the tape needs changing, since there is no way of knowing beforehand how much of what is recorded will be relevant or not. Don't allow the operator to 'get artistic' with camera angles or to decide when to turn the camera on or off.

Selecting data for transcription/analysis

It is unlikely that the researcher will be able, or even want, to transcribe all the data which are collected. For one, in a large scale test administration with hundreds of candidates, this kind of work will be too time consuming. Perhaps a subset of the tapes, based on some preset criteria of representation – gender, proficiency level, L1, etc. – can be selected. Another reason that all the data cannot be analyzed is that at least some of them will be unusable – this is a given. As was mentioned earlier, up to 25% of the tapes I have been asked to transcribe are cut off, too hard to hear, etc. Plan for this ahead of time!

Summary

Care taken at the data collection phase of conversation analysis will pay off when it comes to transcribing and analyzing the data. Institutionalizing data collection procedures ensures that both examiners and candidates are aware that data will be collected and for what purposes. A number of tips to consider before, during, and after collection of audiotaped data were proposed; a few additional suggestions were given for collecting videotaped data. A reminder was made that not all data collected may be amenable to transcription: there may be too much of them or they may not be of sufficient quality. Researchers are urged to plan for this sort of attrition before collecting the data.

It must be noted that this section has discussed data collection in terms of currently available and widely used technology for audiocassette tapes. However, vastly superior forms of technology are on the horizon and deserve brief mention here. The digital format is here to stay, which means that recordings can be made and stored in a format that will not deteriorate. DAT tapes and the recorders for them are widely available. Another option is to record on audio CD or minidisk.

Additionally, a 'wave file recording' can be produced using widely available software. The wave file can then be saved like any other computer file on hard disk, CD ROM, etc. A current UCLES project involves collecting an archive of performance from Speaking tests on traditional and contemporary media. Further research will be undertaken on this archive. Such research might include taking advantage of software functionality to mark sections of speaking test recordings and to store information related to duration of test sections in a database.

Data transcription

Once one has collected some data for analysis, the next step is to transcribe them using some sort of conventional notation. One such system is introduced in this section: the notational system of conversation analysis. Before turning to a description of the actual system, some background on the philosophy and goals of transcription, and the ways in which one can learn and teach the system, is necessary.

Understanding transcription philosophy

Discourse analysts generally agree that the act of transcription embodies one or more of the following characteristics: it is selective in nature, conventional by design, theoretically motivated, socially situated, and methodologically driven (P. Atkinson 1992; Edwards 1993; Fairclough 1992; Goodwin 1981, 1994; Green, Franquiz, and Dixon 1997; Gumperz 1992b; Mehan 1993; Ochs 1979; Roberts 1997).

Ochs (1979) is one of the most frequently cited sources on the situated nature of transcription. In her article 'Transcription as Theory', she points out a number of ways that bias creeps into the transcription process, discussing issues ranging from the privileged status of topmost and leftmost information, so that native-speaker, adult, verbal speech is prioritized over nonverbal behaviour or the speech of children, to some concrete suggestions for setting up less biased transcriptions.

Mehan's (1993) study of the referral process by which students are considered for placement in special education classes in California attempts to 'uncover the discursive and organizational arrangements that create descriptions of students as handicapped' (p. 245). Working within the sociological tradition of ethnomethodology, Mehan was interested in how social structure is constructed, and embodied in everyday interactional practices. Specifically, he was concerned with how 'texts', loosely construed, are derived from discourse generated in a different, prior setting: 'such texts, generated from a particular event in the sequential process (e.g., a testing encounter), become the basis of the interaction in the next step in the sequence (e.g., a placement committee meeting). These texts become divorced from the social interaction that created them as they moved through the system, institutionally isolated from the interaction practices that generated them in the preceding events' (p. 246). I hope that the parallel to discourse-based research on the oral assessment process is clear: the tape of an original assessment interaction is rated at a time and place divorced from its original context, and if it is transcribed and analyzed as well, it is even further removed from that context. Clearly, Mehan's study has direct bearing on the sort of work in which some language testers are engaged.

The 'politics of representation' that Mehan discusses is also of interest to Roberts (1997) and to Green, Franquiz, and Dixon (1997). These authors see transcription as a fundamentally *political* act that involves not just decisions about what to put down on the page, but how participants are represented, why, and towards what end. Although the obvious goal of transcription is 'fixing sound and vision on the page' (Roberts: 168), we are reminded that transcription is not only representational, it is also interpretive in that our values are shown in what we choose to transcribe. Transcripts are never ends in themselves: they are analytic tools produced within a research paradigm for particular purposes. The question then becomes, how do we ensure that readers are aware of these more ideological issues?

Roberts (p. 170) has several suggestions to help us remember 'that we are transcribing people when we transcribe talk:'

1. *Where appropriate, use standard orthography, even when the speaker is using nonstandard varieties to avoid stigmatization and to evoke the naturalness of their speech, and never use 'eye dialect.'[1]*

2. *Work as closely as possible with the informants to gain agreement on how they wish the features of their speech to be represented.*

3. *Think about some experimental ways in which speakers' voices can be conxtextualized/evoked, but do not underestimate the value of robust design principles for maintaining consistency and accuracy.*

4. *Use a layered approach to transcription, offering different versions and different levels – some relatively more ethnographic, some using fine-grained widely accepted transcription systems to give different readings.*

5. *Be more reflexive about the whole process of transcribing.*

Speaking about ethnographic transcription, P. Atkinson (1992) reminds us that 'transcripts of permanent recordings are not "literal renderings". ... There is no possibility of 'literal' and unmediated apperception and recording' (p. 16). Transcription is a process with decisions made each step of the way. He points out that there is no one best method of transcription and none is inherently more 'natural' than any other: all are what he calls 'conventional', meaning that using certain orthography and punctuation involves employing certain conventions to reconstruct and represent speech. Furthermore, we are reminded that 'the choice of conventions is thus a choice about the representation of persons as social and moral actors in the text' (p. 24).

But the problematicalness of transcription really occurs on a more basic level, that of hearing (Goodwin 1981). Hearing and understanding talk is problematic for participants in interaction, as is evidenced by the robustness of the repair system in English as it is deployed in various settings. Talk can and does occur under less than ideal conditions, and transcripts that are produced with background noise are even more difficult to transcribe. Because of this, we need to remember that different people may hear different things on a tape, and may then produce a different transcript from what we ourselves generate.

Understanding transcription goals

What are the goals of transcription? According to Psathas (1995: 11–12), transcription involves the use of an agreed upon system of symbolic notations for describing details of interaction to provide researcher and reader with sufficient information on what and how people were speaking when recorded. Comprehensive transcripts incorporate linguistic, paralinguistic, and nonverbal information (Jacoby and Ochs 1995) and capture as much of the actual sound and sequential positioning of the talk as possible (Atkinson and Heritage 1984). Sacks (1984) notes that 'the phenomena ... are always transcriptions of actual occurrences in their actual sequence' (p. 25). With P. Atkinson's (1992) point in mind about every system being both unnatural and conventional, the transcription system of conversation analysis (CA) tries to preserve some key features that organize the structure of talk-in-interaction, such as pauses, intonation, turn-taking, and the like. Obviously, the CA system is not exhaustive; it doesn't represent every possible feature of speech or interaction, nor does it claim to. In particular, it will probably not be suitable for those interested in the phonemic, prosodic, or intonational aspects of speech production, and has been criticized on these grounds (e.g., Cortazzi 1993). Sacks (1984) maintains that 'the tape-recorded materials constitute a "good enough" record of what happened. Other things, to be sure, happened, but at least what was on the tape had happened' (p. 26). Researchers are, of course, free to broaden the system by adding new symbols to their transcriptions if they find a feature of talk needs to be represented, but lacks a symbol. For example, Chervenak (1996), in her analysis of narrative speech by international teaching assistants, required symbols for representing pronunciation errors and reduced syllables while still using the basically alphabetic system of CA. She ended up enclosing +pronunciation errors+ and &reduced syllables& with additional symbols. Additionally, the researcher may find that some symbols in the system are too detailed for his or her purposes and will not use all the symbols available. Dubois (1991) details and exemplifies a number of useful principles for designing and adapting different transcription systems.

In fact, the major transcription systems of conversation analysis, discourse analysis, etc. are as much about features of speech as they are about the various intellectual commitments of these approaches. Unfortunately, not everyone engaged in discourse analysis uses the same system of transcription (just as with phonetic transcription, there are several systems to transcribe phonemes), and even more unfortunate is that very few writers even tell us which system was used to transcribe the data they present. Psathas (1995) warns us that 'the use of varying and inconsistent notation systems could possibly confuse ... and would not be conducive to the cumulations of findings concerning the same phenomena' (p. 12). Therefore, only one system, that of conversation analysis, is introduced here.

One of the most useful sources on this issue of transcription systems is Edwards and Lambert (1993), in which a number of researchers explain their own transcription and coding schemes. According to Edwards (1993), 'data accountability' is the primary issue in transcription: transcripts need to be true to the nature of the interaction, using conventions that are practical in terms of data management and analysis. Although the system that she proposes and the ones described by the other contributors in the volume deviate in important ways from the system which is described here, her discussion of the many practical decisions involved in transcription is well worth reading. Another interesting perspective is Haarman's (1998) comparative analysis of three transcription systems (conversation analysis, a discourse analysis transcription system, and a sociolinguistic transcription system), which shows how each system is uniquely suited to the analytic goals of researchers working within those areas. Schiffrin (1994) presents four discourse transcription systems in the appendix of her book.

Learning the conversation analysis transcription system

It is a fact that most people who learn the transcription system of conversation analysis do so by studying with researchers who are themselves trained in the system of producing and analyzing transcripts. I can only describe how I teach participants in my graduate seminars on discourse analysis, and how I was taught in similar classes on conversation analysis, to transcribe using this particular notation (but see Hopper, Koch, and Mandelbaum 1986 for suggestions on structuring a group listening activity that can be adapted for individuals).

First, we listen to a brief taped interaction several times without the transcript, pooling our observations. Then, the transcript is distributed and we read and continue to analyze the segment, noting what each of the transcription symbols means.

The next step is a homework assignment. I start out by assigning a transcription of a short excerpt, maybe a minute or so with which I am intimately familiar, through transcription and listening of my own. Students are to produce a transcript using the symbols; I point out that experienced transcribers usually take about one hour to produce a good transcript of five minutes of interaction, so they should not be spending hours on the assignment.

The students then submit these efforts and I mark my own hearing on their pages, suggesting that they go home and listen again with my comments in front of them. They are told from the beginning that we will all hear different things, but the point of the assignment is to try to hear what I have heard on the tape over many, many listenings.

In some respects, this procedure mirrored my own training (although I teach it on a much tighter schedule), where a group of us actually sat in a room, listening to and attempting to transcribe a short segment, over, and over, and over again. We then shared what we heard in order to come up with a transcript that we all agreed on (more or less). It was quite remarkable how our expectations, assumptions, and predictions about what was on the tape shaped our hearing; it was only through repeated listening, discussion, and then more listening that the passage would begin to make sense to me. How much listening is necessary? Hopper *et al.* (1986) suggest 'a) transcribe until things come into clear focus, and b) transcribe until you see things begin to recur over and over' (p. 177). According to Psathas and Anderson (1990: 77), the goal of listening/transcribing is to experience the interactional event as an actual occurrence; to be able to 'hear/see it in his/her head' where the mind becomes a 'replay machine'. While this may sound a little strange, I can attest that when I have listened to a tape enough times, I will be able to recall (and sometimes even reproduce) the speech in just the manner it was produced; I am also reminded of snippets on a tape from time to time when I hear someone use an expression or intonation pattern that was used on the familiar tape.

Two important implications of these anecdotes can be noted. First, it is difficult to learn the system of conversation analysis transcription alone, but if this becomes necessary, it is a good idea to have a transcriptionist experienced with the system check the resulting transcript. With the six or so research assistants that learned transcription from me, all of them had taken one or two of my classes where they had learned to do transcriptions. Even after this training, when the projects they worked on required transcription, I asked them to produce just one transcript initially, which I 'corrected' and used to point out features they needed to pay attention to. Moreover, all the transcripts they produced for the project were checked, for accuracy and for beginning to familiarize myself with the data, when they were finished and before I started any analyses of my own.

This leads to a second implication, which is that transcription is more than a product: it is a process which is inseparable from the conversation analytic endeavor. For this reason, it is generally not a good idea to hire professional transcribers to produce transcriptions, or to expect that secretaries will be able to produce transcripts with the necessary amount of detail in them. As Psathas and Anderson point out (1990: 91), what is needed to do conversation analytic transcription is 'training in the approach and procedures used by conversation analysts, engagement in the research and training process in order to experience repeated listenings/viewings, awareness of the analytic issues involved in the discovery of interactional phenomena, and the effort to produce a detailed transcript of some segment of interaction for oneself.'

Considering the mechanics of transcription

Selecting equipment

The most important piece of advice here is to use a transcriber, if possible. These inventive machines (also known as Dictaphones) have a foot pedal that controls the direction and speed of tape playback, which frees the hands to type or write notes. Sony and Panasonic both produce transcribers that cost about $200–500 US. Of course, it is always possible to use a regular tape player to play back, but this becomes very tedious and is actually quite inefficient because the hands are not free for typing when they are working the recorder. The same problem arises in transcribing from a CD or computer sound file: clicking the buttons which control playing the tape make typing at the same time impossible.

Selecting a typing font

Monospaced fonts, such as Courier, are best for preparing transcripts since they are easiest to align vertically on the page.

Setting up the page format

Here is a sample first page from a CAE (Certificate of Advanced English, UCLES 1997b) transcript:

```
(1) CAE [1]
Godmer House, Oxford [2]
November 1995 [3]
Bentley (148)/Carlson (624)[4]
Tape 1 (18:15) [5]
Candidates Farhad K. (5007) and Tomoko M. (5008) [6]
Transcribed by Erin Chervenak, January 1996 [7]
    1 [8]  IN1:[9]   (my) name's To:m, (.5) and this is my colleague, (.2)
    2             Laura (.2) [%she's (just) going to% (.) listen to you but
    3      IN2:    [hi:
    4--->IN1:    she might talk to you a bit later. (.5) and (.) YOUR names
    5             are?
    6             (.2)
    7      TM:    Tomoko.
    8             (.8)
    9      IN1:    Tomoko?
   10             (.5)
   11      FK:    my name is Farhad
```

Ordinarily, the top left of the first page of the transcript will identify the recording with relevant information, including at least the date and place of recording and the participants. Here, the examination is identified (1), the test site is recorded (2), and the administration date is given (3). The fourth line contains information about the examiners (4), with their names as well as their examiner numbers. Since Bentley is listed first, he is the interlocutor for the particular assessment. In the next line, the tape number is given as well as the length of the assessment (5). Although numbering tapes initially is usually arbitrary, once a tape becomes Tape 1, this is how it is subsequently identified.

The candidates are then listed, by name and by number (6). Obviously, care must be taken to preserve the anonymity of participants once data are made public (and may be required by human subjects protections laws at universities). Either pseudonyms (as are all examiner and candidate names in this book), initials (as shown above for the two candidates), or other identifying features (such as interviewer role as above for the two examiners) may be used to identify participants. It is worth noting, though, that in conversation analysis, at least, '... the mundane nature of most of the kinds of interactional phenomena studied hardly raises any issue concerning privacy. In addition, the fact that most researchers are concerned with interaction in its own right, rather than with the particular persons or places or institutions providing the data, serves to alleviate concerns about privacy' (Psathas 1995: 45). The transcriber might often identify herself and give the date the transcription is prepared (7); this is optional.

The actual set-up of the transcript, including margins, spacing, and alignment, may vary. Here, line numbers are printed down the left hand margin (8). At least four spaces are left between the line number and the speaker identification markers (9) so that arrows, as in line 4, will fit nicely. Note also that there are spaces between the identification markers and the actual speech.

Finally, it is worth pointing out what may seem obvious: that the talk is segmented into turns. In the fragment above, Interviewer 1 has two turns: one that is presented in lines 1, 2, 4, and 5, and the other in line 9. Interviewer 2 has one turn in line 3; the candidates have one turn each, in lines 7 and 11. Remember, turns begin and end at points of speaker transition.

Using the conversation analysis transcription system

Let's look at using the transcription system. Any number of books (e.g., Atkinson and Heritage 1984; Ochs, Schegloff, and Thompson 1996; Psathas 1995) explicate the system, using basically the same features; I have used these features but with examples from my dissertation data (Lazaraton 1991) to illustrate each. A list of symbols can be found in Appendix 2.

A point worth repeating is that not all symbols will necessarily be needed for producing a quality transcript. The transcriber is free to ignore certain symbols, or to create new symbols for features of importance. Nevertheless, the conventional CA thinking is that it is best to put in as much detail as possible in any transcript, for two reasons. First, one does not necessarily know when producing a transcript what research questions might be asked, and answered by the data. Therefore, transcribing as much detail as possible insures that the details will be there if they are needed. Secondly, others who may use these transcripts in the future may need those details; in fact, you yourself may need that amount of detail in some future project.

One more reminder: the transcript should represent speech *as it is produced, not as it is understood* (Zimmerman 1988); don't correct it in any way! This reminder is particularly relevant for transcribing the contributions of nonnative speakers in interaction, which may contain phonological, lexical, and syntactic errors.

A. Pausing

A great deal of research has shown that silence has import for interaction (see, for instance, the chapters in Tannen and Saville-Troike 1985, and Jefferson's 1989 empirical study of silence, which suggests a 'standard maximum' silence of one second in conversation). For example, in my dissertation data, interviewer silence following student assessments of language ability showed, and helped to accomplish, interviewer objectivity in the assessment process. Since participants in interaction *can*, and *do*, produce talk with no hearable silence between turns or as 'latched utterances' (Feature 13 below), silence takes on meaning, particularly a negative meaning, that projects some sort of interactional trouble. Therefore, properly transcribing silences is important, especially for studies of turn-taking and speaker transition. However, the CA transcription system does not strive for some sort of scientific measurement that one would achieve by use of a stopwatch or a metronome; rather, the transcriber aims for internal consistency within a transcript or a dataset, so that a sort of ordinal scale of silence emerges which is internally consistent. In other words, it is the difference between silences of a half a second (.5) versus one second (1.0) that is significant, not whether the half second is really four tenths of a second. It is important to remember that silence lengths cannot, and should not, be compared across different transcriptionists, since we cannot be sure if their personal measurement systems are really the same. Finally, we need to remember that verbal silence does not mean that nothing else of importance is going on at the point – videotape always shows that there is.

1. *Periods of silence* are timed in tenths of a second by counting 'beats' of elapsed time. A convenient method to use is the 'no-one-thou-sand' rule, where each of the four beats in the expression represents about a quarter of a second. So, if during the silence you can say 'no', transcribe (.2); 'no one' (.5), 'no one thou' (.8), and 'no one thousand' as (1.0). Silences appear as a time within parentheses: (.5) or (0.5) is five tenths of a second. For silences over one second, use 'one one thousand', 'two one thousand', etc. Look at the four transcribed silences shown in the fragment below (each feature being explained is shown in bold type):

   (2) CA: uh: I came he:re **(.5)** uh:: **(1.0)** uh:::: nineteen eighty
           ni:ne summer. **(.)** a:nd **(.5)** still I have been here...

'Micropauses', silences of less than (.2) seconds (in other words, those that are less than the 'one' in the 'no-one-thou-sand' counting method) are symbolized (.), as in line 2 above.

One issue that vexes transcribers is how to display silences which appear *between* turns: who 'owns' the silence? This brings up the distinction between a 'pause' and a 'gap', two technical terms that CA employs. If the turn is not yet hearably complete, either syntactically, intonationally, or pragmatically, the silence is considered within-turn and is called a pause. Pauses occur as the first, second, and fourth silence points in fragment (2) above. However, the third silence, the micropause (.) in line 2, occurs after a possibly complete turn unit and is a gap which could be transcribed as shown below:

   (3) CA: uh: I came he:re (.5) uh:: (1.0) uh:::: nineteen eighty
           ni:ne summer.
           (.)
       CA: a:nd (.5) still I have been here...

This shows that this micropause is a *possible* point of speaker transition at the end of the CA's first turn, although the interviewer does not take a turn here. There is no one 'right' way to transcribe a case like this; either works, although the second system will take up much more space on the page.

What *would* be incorrect would be to put a silence at the end of a turn where speaker transition is relevant:

```
(4) CA: I:'m the student in: TESL program (.5)
    IN: you a:re.
```

This is incorrect because CA's turn is a possibly complete TCU, and the silence therefore does not 'belong' to her; the gap, as it is called, should be on its own line:

```
(5) CA: I:'m the student in: TESL program
        (.5)
    IN: you a:re.
```

Don't confuse end of *turn* gaps with end of *line* pauses – remember that the physical layout of the page may force one to place a silence at the end of a line:

```
(6) CA: I just .hhh went in front of the class n then .hhh (.8)
    do: impromptu speech
```

Finally, it should be noted that other transcription systems may use a combination of + signs and/or dashes to show silences, or, if the transcription is very rough, pauses may be shown as untimed:

```
(7) CA: I just .hhh went in front of the class n then .hhh ((pause))
    do: impromptu speech
```

B. Features of speech production

Although even a rough transcription can show what was said, only a detailed system such as CA notation can indicate how something was said. A rough transcript may represent the word 'okay' just as 'okay', using standard orthography. However, this will mask the different ways that 'Okay' can be said: 'O::ka::y', 'Okay?', 'Okay!', each of which has potentially different meanings. Therefore, it is important to transcribe the features of speech production that may figure centrally in any analysis.

2. A *colon (:)* represents a lengthened sound or syllable; more colons prolong the stretch. One can use the 'no-one-thou-sand' system to transcribe multiple colons, if necessary. Whereas the vowel in line 5 below gets lengthened only a little, the vowel in line 3 gets elongated a great deal more:

```
(8) CA: I (.5) transfer to UCLA two years ago .hhh (so) altogether
        .hhh I have been in this country for six yea:rs
    IN: o:::h
        (.5)
    IN: wo:w.
```

Be careful not to confuse colons with spaces inserted in words in order to fill an overlap or align text: this formatting convention says nothing about how the word was pronounced:

```
(9) IN: wutz yr last name?=
    CA: =Marietti [M.  A.  R.  I.  E.        ] TT I
    IN:           [%marieti% yeah no problem.]
```

Here the letters of the candidate's name were spread out in the overlap space so that it would appear balanced with the interviewer's overlapping turn.

3. *A dash (–)* shows a cut-off of the prior sound or word, often a self-interruption; its termination is noticeable and abrupt:

```
(10)    IN: are you thinking about thirty four then for— as a
            course or—
```

4. *Inward arrows (> <)* indicate that the talk speeds up, is compressed, or is rushed; *outward arrows (< >)* show the talk slows down, is spaced out, or said slowly:

```
(11)    IN: uh:- (.) in: the:se particular cla:sses (.) <I think it's
            like fi:ftee:n or tw:e::nty maximum.>
```

```
(12)    IN: why don't you tell me something about yourself like
            country of origi:n la:nguage uh pro:gram you're in: an: (.)
            >things like that<.
```

5. *Underlining* or *CAPS* denotes a word or SOund is emphasized or spoken more loudly. Some systems may use italics for this purpose.

```
(13)    IN: uh:- (.) in: the:se particular cla:sses (.) <I think it's
            like fi:ftee:n or tw:e::nty maximum.>
```

```
(14)    IN: uh:- (.) in: THE:se particular cla:sses (.) <I think it's
            like fi:ftee:n or tw:e::nty MAXimum.>
```

6. *Per cent signs (% %)* represent quiet talk. Degree signs may also be used for this purpose:

```
(15)    IN: mbye
        CA: %bye%
```

```
(16)    IN: mbye
        CA: °bye°
```

7. *A psk* indicates a lip smack; *tch*, a tongue click:

```
(17)    IN: psk! (m)- wu- where are you from.

(18)    IN: tch! alright .hhh wu-  u- is: what is: your native
            la:nguage.
```

C. Features of aspiration

The letter 'h', alone or in multiples, is used to represent inhalation, exhalation, and laughter. While transcribing these finer details of speech production may seem pointless, it should be remembered that inhaling and exhaling have implications for speaker transition: in-breaths in particular can indicate that someone is beginning to speak; exhalation may indicate holding a turn or the end of a turn. Finer transcriptions may use one, two, four, or more or 'h's to accurately represent the sound produced, but I use three 'hhh's all the time:

8. *A .hhh* shows an inbreath; *.hhh!* represents strong inhalation:

```
(19)    IN: .hhh u:m ((sniff out)) (.8) are you pla:nning to be a
            teaching assistant at any point?
```

9. hhh shows exhalation; hhh! represents strong exhalation:

```
(20)    IN: because yur la:nguage is really (.) not (.) the problem
        CA: hhh! t(hhh!)hank y(hhh)ou
```

10. *(hhh)* indicates breathiness within a word:

```
(21)    IN: because yur la:nguage is really (.) not (.) the problem
        CA: hhh! t(hhh!)hank y(hhh)ou
```

11. *hah, huh, heh, hnh* all represent 'laugh particles' (Jefferson 1985), and are used depending on the sounds produced. All can be followed by an (!), signifying stronger laughter:

```
(22)    IN: I'm sure that you- (.) got something out of it
        CA: hhh! huh! heh! [I don't know] huh! huh! .huh!
        IN:              [heh!     huh!]
```

Some rough transcriptions may just use ((laugh)):

```
(23)    IN: I'm sure that you- (.) got something out of it
        CA: ((laugh)) [I don't know] ((laugh))
        IN:           [ ((laugh))   ]
```

D. Features of intonation

12. *Traditional punctuation marks* are used to indicate intonation. They do not show clausal structure and should not be taken to indicate syntactic or grammatical forms like sentences or questions.

a) *A period (.)* represents falling intonation, and may or may not signal the end of a sentence:

```
(24)    CA:   uh: I came he:re (.5) uh:: (1.0) uh::::: nineteen eighty
              ni:ne summer.
```

b) *A question mark (?)* indicates rising intonation, and may or may not signal an actual question:

```
(25)    IN:   .hhh u:m ((sniff out)) (.8) are you pla:nning to be a
              teaching assistant at any point?
```

c) *An exclamation mark (!)* shows animated talk:

```
(26)    CA:   I'm too shy to [try it
        IN:                  [n(hh)o no! no! no! no! no!
```

Finer transcriptions may also use a question mark followed by a comma (?,) to represent rising intonation which is weaker than that shown by a (?), and a comma (,) to show continuing intonation.

d) To show a marked rising shift in pitch on a word or sound, a carat (^) (or sometimes an arrow, (⇧) is used:

```
(27)    CA:   ...I:'m .hhh in my fourth ye:ar n expecting to graduate
              this su:mmer.
              (.2)
        IN:   ^o::h, uh huh? oh good
```

E. Turntaking

One of the features that all CA transcripts share is a careful representation of the features of turntaking. This means showing timed silences between utterances as well as utterances which overlap or latch. I personally find this the most frustrating and difficult mechanism to transcribe – it often seems to me that each time I listen to a tape I hear something slightly different in terms of overlap and latching. On the positive side, unless one's analysis depends crucially on some feature of turntaking, we do the best we can with these features. (And, many transcripts I have seen do not even attempt to show turntaking behaviour – they represent talk as if the exchange of turns is neat and orderly with no gaps, latches, or overlap!)

13. *An equal sign (=)* denotes a latched utterance, with no interval between utterances:

    (28)   IN: wutz yr last name?=
                CA: =Marietti

14. *Brackets ([ ])* show overlapping talk, where utterances start and/or end simultaneously. Left brackets show the start of an overlap – sometimes this is all that is transcribed:

    (29)   CA: I'm too <u>shy</u> to [try it
                IN: [n(hh)o no! no! no! no! no!

Right brackets show the end of an overlap:

    (30)   IN: wutz yr last name?=
                CA: =Marietti [M. A. R. I. E.   ] TT I
                IN: [%Mari<u>eti</u>% yeah no problem.]

F. Transcriptionist conventions

15. *Capitalization:* generally speaking, CA transcripts use capital letters for proper nouns like names, the first letter of the first word in the sentence, and the like. Some transcribers eschew this and allow capitals to stand only for increased volume.

16. *The arrow (--->)* shows a feature of interest to the analyst:

    (31)--->CA: I would like to have some more (funny) (.) stuff

17. Words within *empty parentheses ( )* are doubtful or uncertain. Empty parentheses mean that no reliable hearing could be made for talk at that point:

    (32)   CA: I would like to have some more **(funny)** (.) stuff

    (33)   CA: I would like to have some more (   ) (.) stuff

Sometimes alternative hearings are shown:

    (34)   IN: <u>this</u> is your– <u>this</u> is your [last name
                CA: [**(oh right there/uh huh)**

This notation can indicate disagreement or possible hearings by co-transcribers or double hearings by one transcriber.

18. *Double parentheses* (( )) give a description of non-vocal action, or details of scene, such as coughs, snorts, sniffles, telephone rings, throat clearing, etc.:

```
(35)   CA: yeah(hh). .hhh [n (.)       ] so (.) that's why I take
                           [((feedback))]
             this course.

(36)   IN: ((sniff)) .hhh a:nd uh what's your ma:jor?

(37)   IN: .hhh u:m ((sniff out)) (.8) are you pla:nning to be a
           teaching assistant at any point?

(38)   IN: you certainly don't sou:nd like you've only been here
           a wee:k [you sound
       CA:         [((snort)) hhh huh!

(39)   IN: okay so [hello
       CA:         [((clears throat))
```

19. *Ellipsis* ... indicates that part of a turn has been omitted:

```
(40)   CA: ... I:'m .hhh in my fourth ye:ar n expecting to graduate
           this su:mmer.
```

Vertical ellipsis shows that some intervening turns have been omitted:

```
(41)   IN: a:nd um: (.5) tell me som— (.2) where are you fro:m n
           what's your native language

       .
       .   ((5 pages of transcript))
       .

       IN: that's good. hhh do you have any questions for me?
```

20. *Numbering of lines:* Line numbering is done for convenience or reference, and should NOT be used as measures of timing, number of turns, number of utterances, etc. It is recommended that every line, including silences, be numbered. Look at the examples below:

```
(42)   1 CA: I (.5) transfer to UCLA two years ago .hhh (so)
              altogether .hhh I have been in this country for six
              yea:rs
       2 IN: o:::h
              (.5)
       3 IN: wo:w.
```

With this sort of numbering, it is more difficult to locate and describe features that occur in CA's first turn. For example, if I want to talk about inbreaths, I can distinguish between the first and second in the first two lines, but this gets much more difficult in longer turns of many lines (as in a monologue, for example). For this reason, the numbering system below is preferred:

```
(43)   1 CA:  I (.5) transfer to UCLA two years ago .hhh (so) altogether.
       2      .hhh I have been in this country for six yea:rs
       3 IN:  o:::h
       4      (.5)
       5 IN:  wo:w.
```

Finally, it is usually best to number lines continuously throughout the pages of a transcript, but sometimes the numbering is done page by page. If the latter is chosen, one will need to indicate which page the line comes from, since each page will have a line 1, 5, etc.

To conclude, it should be noted that there are other transcription symbols that have not been described here, simply because I have not used them very often. For example, there are more detailed ways of transcribing pitch – see Psathas (1995: 75) or Ochs, Schegloff, and Thompson (1996: 464). For an explanation of transcribing applause, see Atkinson and Heritage (1984: xv–xvi).

Transcribing languages other than English

A number of thorny issues arise with respect to analyzing data from languages other than English. Primarily, the lack of baseline data in other languages makes it difficult to make sense of findings that are compared with English. This paucity of cross-linguistic information on various interactional features was noted by Egbert (1998), who despaired that in order do a proper conversation analysis of the feature of repair in her German as a second language assessment data, she would need, among other things, a) benchmark data on repair in conversational English and in conversational German, b) data on repair in other interview settings with which to compare language interview data, and c) data on repair between native speakers and nonnative speakers of German. These data as of today do not exist, in German or any other language besides English, so cross-linguistic comparisons are severely limited.

More to the issue at hand is how to represent data from other languages. The simplest way, especially for a language like Spanish, is used by Koike (1998), who presents all her data in Spanish in her paper and the translation into English in an appendix.

If one chooses to present the languages simultaneously, several options exist. One format is to present the English translation in italics in the next line:

```
(44)   (1)   Other-initiated repair by native speakers of German
             (from Egbert 1998: 153)

    1   H:  boh äj der Stu:hl hat aber gelitten.
            wow the cha:ir has suffered.
    2       (1.0)
    3--->M: welcher.
            which.
    4   H:  dieser hier
            this one here
```

Another option is to use a three line format – the first line in the other language, the second a direct translation, and the third the everyday expression in English. An explanation is usually included in an appendix or glossary of the direct translation terminology. This technique is used by Sorjonen (1996) for Finnish; Fox, Hayashi, and Jasperson (1996) for Japanese; and Kim and Suh (1998) for Korean. Here is an example from Kim and Suh (1998: 323):

```
(45)   (13) From the interview with LN, a low-intermediate speaker

    1   IR: chohaha—nun cakka iss    —eyo?
            like    —ATTR writer exist—POL
            Do you have any favorite writer?
    2   NNS:cakka?
            writer
            cakka (writer)?
    3   IR: ney. writer
            yes writer
            Yes. Writer
    4       (0.8)
    5   NNS:eng (.) cikum eps    —eyo.
            filler now not:exist—POL
            Uh, I don't have any for now.
```

A more complicated format was employed by Egbert (1997: 39), who illustrated how 'schisming' occurs in German conversation. Her task then became showing both the German and English glosses as well as the two tracks of the conversation; other examples in the article show how nonverbal behaviour can be encoded as well:

```
(46)   #7 German original [FAC-anna? kaffee?]

    1   Mata: =der hat grad inge
    2         gesacht          Bea:    anna? kaffee?
    3         (0.5)            Anna:   ja bi=
    4   Inge: der sacht                =tte:
    5         momentan...


       #7 English translation [FAC-anna? kaffee?]

    1   Mata: =he just said
    2         inge             Bea:    anna? coffee?
    3         (0.5)            Anna:   yes pl=
    4   Inge: he says                  =ea:se
    5         at the moment...
```

In any case, if the readership of the material in another language is only conversant with English, which is almost always the case, a translation will have to be provided; any of these three methods is acceptable.

Transcribing nonverbal behaviour

We have already discussed the importance, and the difficulty, of collecting and analyzing data on nonverbal behaviour. Technical issues aside, transcribing even small segments of nonverbal behaviour can be time consuming and unwieldy. Unfortunately, technology does not offer any solutions to this problem as of yet, and it is not logistically possible to include videotapes or diskettes with research reports. As a result, researchers (including myself) who collect videotaped data usually give it a careful, but in no way systematic, examination.

Nevertheless, if one chooses to describe nonverbal behaviour, different representations are possible. Probably the most common method is what is known as a 'second-line' transcript, where the nonverbal behaviour is set off (by italics, parentheses, etc.) from the verbal channel:

```
(47)    (5) RO LAB (1-3) (from Ochs, Gonzales, and Jacoby 1996: 338)

     Ron:[If this were a first order [pha:se transition, (0.2)
          [((moves to board; points to diagram)
                                       [((looks at Miguel))
     Miguel: Mm hm?
     Ron:    [Then that means.    [that- that- this system has no
             [((looks at board))  [((Miguel looks at board))
             knowledge of [tha:t system.
                          [((looks at Miguel))


(48)    (ID 28) (from Dore and Dorval 1990: 85)

     T:   Really? (pronounced intonation, contorted look)
          (.3)
     R:   That's 'is name. I jus thought of that right now.
          (smiling, looking off, enthused staccato)
          (4.4, Richard's smile fades, he exhales, eyes begin moving)
```

There are also transcription symbols for nonverbal behaviour, attributed to Charles Goodwin (1981) and used by others working within the CA framework (e.g., Heath 1984; Maynard and Marlaire 1992; Schegloff 1984a). The following fragment from Goodwin (1984: 230) shows how gaze can be represented:

```
(49)    X= point where gaze reaches the other
        ...transition from nongaze to gaze
        _____gaze at the other
        Beth is the speaker, her gaze is above
        Don is the listener, his gaze is below

     Beth:     [X _____
           Terry-[Jerry's fa[scinated with elephants
     Don:      [. . . . . [X_____
```

Or, here is some notation (Schegloff 1984a: 294) for showing gesture:

```
(50)    o=onset of movement that ends up as a gesture
        c=body part 'cocked' or 'poised' for release of gesture
        t=thrust or peak of energy animating gesture
        ...=extension in time of previously marked action

     #11 (Auto Discussion)

                      o.........................
        Mike:   ...settin there en 'e takes iz helmet

        c......t...
        off 'n clunk it goes on top a' the car
```

Other methods that have been used are diagrams showing participant position and gaze (Egbert 1997); drawings (McIlvenny 1995; Tannen 1990); and reprints (Maynard and Marlaire 1992) or tracings (Goodwin 1981) of video frames.

Summary

It is worth remembering that the transcripts we produce are an analytic tool, a 'post-seeing/hearing depiction' (Anderson and Psathas 1990). Transcripts are written discretely, organized serially, and read line by line. They can be read in ways that are not like the original data source tape, no matter how good the transcription is. As Anderson and Psathas conclude, the transcript is 'subject to all the vagaries of interpretation which a reader may choose to bring to the reading, despite what the transcriber/analyst offers as the "the way" to interpret the transcript. It reveals the extent to which we are limited in our understanding/comprehension of lived interaction, occurring in real time, by the necessities of representing and transforming that interaction for purposes of analysis, record keeping, and presentation' (pp. 90–91).

Conclusion

Since these methodological steps, collecting quality data and transcribing them carefully, are so much part of the discourse analytic process, it is unfortunate that most of the published empirical studies of test discourse and interaction have failed to describe the procedures that were used to collect and transcribe the data presented. This is perhaps exacerbated by publications that are short on space and view this information as 'obvious' or 'extra'. It would be useful to have this information since the counterparts of reliability and validity in qualitative research in general are 'credibility' and 'transferability' (Davis 1992; Johnson and Saville-Troike 1992); a 'thick description' of data collection and transcription procedures would allow us to make more informed judgments about these matters.

Notes

1. 'Eye dialect' refers to transcribing words as they sound: 'gonna', 'wuz yer name', and the like, a practice which conversation analysts generally use. See also Schiffrin (1994) on this matter.

4 Data analysis and presentation

- Reflecting on six methodological issues

  - Real, recorded data
  - Unmotivated looking
  - Units of analysis
  - Single cases, collections, and deviant cases
  - Sociological variables
  - Coding and quantifying data

- Working with interactive data

  - Five 'analytic tools'
  - A worked example

- Working with monologic data

  - Rhetorical analysis
  - Functional analysis
  - Structural analysis

- Presenting data and reporting results

  - Rationale
  - Guidelines for presenting data
  - A research report format
  - Guidelines for evaluating other studies
  - Conclusion

- Practice problems

The last chapter covered the first steps in qualitative discourse analysis, namely, how to collect and transcribe data. The separation of data transcription from data analysis is somewhat artificial, since the analyst is apt to notice and to begin characterizing interesting features while transcribing. In fact, one of the hallmarks of qualitative research in general is the recognition that every stage of the research process is both connected and interpretive (Riggenbach 1999). Yet, there are times when one analyzes data that one neither collected nor transcribed, or when the analysis takes place long after the transcription is completed. This chapter presents a rationale for the conversation analytic method of data analysis. A number of methodological issues with which the conversation analyst grapples are discussed; it will be up to each reader to determine whether these decisions are consistent with the variety of research goals that oral test validation encompasses. Then, actual data analysis procedures are demonstrated with both interactive and monologic oral test data. A number of analytic 'tools' and suggestions are detailed to guide the data analysis process. Finally, some relevant issues about and suggestions for data presentation, reporting results, and writing reports are addressed.

Reflecting on six methodological issues

In order to contextualize the actual data analytic techniques presented later in this chapter, six important analytic decisions which are customarily made by the conversation analyst are discussed first. These decisions include:

1 using authentic, recorded data;
2 using 'unmotivated looking' rather than pre-stated research questions;
3 employing the 'turn' as the unit of analysis;
4 analyzing single cases, deviant cases, and collections thereof;
5 disregarding ethnographic and demographic particulars of the context and participants;
6 eschewing the coding and quantification of data.

Real, recorded data

Conversation analysts insist on the use of real, recorded data. As Jacobs (1990: 247) puts it, 'taping is a comprehensive and impartial process' that does not rely on memory (as with field notes), intuitions (as with verbal reports), or interpretations (as with idealized or invented examples). Psathas (1995: 47) states that 'recalled or imagined instances are not admissible as proof or support or corroboration of claims about the actual phenomena. Rather, only repeated instances of demonstrably similar empirical instances are admissible, provided they are also available in recorded form.'

Also excluded are reports from interactants about what they 'meant', since there is no proof that this kind of knowledge is conscious or available for analysis (Pomerantz 1990). As Wootton (1989: 253) explains, 'uncovering the interactional significance that people attach to moves in conversation is complicated ... excavating the implicit analysis which parties in interaction make of each other's talk is then a technical task: one which, for example, though it does not preclude consulting with people about what they think they are doing, has to be grounded in close exploration, analysis, and documentation from the behavioral details of the exchange in question.'

Finally, the conversation analyst asserts that only interactions which would have occurred even if someone had not been there to record them are useful for analysis. This means that interactions that emerge from experimental situations are not suitable for study.

Unmotivated looking

In general, CA researchers do not posit explicit research questions before collecting data. Rather, they attempt 'unmotivated looking'; consider Harvey Sack's (1984) comments on this approach:

> *Now people often ask me why I choose the particular data I choose. Is it some problem that I have in mind that caused me to pick this corpus or this segment? And I am insistent that I just happened to have it, it became fascinating, and I spent some time at it. Furthermore, it is not that I attack any piece of data I happen to have according to some problems I bring to it. When we start out with a piece of data, the question of what we are going to end up with, what kind of findings it will give, should not be a consideration. We sit down with a piece of data, make a bunch of observations, and see where they will go.*
>
> *Treating some actual conversation in an unmotivated way, that is, giving some consideration to whatever can be found in any particular conversation we happen to have our hands on, subjecting it to investigation in any direction that can be produced from it, can have strong payoffs. Recurrently, what stands as a solution to some problem emerges from unmotivated examination of some piece of data, where, had we started out with a specific interest in the problem, it would not have been supposed in the first instance that this piece of data was a resource with which to consider, and come up with a solution for, that particular problem.*
>
> *Thus, there can be some real gains in trying to fit what we can hope to do to anything that happens to come up. I mean not merely that if we pick any data we will find something, but that if we pick any data, without bringing any problems to it, we will find something. And how interesting what we may come up with will be is something we cannot in the first instance say.*
>
> (p. 27)

However, while the interactional phenomena and characterizations of them that emerge from CA are not based on 'preformulated theorizing' (Psathas 1995: 45), this is not to say that we must (or that we can) approach our data with no preconceived notions whatsoever. Much of my own work on spoken interaction is based on the broad analytic categories CA postulates (sequence structure, repair, etc.), but these 'components' of interaction generally emerge from the total reality of the data as my work progresses. Often, I make an informed guess, based on the relevant literature that I have read, the empirical studies conducted by others, or my own prior experiences with similar data, about which interactional features might be particularly interesting to study. For example, in my dissertation (Lazaraton 1991), I hypothesized that three organizational systems of conversation, namely, sequence structure, turntaking, and repair, would surely be worth analyzing in the oral interview data I had collected. Yet, during the long, involved transcription process and some initial analyses, I became aware of other phenomena that I could not have known about before undertaking an in-depth, continuous examination of my materials. For example, the findings on ability assessments (where candidates talk negatively about their language ability) reflect a practice that I discovered only after I had begun to transcribe and analyze the data. On the other hand, the system of repair, and to a lesser extent, that of turntaking, turned out to be less analytically fruitful than I had originally expected. This is not to say that the turntaking and repair in these oral interviews was 'uninteresting', only that they did not seem to 'pan out' as I originally hoped they might. Likewise, an interactional practice that I had never planned to study (namely, interviewer question design which is responsive to student trouble) turned out to be a rewarding phenomenon to examine and this feature warranted a whole chapter in the thesis.

The basic advice is: try to keep your preconceptions about what will be found, important, etc. to a minimum. Let the data drive your questions, rather than the reverse.

Units of analysis

A fundamental decision that needs to be made in order to undertake any sort of discourse analysis of some text is what the 'unit of analysis' for the study will be. It was mentioned in previous chapters that the primary focus of CA is *social action*, as encoded in *turns* that constitute *adjacency pair sequences*. We can define a turn as the primary organizational unit of interaction, composed of one or more *turn constructional units* (TCUs) (Schegloff 1996). Furthermore, each TCU must exhibit features of syntactic, intonational, and pragmatic completion (Ford and Thompson 1996; Heritage and Roth 1995). Still, it is worth considering briefly some other analytic units that are used in oral language analysis and that reflect different research goals.

A number of analytic units considered potentially appropriate for oral discourse analysis in applied linguistics are reviewed by Crookes (1990), including a) sentences, b) t-units and their variations, c) communication units, d) idea units, e) tone units, f) utterances, and g) turns. The *sentence*, a grammatical unit based on writing, is rejected by Crookes as a possibility since it has not been developed, or described, for speech. The *t-unit*, and variations of it, stem from Hunt's definition (cited in Crookes p. 184) as 'one independent clause plus any number of subordinate clauses that are attached to or embedded in it.' So, clauses connected with coordinators like 'and' are considered two t-units (I like baseball and she likes basketball), while (I like baseball although she doesn't) consists of one t-unit, where 'although she doesn't' is embedded in the main clause. The *communication unit*, or c-unit (Loban 1966, cited in Crookes, p. 184), allows for incomplete grammatical clauses that carry meaning to be coded as well (such as 'no thanks', 'over there'). Crookes also describes the *idea unit* (Kroll 1977 cited in Crookes p. 184), which is 'a chunk of information which is viewed by the speaker writer cohesively as it is given a surface form ... related to psychological reality for the encoder.' While t-units, c-units, and idea units have been fruitfully employed in any number of applied linguistic studies (e.g., Campbell 1990; Duff 1986; Yoshida-Morise 1998; Young and Halleck 1998), their primary focus on form rather than interaction make them unsuitable for the type of discourse analysis being proposed here.

A completely different unit of analysis derives from work on the grammatical nature of spoken L1 English, the *tone unit*, the basic prosodic unit in speech. Tone units are identified by pitch prominence, intonation, pausing, and phonetic modifications to produced speech.

Crookes then describes the *utterance*, the unit that he prefers, as 'a stream of speech with at least one of the following characteristics: (1) under one intonation contour, (2) bounded by pauses, and (3) constituting a single semantic unit' (p. 187). Finally, Crookes describes the *turn* as 'one or more streams of speech bounded by speech of another, usually an interlocutor' (p. 185).

Crookes proceeds to show how these units are related to one another and to evaluate each unit based on its reliability and validity. In other words, problems may arise if units are not identified correctly (an issue of reliability) or if the units chosen don't reflect the relevant processes under investigation (whether they be psychological, socio-interactional, or whatever). On these grounds, Crookes rejects the tone unit as tenable on grounds of reliability – even trained linguists do not always agree on the segmentation of text into such units (see also Schiffrin 1994 on difficulties that may be encountered in trying to identify other structural constituents of a text). As for the validity of the seven units described, he contends that 'In general, structural investigations of SL [second language] discourse are concerned with the results of psychological processes of language production ... the demand for instrument validity is particularly served if the basic unit of a discourse analysis system corresponds to, or directly reflects such processes' (p. 191). On these grounds, he rejects the turn as utile, since it is based on social–interactional, rather than psychological processes; in addition, it is a meaningless unit for monologic speech. He concludes that the utterance (defined as per above) is the unit best suited to his particular endeavors. Interestingly, Schiffrin (1994) also adopts the utterance as the most appropriate segment for discourse analysis, but her definition is much broader than Crookes': utterances are 'units of language production (whether spoken or written) that are inherently contextualized' (p. 41) and that are constructed to meet sequential, semantic, and pragmatic goals in actual communication. In fact, the terms 'utterance' and 'turn' are sometimes used interchangeably, but Linnell and Markova (1993) believe that the utterance should be reserved for sentence- or clause-based structures, rather than interactional ones.

Schiffrin (1987) also reviews these and other analytic units, but comes to the conclusion that all such units are inherently problematic: 'deciding which discourse unit to study, how to define that unit, and how to select data are often tasks which do not receive much guidance from previous analyses ... because of the vast and ambiguous nature of discourse analysis' (p. 48). Schiffrin doesn't see this situation as necessarily negative, since discourse analysis assumes 'reciprocal relationships ... among theory, analysis, and data' (p. 48). That is, the data we are analyzing, the theoretical framework in which we are working, and the analytic goals and techniques we are using make it difficult to decide a priori which of these units is most appropriate in any given context.

Thus, while other units of analysis have been and can be usefully employed in analyses of discourse, we will continue to use the turn, composed of at least one turn-constructional unit, as the basic building block of adjacency pair sequences which encode social actions.

Single cases, collections, and deviant cases

Conversation analysis is a method that looks at 'instances', or 'occurrences', as the focus of analysis. These instances, though, are not samples in the statistical sense – they just happened to occur in the data under investigation. In fact, in looking at data, the analyst tries to approach the data with as few preconceptions – about what 'should' be there – as possible. CA uses an analytic induction approach, a methodology which claims 'no standard research designs, no widely accepted criteria for validity or observation, no body of principled or practical wisdom to guide selection of cases' but which is a powerful 'way of generating arguments about empirical claims rather than a set of procedural guarantors of truth' (Jackson 1986: 133).

Once an interesting 'instance' is found, the analyst, using these analytic induction procedures and 'more or less conceptually informed "hunches" about the uses and organizational properties of particular conversational practices' (Heritage 1995: 399), works to discover the 'machinery' that produced the instance in the interaction, as it happened. Jacobs (1990) uses the term 'structural corroboration' to describe how 'convergent lines of analysis' are 'drawn from a variety of different kinds of observations' (p. 244). That is, conversational 'order' can be found and explained by interpretations that are 'the most consistent with the widest variety of different kinds of facts' (p. 244).

Unlike the traditional social scientist, the conversation analyst is not interested in the *frequency* with which the practice occurs, but whether an *adequate description* of its machinery has been, or can be, provided. More instances cannot be taken as 'proof' of an adequate analysis of the machinery; what they can do is provide more examples of the machinery itself in action. Single case analysis 'may yield a specification of interactional considerations bearing on it which can prove valuable in shaping our ideas about the nature of particular phenomena contained within it. Furthermore, detailed analyses of single data extracts can be undertaken with a view to demonstrating how a variety of different forms of conversation organization intersect in a given instance' (Wootton 1989: 256).

Generally, however, the analyst aims towards developing a collection of instances (Psathas 1995; Heritage 1995; Wootton 1989), since such collections can 'reveal transcontextual properties of the phenomenon in question, properties which inform both its production and comprehension across the variety of particular sequences within the collection' (Wootton p. 255). In addition, considering multiple instances increases the likelihood of locating what are referred to as 'marginal cases' and 'deviant cases', both of which can aid in delimiting the exact parameters of some interactional 'practice'. That is, collections may 'reveal that the original phenomenon is more complex than first noted; or that a second instance is found to be not an instance like the first, but rather a different phenomenon in itself' (Psathas 1995: 52).

And what happens when one finds an instance that does not follow the already understood machinery? Unlike other research approaches that may disregard or discard outliers as uninteresting or problematic, CA actually thrives on such 'deviant cases' (Clayman 1995; Clayman and Maynard 1995; Heritage 1995; Psathas 1995). The analyst may decide that in a particular deviant case, the participants have noticed its oddness and shown that it is somehow deviant, therefore in line with the proposed machinery. Or, the analyst may decide to replace the initial formulation of the machinery with something more general that accounts for this new case. Or, another possibility is that this deviant case in fact warrants a new machinery of its own. Clayman and Maynard (1995: 9) state that 'CA has developed a data-driven methodology that places a high priority on working through individual cases to obtain a comprehensive analysis of the available data. In several ways, coming to grips with deviant cases has been part of the methodology.'

So, for example, according to Benson and Hughes (1991: 132) '... the description of the turntaking machinery in conversation describes ... the methods members use for organizing the sequential order of turns at talk, and can be shown in many, many cases of naturally occurring conversation not as an empirical generalization to the effect that, as a matter of fact, in a very large number of cases conversation has been found to be organized this way, but as a "mechanism", a set of a priori methods, members orient to and use in order to producing naturally occurring conversation in the "way conversation happens". The frequency is not the point: this is the way members produce conversation as an orderly phenomenon.' Benson and Hughes go on to use two very useful analogies for understanding the goal of single case analysis. The first is the rules of the game of chess: the rules which are used are not based on the frequency with which they are used in chess games. The rules structure and define play; if the rules aren't adhered to, then the game is not really chess. A second useful analogy is the analogy of human anatomy – in order to understand and describe the structure of the human body, one body suffices – multiple corpses are not really necessary.

Sociological variables

Unlike much research in applied linguistics, and many forms of discourse analysis, the conversation analyst places no a priori importance on the sociological, demographic, or ethnographic details of the participants in the interaction or the setting in which the interaction takes place (Psathas 1995). In other words, the practices that are analyzed in CA 'are fundamentally independent of the motivational, psychological, or sociological characteristics of the participants. Rather than being dependent on these characteristics, conversational practices are the medium through which these sociological and psychological characteristics manifest themselves' (Heritage 1995: 396). So, for example, other sorts of research (e.g., Tannen 1985; West and Zimmerman 1983) have reported differences in interruption patterns in conversation due to ethnic style and/gender differences. In contrast, the conversation analyst works first on locating and describing the structural organization of a social practice such as interruption, and then, and only then, if at all, is it 'meaningful to search for the ways in which sociological factors such as gender, class, ethnicity, etc. or psychological dispositions such as extroversion or a disposition to "passive-aggressive" conduct, may be manifested – whether casually or expressively – in interactional conduct' (Heritage 1995: 396).

Furthermore, the conversation analyst makes 'no assumptions ... regarding the participants' motivations, intentions, or purposes; nor about their ideas, thoughts, or understandings; nor their moods, emotions or feelings; ... past relationships, biographies, and interests; as well as about their past beliefs, thoughts, or hopes, and so on; except insofar as these can be demonstrably shown to be matters that the participants themselves are noticing, attending to, or orienting to' (Psathas 1995: 47). Schegloff (1999) sees a 'central concern ... is the further development of our understandings of the organization of talk and other conduct in interaction itself, at the most general level at which it can be described. Not only those features that are specific to particular settings or for particular functions, not only those modifications that serve to constitute distinctive and specialized speech exchange systems, not only features that characterize particular language, discourse, or speech communities, but, if there is such thing, that organization of talk-and-other conduct-in-interaction that is ours as humans, as members of this social species' (p. 142).

Coding and quantifying data

It has been noted more than once that CA fundamentally differs from the methods and techniques used in traditional social science. One contrast is that conversation analysis does not use preformulated coding systems to categorize data. Psathas (1995: 8) lists four reasons for eschewing this sort of analytic tool:

1. Category systems, because they were preformed or preformulated in advance of the actual observation of interaction in a particular setting, would structure observations and produce results that were consistent only with their formulations, thereby obscuring or distorting the features of interactional phenomena.

2. They were reductionistic in seeking to simplify the observer's task by limiting the phenomena to a finite set of notated observables.

3. They ignored the local context as both relevant for and inextricably implicated in meaning production, and instead substituted the theoretical assumptions concerning 'context and meaning', which were embedded in the category system itself.

4. They were quantitatively biased in that they were organized for the production of frequency counts of types of acts, and thereby were willing to sacrifice the understanding of locally situated meanings in order to achieve quantitative results.

In fact, according to Wieder (1993), CA and 'constructive analytic social science' are actually 'incommensurable' enterprises: the sorts of coding schemes that are employed in traditional social science will miss critical features of CA phenomena altogether. Heritage and Roth (1995), in their empirical study of questioning behaviour in news interviews, found that coding questions based on grammatical criteria could only 'capture the recognizability of questioning but not its complex dynamics' (p. 48).

However, according to Goodwin and Heritage (1990), a common misunderstanding about CA is that it uses *no* categories for analysis. This is untrue, but: 'CA insists that the categories used to describe participants, action, and context must be derived from the orientations exhibited by the participants themselves ... The fundamental issue from which this stance derives is the problem of **relevance**: showing that the categories proposed for analysis are oriented to by the participants themselves, in and through the production of their actions' (p. 295). That is, even if it were possible to create a perfect coding system for interactional behaviour and to teach analysts to use the system perfectly, it is likely that what results will 'not be isomorphic with the sense-making categories as employed by members of society; and even if it were then the sense attached to the various categories by them would remain to be explicated' (Wootton 1989: 239). Of course, determining participant understandings of actions in interaction is a major goal of conversation analysis, and is no straightforward manner.

In fact, though, studies exist within the CA paradigm where data are coded. In their study of repair in English and Japanese, Fox, Hayashi, and Jasperson (1996) coded instances of repair, but explicitly state what they see as the inherent risks of this decision: 'choosing syntactic categories for analyzing such data obviously poses several risks. First, it is not possible to know at the outset whether the phenomenon in question is organized according to syntactic categories. ... Second, it is possible that the categories we used, while widely accepted by linguists, would not be the *appropriate* syntactic categories; that is, it is possible that repair is organized thorough syntactic categories, – just not the syntactic categories typically recognized by linguists ... choosing syntactic categories that are appropriate for two typologically divergent languages is also complex' (p. 194).

Heritage and Roth (1995) not only coded, but quantified their data on the nature and extent of interviewer questioning in a corpus of 12 U.S. and 36 U.K. news interviews, comprising over 600 interviewer turns at talk. One goal was to develop, operationalize, and evaluate a coding scheme to categorize interviewer questions. An initial attempt to use grammatical criteria to identify questions proved to be too limited, so other practices that accomplish questioning, such as 'question delivery structures', were required to account for the questioning practices in the data. In evaluating their efforts, Heritage and Roth explain that locating interviewer questions, as social actions, was fairly straightforward, because questioning is what interviewers are supposed to do. Nevertheless, they found cases where question forms did not accomplish questioning, and where other forms did. (See Schegloff 1984b for more on this point.) While they found that 'a very substantial majority' of interviewer turns were formatted as grammatical questions, they are aware that coding turns at talk 'decontextualizes the conduct, social action is rendered as atomistic behaviour, and collaborative achievements become construed as the monolithic products of individual intentions' (p. 56).

And what of quantification? CA, for the most part, steers clear of quantification of data (Heritage 1995; Heritage and Roth 1995; Jacobs 1990; Schegloff 1993). The most cogent argument about this issue is made by Schegloff (1993), who believes that the quantification of conversational data is premature, given our incomplete understanding of both the features we may wish to count and the environments in which they occur. So, for example, if we were interested in how participants in conversation initiate repair, we would first have to know all the methods and the forms that can be used to accomplish this action. Even though a great deal is known about repair, we still don't know all there is to know. Furthermore, we would need to understand not just whether participants do initiate repair, but whether they *should*; that is, is such an action relevant at any given point in an interaction?

Schegloff, as one who advocates single case analysis, argues that quantification depends on aggregating multiple single cases, and unless each single case is fully understood, aggregation can be misleading, if not wrong. He approaches his argument against quantification in three ways, using the two parts of the classic ratio and the context in which the ratio is figured as just three possible sources of difficulty. The ratio in discourse analysis is often meant to express ideas such as x out of y times, N% of the time, rate per thousand words, s-nodes per t-unit, laughter per minute, or self-corrections per turn. First, he points out that the denominator in each of these instances reflects environments of *possible relevant* occurrences, the stress on relevant. Taking the ratio 'laughter per minute', he points out that participants in interaction '... do not laugh per minute. Laughter is among the most inescapably *responsive* forms of conduct in interaction' (p. 104). It is relevant (and seen as missing if not done) during and after a joke, but inappropriate (and seen as such) during troubles telling. That is, 'positioning matters' (p. 104). Schegloff's point is that laughter (and other aspects of talk-in-interaction, such as continuers like 'uh huh' and 'yeah') analytic relevance, and an organizational relationship to other talk. So, other responses are possible and may be found during the telling of a joke. In fact, '... not every place that something may not be found is a place at which it is missing' (p. 106). It is only through analytically grounded analysis that we will be able to determine if such nonoccurences are relevant, and thus countable.

Schegloff's second point has to do with the numerator of the ratio. What exactly counts as an occurrence? Even a category as apparently commonsense as continuers (also referred to as backchannels) is fraught with problems in determining its membership. Even if we limit this category to 'uh huh', 'mm', 'yeah', and head nods, these may be deployed in different ways in interaction. An additional problem which Schegloff notes is that of avoidance of certain forms, of reference to persons, for example: '... alternative realizations are not necessarily similar sorts of objects ... we will need to figure out how to incorporate all the possible forms of the occurrences' as well (p. 109).

Finally, Schegloff discusses the issue of context: 'the domain or universe from which our data are drawn, for which our claims are made, and to which they are responsible' (p. 110). I stressed this issue in Chapter 1 when mentioning cases where researchers seemed to confuse, both the terms and the communicative events, 'conversation' and 'interview'. That is, '[t]he issue is not, or is not *merely*, a taxonomic one. These domains need to be discriminated when we believe, and *because* we believe that interactants conduct themselves differently, are oriented to different sets of relevancies, and therefore produce and understand the conduct differently in these different domains' (p. 111). Schegloff (and I) are concerned that data drawn from one context (such as an interview) will be used to make claims about another (such as a conversation), or about 'discourse' in general. Moreover, even within the category 'interview', there are clearly different types of interviews that may employ different turntaking systems or may alter other features of talk in systematic ways (see, for example, Lazaraton's 1997a findings on preference structure in her corpus of language assessment interviews).

Schegloff concludes by remarking that 'quantification is no substitute for analysis. We need to know what the phenomena are, how they are organized, and how they are related to each other as a precondition for cogently bringing methods of quantitative analysis to bear on them' (p. 114). Does this mean that Schegloff sees no role for quantification in the study of conversation? Only if such analysis is 'distinctive' (that is, importantly different from single case analysis), 'defensible' (that is, it is answerable to the issues of the ratio and domain described above) and 'comparative' (see Heritage and Roth on this last point). Until that time, 'informal quantification' represented by the use of terms such as 'occasionally', 'frequently', and 'ordinarily' may be preferred. The use of these terms in CA 'reports an experience or grasp of frequency, not a count; an account of an investigator's sense of frequency over the range of a research experience, not in a specifically bounded body of data; a characterization of distribution fully though tacitly informed by the analytic import of what is being characterized' (p. 119).

This stance is generally agreed upon by most working within the CA tradition, but there are exceptions. Heritage and Roth (1995) point out that most research in CA, even to this day, uses 'informal quantification' terms such as 'regularly', 'massively', 'seldom', and the like. Such 'informal distributional claims' were adequate for the sorts of initial descriptive analyses of conversational organization in which the conversation analyst generally engages. In fact, they go on to say, working with single cases is justified, even required, since 'order at the level of the single case is the primordial basis for concerted talk-in-interaction', and understanding this local order is 'a prerequisite to quantification' at the aggregate level (p. 43).

Furthermore, they acknowledge that coding and quantification in CA is quite controversial: 'from its inception, [CA is] an approach based on detailed explication of single cases and on collections of these. Few if any CA questions require specifically quantitative solutions. CA can and will continue to advance without recourse to quantitative analysis' (pp. 51–52). Heritage (1995: 406) continues:

> *Quantitative studies have not, so far, matched the kinds of compelling evidence for the features and uses of conversational practices that have emerged from 'case by case' analysis of singular exhibits of interactional conduct. It does not, at the present time, appear likely that they will do so in the future. For quantitative studies inexorably draw the analyst into an external view of the data of interaction, draining away the conduct-evidenced local intelligibility of particular situated actions which is the ultimate source of security that the object under investigation is not a theoretical or statistical artifact. In sum, statistical treatments of evidence for conversational procedures have yet to prove to be central or significant as resources for analysis. Significant methodological problems inhibit their implementation at the present time.*

However, Heritage and Roth (1995) part ways with Schegloff here; they believe that some interests in CA cannot be served by this hard line position on quantification. Heritage (1995) seems to be in general agreement with Schegloff about proceeding cautiously, if not delaying quantitative analyses of CA data, but he does not believe (as Schegloff appears to) that statistical analysis is an impossibility. Rather, our expectations about the payoffs of deploying statistics must be tempered by our realization that quantification 'is likely to be more successful in relation to well defined elements of talk and with respect only to a relatively limited range of goals' (p. 404). And one such goal, for Heritage, is the explication of institutional talk, including interviews. Such 'constructive' uses of quantification in conversation analysis include 'sensitizing' the analyst to interesting phenomena for later study, verifying intuitions about an already well understood interactional practice, and, as above, accounting for social and psychological factors, such as age, gender, etc. in talk. Moreover, Heritage agrees that the analysis of single and deviant cases has proved extremely fruitful for understanding some conversational practices, such as turntaking. Yet, other aspects of interaction, especially institutional talk, may not be as easily understood using these techniques. As a result, the use of quantitative procedures will necessarily increase 'if only because the relationships between particular social identities and the implementation and outcomes of particular social practices is more significant (in this type of research). While the strictures on the use of quantitative methods mentioned above remain in place in institutional domains, there is an undeniable incentive here to advance the analysis of conversational procedures as a precondition for the development of better focused analytic tools in this endeavor' (p. 410).

Heritage and Roth (1995) conclude with a nice resolution in the form of an analogy: 'the products of coding offer a macroscopic snapshot of "order in the aggregate." They are not designed to, and cannot, compete with the sensitivity and specificity of single-case analyses of which they are properly aggregates. Rather, they are approximate, but informative, complements to such analyses' (p. 53). The use of both the interpretive 'microscope' of CA and the statistical 'telescope' can have a place in our analyses (Heritage 1995). As Heritage (1999) points out, 'part of the claim of any framework worth its salt is that it can sustain "applied" research of various kinds ... just as an architect can shift from a vertical to a horizontal view of a building, so ... it seems to be possible to shift from basic CA to "applied" analysis and back again' (p. 73).

Summary

A review of these six analytic issues sets the stage for explicating the analyses which follow. Only the reader can decide if using real, recorded data that are segmented into turns, analyzing single cases and collections thereof, and refraining from posing before-the-fact explicit research questions, from considering sociological variables, and from coding and quantifying data, are legitimate decisions for any particular oral test validation question.

Working with interactive data

Now that some of the important methodological decisions that are made in conversation analysis have been discussed, it is time to show how this sort of data analysis is accomplished.

Pomerantz (1990) explains that the conversation analyst is interested in making three sorts of analytic claims, including *characterizing actions* (that is, explaining how speakers 'do' actions, identities, and roles); *proposing methods* (describing the ways in which interactants accomplish actions), and *proposing features* (explaining how methods work, sequentially). Much preliminary analytic work involves making observations that become *characterizations*, which require the analyst to use world knowledge about language, culture, and social practices. Characterizations are not analyses themselves; rather, they are provisional descriptions that serve as means to that end. 'The thrust of an analysis is to explicate how methods of accomplishing actions work rather than with finding the right names with which to label actions' (Pomerantz 1990: 232).

Five 'analytic tools'

Pomerantz and Fehr (1997), in a useful introductory article on conversation analysis, present a concise list of analytic 'tools' which can assist in CA's stated goal of 'illuminat[ing] understandings that are relevant for the participants and the practices that provide for those understandings' (p. 71). Specifically, these tools, and the analysis that they help to generate, should describe a conversational 'practice' and the knowledge that conversational participants employ in conducting the practice. These five tools are explained and employed to analyze two data fragments taken from a dataset of ESL course placement interviews (Lazaraton 1991).

1. Select a sequence of interest by looking for identifiable boundaries.

The first step is to choose somewhere in the discourse to begin focusing. Although it may be tempting to look for humorous, problematic, or exceptional sequences, it is not necessary to do so: uncovering the machinery of seemingly mundane sequences can be equally rewarding. Recall that sequences are composed of at least two turns that accomplish some action, but just one turn that is initially interesting can prompt the analyst to 'unpack' the sequence in which it resides. Look at these data below (from Lazaraton 1991):

```
(1)     MC  (2:29-42)  IN=Interviewer    CA=Student¹

  1  IN: an:d um: (.5) tell me som- (.2) where are you fro:m n
  2      what's. your native langua[ge
  3  CA:                           [u:h: m:y na:tive language is
  4      Mandarin Chine:se I'm from: Taiwa:n
  5      (.2)
  6  IN: mmhmm?
  7      (3.5)
  8  IN: (now) yer English is already very goo:d
  9      (.8)
 10  IN: ob[viously: you know that.
 11  CA:   [eh
 12      (.2)
 13  CA: yes: b[u:t-
 14  IN:       [but where do you learn it?
```

Here, a number of possibilities for analysis present themselves. One could look at the question–answer sequence in lines 1–4; the compliment in line 8 (and try to determine what else belongs in that sequence); the candidate's responses in lines 11 and 13; or the IN's question in 14. Each of these would be sure to bear analytic 'fruit'.

Once an interesting sequence has been located, the next step is to search for its boundaries. Sometimes boundaries are easy to spot, and other times they are not. To find the beginning of a sequence, look for where some action or topic was initiated. Similarly, the end of a sequence is the place at which participants no longer respond to the prior action or topic. Again, this is not always as easy as it sounds. Recall that sequences, and the practices they represent, are negotiated in interaction, and their 'accomplishment' can only be said to have happened if both participants 'orient to' the practice underway. Remember, the analyst attempts to model participant perspectives, so that when the participants note the beginning or end of a sequence, the analyst can feel confident in doing so as well. The reverse, however, is not true!

Referring to the data above, how can we determine the beginning and end of any particular sequence? Let's say that we were interested in looking at the question–answer sequence in lines 1–4. Although the prior talk is not given, the participants were discussing course preferences, the candidate saying that she prefers the higher level course, ESL 34. An eight-tenths of a second pause immediately precedes line 1; the beginning of the IN's turn is not only topically disjunctive with what went before, it is disfluent, and what follows is a different question in line 1. Therefore, it appears that this sequence begins in line 1. As for its ending, the first-pair-part question suggests a second-pair-part answer, which is what occurs in lines 3–4. And what follows that is a brief silence in line 5, a continuer in line 6, and a long silence in line 7, all of which are then followed by what appears to be a topically disjunctive comment in line 8. Therefore, we should feel comfortable in a preliminary definition of the boundaries of this sequence as lines 1–4.

2. *Characterize the actions in the sequence by answering the question,*
   'What is the participant doing in this turn?'

The second suggested step in a CA analysis is to determine the actions which
are being undertaken in the sequence. Pomerantz and Fehr state that actions
are the 'fundamental part of the meaningfulness of conduct' and that they can
be labeled by asking, 'What is this participant doing in this turn?' (p. 72).
Greeting, complaining, giving bad news, and changing topics are all examples
of 'actions' in the CA sense. Recall though, that in answering the fundamental
CA question, 'Why this now?', the analyst is modeling participant
understandings, and s/he cannot 'look ahead' in the discourse to understand
actions; all that is available for inspection is what has been said and done up
to any particular point. That is, explanations about the meanings of actions
can only be made by direct examination of 'what happened before' and 'what
follows next'.

Once this step is completed, the analyst should have identified an action for
each turn in the sequence. There is nothing wrong with finding that a turn
accomplishes several actions at once. Also, note that actions are structurally
related in many sequences, so that a turn that acts as a request 'projects' a
subsequent turn which responds to that request. In the example above, the IN
requests information (in the form of a question) from the candidate in lines
1–2, indicated by the 'tell me' and the two wh-questions. This action of
requesting information is responded to by the candidate, who provides this
information in lines 3–4.

3. *Consider how the packaging of actions, that is, how they are formed and*
   delivered, provides for certain understandings.

The next phase involves looking at how the actions identified in the second
step are formed and delivered. Pomerantz and Fehr refer to the formation and
delivery as 'packaging', and they point out that packaging choices that
participants make are rarely conscious decisions. Rather, different packages
are 'alternative items in a class' (p. 72).

In addition to considering how actions are packaged, the analyst should
undertake to explicate the sorts of understandings that different forms of
packaging imply, and the sorts of choices they give to the recipients of such
actions. Specifically, Pomerantz and Fehr suggest these questions as relevant
to this task (p. 73):

- *What understandings do the interactants display (and you have) of the action?*
- *Do you see the interactants treating the matter talked about as important, parenthetical, urgent, trivial, ordinary, wrong, problematic, etc.?*
- *What aspects of the way in which the action was formed up and delivered may help provide for those understandings?*
- *What inferences, if any, might the recipients have made based on the packaging?*
- *What options does the packaging provide for the recipient? In other words, what are the interactional consequences of using this packaging over an alternative?*
- *Finally, what are the circumstances that may be relevant for selecting this packaging over another for the action?*

For example, imagine that I am moving on Saturday and I need help. Consider the differences in these request formats (that is, their packaging):

- What are you doing this weekend?
- Are you busy Saturday?
- Do you have a spare hour on Saturday?
- Can you help me move on Saturday?

The first three are structured in such a way as to allow you to give me information (perhaps that you are going to a wedding that day) that would imply rejection without actually rejecting my request; the fourth does not. Additionally, while the second and third are formed as 'pre-requests', the first is ambiguous – it could be nothing more than asking you to give me an account of noteworthy future happenings. And only the last is a direct request. In each case, however, the recipient must determine what is being asked for, how it is accomplished, and what sorts of responses are options as a result.

4. *Consider how timing and turntaking provide for certain understandings of actions and the matters talked about.*

An understanding of how turns were obtained by each participant (by self-selection or being selected), started (in overlap, latched, after a silence), and terminated can help make clear the actions that have been identified in earlier steps. For example, turning down a request, as a dispreferred action, may be done after a silence, which 'projects' a dispreferred response and allows the requester to 'jump in' the silence and deflect such a negative response. Using the data fragment above once more, while the request for information in lines 1–2 is followed promptly (in fact, in overlap) by the candidate's response in lines 3–4, the IN's compliment in line 8 is followed by an eight-tenths of a second silence, indicative of a dispreferred response to follow. The IN follows up with a second TCU to the first after this silence, and one which narrows the CA's response options considerably.

5. *Consider how the ways the actions were accomplished suggest certain identities, roles, and/or relationships for the interactants.*

Although it was noted earlier in this chapter that CA avoids a priori appeal to demographic information on participants to understand their interactional behaviour, this is the point at which it may be appropriate to search for evidence of various relationships, roles, and statuses being actualized in the discourse being analyzed. Particular ways of talking and acting, of referring to people, places and things, of packaging and timing actions, may indeed 'implicate particular identities, roles, and/or relationships' (Pomerantz and Fehr 1997: 74).

Briefly, using the example above one more time and targeting the candidate's lack of response to the compliment in line 8 – are there any features of the context that could account for her lack of uptake? In fact, since compliments are generally responded to promptly (and affirmatively) in conversation, we can guess that some aspect of this encounter has altered this normal state of affairs. In fact, because agreeing to and accepting the compliment is tantamount to admitting no need for the desired ESL course, candidates in this encounter (at least the ones who were complimented on their language ability) *routinely* behaved in this manner, showing how conversational behaviour may vary by interactional context. This point will be taken up further in the worked example below.

A worked example

Let's use these tools on another segment of talk obtained from the ESL oral skills course placement interviews at UCLA (Lazaraton 1991).

1. *Select a sequence of interest by looking for identifiable boundaries.*

While examining this corpus of data, an interesting feature emerged in some of the interviews, namely, student self-deprecations of their own English language ability. These were intriguing to me, given that the purpose of the interview itself was to evaluate language ability – why would a potential student want to judge herself this way? Therefore, I undertook an analysis of all the interviews in which these self-deprecations occur. One such sequence occurs below:

```
(2a)   HN   (1:26-40)        IN=Interviewer    CA=Student

 1 IN:psk! so: Hank why don't you tell me something about
 2     yourself.
 3     (.8)
 4 CA:myself? ((sniff out)) [.hhh!
 5 IN:                      [mmhmm?
 6     (.2)
 7 CA:uh: I came he:re (.5) uh:: (1.0) uh::::: nineteen eighty
 8     ni:ne: summer. (.) a:nd (.5) still I have been here
 9--->  .hhuh: about uh: one n half years (.5) but (.5) I cannot
10--->  sp(huh!)eak .hhh English (.2) e:m (.8) uh:: fluently.
11     (.2) so I: ha:ve ma:ny uh: (.5) I feel many uh
12          troublesome:(.5) uh: to: conversate- (.) to converse with
13     m- my:pro:fessor .hhh (mm)
14     (1.0)
15 IN:psk! (m)- wu- where are you from.
```

How were these boundaries determined? In other words, why did I present just this much data? In this case, the interview agenda makes this task easy: 'why don't you tell me about yourself' is the first question on the agenda and 'where are you from' is the second.

2. *Characterize the actions in the sequence by answering the question, 'What is the participant doing in this turn?'*

The next step is identifying the actions that are undertaken by each of the participants. Lines 1–2 show the IN *requesting information*. Line 4 is a repetition by the candidate that checks hearing and/or understanding, and can be considered a *next turn repair initiation*. In line 5, the IN confirms the *hearing/understanding;* this 'insert' repair sequence will not be considered further. Then, in lines 7–13, the candidate responds to the interviewer prompt to 'tell me something about yourself' (lines 1–2), by *providing some factual information* on his background (when he arrived in the US), and then by *deprecating his English language ability*, 'I cannot sp(huh!)eak .hhh English (.2) e:m (.8) uh:: fluently'. These actions can be shown schematically as follows:

```
     (2b)   HN  (1:26-40)      IN=Interviewer   CA=Student

 1 IN: psk! so: Hank why don't you tell me something about   INFO REQUEST  ⌐
 2     yourself.
 3     (.8)
 4 CA: myself? ((sniff out)) [.hhh!          NEXT TURN REPAIR INITIATION ⌐
 5 IN:                       [mmhmm?                        CONFIRMATION ⌐
 6     (.2)
 7 CA: uh: I came he:re (.5) uh:: (1.0) uh:::: nineteen eighty INFORMATION⌐
 8     ni:ne: summer. (.) a:nd (.5) still I have been here      │ GIVEN
 9     .hhuh: about uh: one n half years (.5) but (.5) I cannot │ SELF-
10     sp(huh!)eak .hhh English (.2) e:m (.8) uh:: fluently.  DEPRECATION ⌐
11     (.2) so I: ha:ve ma:ny uh: (.5) I feel many uh troublesome:
12     (.5) uh: to: conversate- (.) to converse with m- my:
13     pro:fessor .hhh (mm)                                              ←
14     (1.0)                                                             ⌐
15 IN: psk! (m)- wu- where are you from.          INFORMATION REQUEST   ⌐
```

3. *Consider how the packaging of actions, that is, how they are formed and delivered, provides for certain understandings.*

This step suggests that we look into turn construction (that is, the formatting of the actions taken) in more detail. First, IN's information request, 'why don't you tell me something about yourself' is a scripted agenda question that the interviewers felt would elicit the required factual information about the candidates and a speech sample that would allow for an assessment of language competence. Sacks (1992) saw that a similar first question from some psychiatric data ('What brings you here?') analyzed by Pittenger, Hockett, and Danehy (1960), actually functioned to allow the potential patient to provide grounds for being accepted into therapy. Therefore, it is likely that 'tell me something about yourself' is or should be understood by these students as an invitation to provide grounds for being accepted into the elective ESL courses. And one sort of ground that is relevant in this context is either a demonstration of or a statement about poor language ability, or both. Grounds that would not be relevant include being a football fan, coming from a family of five, etc.; no candidates provided this sort of information, which implies that they were able to interpret the request as one of a very specific sort.

As for CA's response in lines 7–13, he constructs it in such a way as to provide grounds for judging his upcoming deprecation, namely, the seeming incongruity of his length of stay in the country ('still …') and his perceived ability (…'but'). Note also that the deprecation itself comes out in two pieces, 'I cannot sp(huh!)eak .hhh English' and then after some hesitation, 'fluently.'

4. *Consider how timing and turntaking provide for certain understandings as well.*

It was noted above that the CA's self-assessment of language ability comes out in two chunks. It is interesting that what the candidate says about himself is shown in how he says it – nonfluently, with numerous pauses. One cannot imagine a more uniquely suited turn construction for this encounter! And what is the IN's response to this self-deprecation? Nothing, so to speak. His next topically disjunctive question is delivered after a silence and disfluently; the self-deprecation is left to hang.

5. *Consider how the ways the actions were accomplished suggest certain identities, roles, and/or relationships for the interactants.*

In this small segment, both IN's and CA's actions characterize and instantiate their assigned 'roles' in this encounter. IN behaves 'like an interviewer' by sticking carefully to the agenda, which requires him to elicit information only; this requirement allows him to avoid responding to the deprecation and allows him to 'maintain objectivity' in the encounter. The candidate 'behaves like an interviewee' by providing the requested information, but in a way that both says and shows that he is in need of the assistance the desired courses provide.

Summary

This section has overviewed a five-step process for analyzing interactive oral test data. By selecting a sequence and identifying its boundaries, characterizing actions in the sequence, and considering how the packaging, timing, and turntaking of the actions lead to various understandings about the context, and participant roles and relationships, the analyst has moved from observations, to characterizations, and finally to empirical claims, which can be evaluated by an inspection of the data on which the claims are based. This form of 'argument from example' is taken up later in the chapter.

Working with monologic data

Some oral test validation work obviously involves analyzing the production of an individual candidate, or a candidate, who, by virtue of the test format, has no interaction with either an interlocutor or with another candidate. In these cases, the tools that Pomerantz and Fehr (1997) propose for analyzing interactive discourse will generally not apply to monologic talk (since monologues do not occur in sequences, for example, and there is no turntaking). As far as I know, there is no one accepted way of analyzing this type of speech – it will always depend on the particular analytic goal. While a complete discussion of approaches to analyzing monologic data is beyond the scope of this book, several approaches that have the potential to be useful to the test validator are overviewed below. The interested reader is urged to consult Hatch (1992) for more complete information.

Rhetorical analysis

One set of approaches to monologic text falls under the heading of rhetorical analysis, which subsumes at least two sub-approaches: text structure theory and genre analysis. *Text structure theory*, which is not dealt with further here, is a cognitively oriented approach to discourse that attempts to understand how the structure of discourse reflects the intentions and goals of a speaker via an analysis of relations present in the text.

On the other hand, *genre analysis* has been used a great deal by applied linguists to understand actual discourse, including the typical rhetorical genres of narration, description, comparison–contrast, cause–effect, and opinion. Since a number of oral tests require candidates to produce language within these genres, it will be worthwhile to look at two such produced texts and to explore ways in which they can be analyzed.

A. Narration

In a tape-mediated oral skills placement test administered at UCLA, Lazaraton and Riggenbach (1990) rated ESL students' oral production on five rhetorical tasks using two four-point scales: one for linguistic skills and one for task completion. Some of the most interesting data were generated in the narrative task, a sample of which is reproduced below. Students responded to a four-picture set, entitled 'A Clever Dog', which showed first, two boys and a dog in a park; second, the boy throwing a shoe into the woods and the dog running after it; third, the dog coming back with the shoe and the boys being pleased; and fourth, a man running out from the woods who is missing a shoe. Students were instructed to plan their story for one minute, and then to tell it in 90 seconds. Candidate SH, a female from Taiwan, produced this:

```
(3a)   Lazaraton and Riggenbach speaking test

 1 uh John and Tom uh they're in the park. and John's doggie um— his
 2 name u— John's doggie its name is uh...Lily.  and John say to Tom
 3 that 'oh my Lily is (a) very clever dog.' Tom said '(o)h prove that.'
 4 uhn then John say 'okay.' then they went to a trash can uh John
 5 pick up a— a broken (a) used shoes from the trash can and threw it.
 6 into the woods to the trees to far away. and Lily running to find.
 7 the shoes. and after few seconds Lily did come and— uh take a with
 8 a shoe. but it's not the really shoe John throw. it's a (brind) new.
 9 shoe and also they find a man very angry coming here and shout
10 'where's my shoe? (oh) Lily really a clever dog.
11 he got a brand new shoe from... from angry man.
```

Now, Lazaraton and Riggenbach used two approaches to develop the task completion scale for responses: first, they adapted Labov and Waletsky's narrative template (1967), which proposes abstract (such as a title), orientation (the 'when', 'where', and 'who' of the story), complicating event (that is, the main actions in the story), resolution (the climax, what happened), and coda (a concluding comment or moral) as components to construct the scale. Second, they collected data from a small group of native speakers performing the task. The ratings were completed long before the tapes were transcribed, but it is interesting that the rater impressions of task completion (the candidate was awarded the top rating of 4) are consistent with the components present in her story, which are evident in the transcript:

(3b)   **Lazaraton and Riggenbach speaking test**

```
1  uh John and Tom uh they're in the park. and John's doggie um— his
   (orientation to setting and characters)
2  name u— John's doggie its name is uh...Lily and John say to Tom
3  that 'oh my Lily is (a) very clever dog.' Tom said '(o)h prove that.'
   (use of quoted speech to animate characters; sets out complicating
   event)
4  uhn then John say 'okay.' then they went to a trash can uh John
   (shows time reference with 'then')
5  pick up a- a broken (a) used shoes from the trash can and threw it.
6  into the woods to the trees to far away. and Lily running to find.
7  the shoes. and after few seconds Lily did come and— uh take a with
   (more time expressions to show ordered steps) (resolution)
8  a shoe. but it's not the really shoe John throw. it's a (brind) new.
9  shoe and also they find a man very angry coming here and shout
10 'where's my shoe?' (oh) Lily really a clever dog.
   (characterizes man's emotions, uses quoted speech)
11 he got a brand new shoe from... from angry man.
   (ties story to title; tells how goal of proving dog to be clever met)
```

Obviously, there are many other interesting features that could be analyzed in such texts. One possibility would be to look at the relationship between task completion and linguistics skills ratings by analyzing the discourse further. Chervenak (1996) pursued a similar line of inquiry in looking at narratives, produced on a modified version of the SPEAK test by international teaching assistants, in terms of their ratings and their discourse features of pausing, self-repair, grammar, pronunciation, and word stress.

B. Description

A similar analysis was attempted with some monologue data from The Cambridge Assessment of Spoken English (CASE: UCLES 1992). In one part of the test, candidates are asked to produce a long turn of one minute; the task for some was to describe a movie they enjoyed. To analyze the sufficiency of the descriptions produced, graduate students (in a discourse analysis seminar at George Mason University in 1999) used one of two approaches: either they analyzed three film descriptions produced by native speakers to come up with components with which they judged the candidate's descriptions, or they intuited desirable components to evaluate candidate descriptions. Both groups generally agreed that a good movie description would contain: an orientation that mentions the title and possibly the year of the film, the actors, director, and/or film genre; an optional description of the action and/or the plot and/or the moral of the movie; and either reasons why one liked the movie or a recommendation to see the movie. This description was produced by a Japanese female (from Lazaraton 1993):

```
(4)    CASE — Candidate 14 (2:32-39) Examiner W Phase 2: Presentation [2]

1   .hhh %mmm% (last) day I saw (.) Hook. (.) mmm it is Steven
                                    (title)
2   Spielberg's film. (.) I (.) I wanted (.) wanted to see it because
         (director)              (reason to see)
3   mmm I like Robin William. (.) %mmm% (.) .hhh this film is (.)
             (actor)
4   mmm the story that (.) mmm Peter (.) Pan .hhh <who have grown
                            (story plot) --->
5   grown up.>(.) %mmm% (7.0) he (.) he (hh)has for- forgotten (.)
6   that he's Peter Pan. that he was Peter Pan. but he mmm remembered
7   (.) to help (.) his: children. so he mmm (.) he he could he can
8   fly?, and (.) became strong. (2.0) .hhh %mmm% it is very mmm
         --->                        (evaluation)
9   fantastic %mmm%
```

While the linguistic skills displayed may be weak, the description itself conforms nicely to the template that the student discourse analysts proposed.

Functional analysis

A more macroanalytic view of genre can be found in the functional analyses of Lazaraton and Frantz (1997), who examined monologic discourse produced on the FCE (UCLES 1998a). They inspected the different speech functions produced by 28 candidates on a 1996 administration of the test. A total of 15 speech functions were identified in the data, a number of which were ones UCLES had identified as expected candidate output functions. For example, in Part 2, where candidates are required to produce a one-minute long turn based on pictures, UCLES hypothesized that candidates would engage in *giving information* and *expressing opinions through comparing and contrasting*. While these speech functions did occur in the data analyzed, candidates also engaged in *describing, expressing an opinion, expressing a preference, justifying (an opinion, preference, choice, life decision) and speculating*. In the fragment below, the candidate spends most of her time speculating about the feelings of the people in each picture, as she is directed, but does not compare or contrast. Here is how Lazaraton and Frantz analyzed this response:

(5) FCE — Candidate 43 (2:140-153) Examiner 377, Part 2

(Task: Couples: I'd like you to compare and contrast these.
pictures saying how you think the people are feeling)

```
 1 yeah (.2) from the first picture I can see .hhh these two (.)
                           (description)
 2 people they: seems not can:: cannot enjoy their .hhh their meal
       (speculation)
 3 (.) because these girl's face I think she's: um (think) I think
       (justification)
 4 she's: .hhh (.2) an- annoyed or something it's not impatient and

 5 this boy: (.) she's also (.2) looks boring (.2) yeah I I think
                      (speculation)
 6 they cannot enjoy the: this atmosphere maybe the: .hhh the::
                           (justification)
 7 waiter is not servings them (.) so they feel so (.) bored or (.5)
                      (speculation)
 8 or maybe they have a argue or something like that (1.0) yeah and

 9 from the second picture (.8) mmm::: this: rooms mmm: looks very
                           (description)
10 warm (.) and uh .hhh (.2) mmm these two people? (.) they also

11 canno— I think they are not talking to each other .hhh they just
              (speculation)
12 (.) sit down over there and uh (.5) these gentleman just
       (description)
13 smoking (.) yeah and this woman just look at her finger
```

Structural analysis

Structural analysis is a broad category of micro-analytic approaches that subsumes analyses of the traditional linguistic features of phonology, lexis, and syntax, as well as more discourse-oriented features like communication strategies and discourse markers. For example, Halliday and Hasan (1976) propose five means by which texts become cohesive: reference, substitution, ellipsis, conjunction, and lexical ties. In a report on candidate performance at different band scores (ranging from 1–9) on IELTS (UCLES 1999a), Lazaraton (1998) found some interesting differences in candidate ability to use these cohesive markers. For instance, candidates at the lowest Band score 3 made only limited use of conjunctions. Here, the candidate uses a listing strategy in conjunction with 'and':

(6)   IELTS — Candidate 9 (3:79-82) Part 2

```
E: okay what about the Olympic Games are you interested in
   that kind of sport or
C: mm yeah.
E: yeah
C: Yes I inlested in ah football mm and swimming tennis
   .. yeah.
```

However, 'and' above and the 'but' and 'because' below are not used to link sentences, per se:

(7) IELTS — Candidate 9 (4:92) Part 1

C: but I dink soccer is better

(8) IELTS — Candidate 9 (1:23-26) Part 1

E: what do you like most Sydney or Bangkok?
C: Sydney.
E: why?
C: because mm in Sydney it have (a rarely) traffic jam

On the other hand, another candidate at this level was able to link two relatively well-formed (albeit simple) sentences with the conjunctive marker 'because':

(9) IELTS — Candidate 2 (5:148-150) Part 4

C: I want to improve my country because my country is many pollution

and with 'when':

(10)   IELTS — Candidate 2 (4:82-84) Part 2

C: when I am finished from my city when I want to study continue I am going to study in Bangkok.

In contrast, a candidate at a higher Band score of 7 readily used cohesive ties to connect sentences to produce extended discourse:

(11)   IELTS — Candidate 20 (7:166-172) Part 4

C: in one week I leave ah Australia but I intend to stay in Australia in Jinuree. so I will um I applied a for um to to participate ah in a course here at the university and um if I get in into it into this course I will come back but at first I have to return to Switzerland. to to join the army.

In sum, structural analysis can be used to isolate and evaluate specific textual features of interest. This approach has been used to analyze the speech of international teaching assistants by Wagner (1994a) for their use of discourse markers (so, okay, etc.) in graded oral presentations.

Summary

In summary, this brief discussion of these approaches to analyzing monologic speaking test data is not meant to be comprehensive, but to alert the reader to the various possibilities for dealing with such data. Few empirical studies to date have analyzed monologic data taken from oral examinations; just as we have seen more research on the interactive discourse of oral interviews, it can be hoped that this interest will extend to the monologic talk produced in other oral assessment contexts.

Presenting data and reporting results

This final section addresses issues in and suggestions for presenting data and reporting results of conversation analytic research. First, a rationale for 'argument from example' (Jacobs 1986) is outlined. Then, concrete suggestions for how to present transcribed data, describe a study, and report results are put forward. A few ideas on how to critique other studies using this approach are also brought up.

Rationale

Earlier sections of this chapter described how one goes about coming up with an analysis of a sequence in a data fragment, or of a fragment itself. While a report may deal with just one sequence only, it is more likely that the conversation analyst will present a number of data fragments and describe some particular feature (or features) present in them. That is, conversation analysts 'work though the details of conversational fragments together with intuitions about those details to reflect the rules and procedures that generate the sense and order found in the examples' (Jacobs 1988: 437). So the question arises, what is the role of examples in conversation analysis? How does one go about choosing examples to display in reports? And, how can examples suffice as evidence for analytic claims?

According to Jacobs (1986), 'the most distinctive feature of discourse analytic studies is the method of argument from example' (p. 149). After comparing and contrasting examples, the analyst presents and documents some claim about a practice. And what is this claim? According to Jackson (1986), all reports should contain a thesis explaining what was discovered (as opposed to attempted, noted, or exemplified). Also excluded from the class of 'empirical claims' are the goals of a study, remarks about a theory's value, definitions of terms, and proposals about rules. 'An empirical claim must commit the speaker to defending the existence of some state of affairs' (p. 137). In all cases, examples, while serving to illustrate the practice in question, do more: 'The specific features intuited in the examples will have served as evidence for the existence (or nonexistence) of the properties in question' (p. 149). However, examples suffice as evidence if and only if an empirical claim has been put forward which can be checked against the data; that is, 'Conclusions are justified by what examples show' (Jacobs 1988: 435).

So what sorts of fragments should be used? Jacobs (1986, 1988), like other researchers mentioned earlier, suggests paradigm cases, fringe cases, and deviant cases should all be presented as evidence of an analytic claim. Examples that are paradigm cases are prototypical and provide evidence of a pattern or feature. Fringe cases should be analyzed in their own right, and should not be forced into or out of already established categories; rather, the analyst should explicate the details that give rise to their fringeness. Finally, deviant cases can be used to show when and how the pattern fails. The important point is that the analyst should not make a claim and present only confirmatory examples; contrastive examples are needed as well (Jackson 1986).

In other words, examples are used to justify characterizations of interactional patterns. The examples aren't the characterization, or the pattern, itself, but are employed to justify a technical description of that pattern or practice (Jacobs 1986). It is customary to provide several examples for any claim being made, not because more is better, but because additional data may help the analyst to explain both the form and the logic behind the practice. The purpose of presenting examples to support an analytic claim is to affirm the claim's consistency over the scope of examples that are exhibited. Examples, however, are not well-suited to claims about frequency of occurrence, since showing examples does not prove that they occur regularly: prototypes are not necessarily typical (Jacobs 1986, 1988).

Jackson (1986) is well aware that some will question whether we should feel confident that what amounts to an analyst's intuitions about examples can really count as evidence of an empirical sort. It should be recalled that conversation analytic claims are not meant to explicate 'regular' occurrences, but to provide a description of a pattern or practice. Such 'claims are warranted by the fact that the pattern and its features are intuitively recognizable in some collection of examples of that pattern' (Jacobs 1986: 156). That is, it is assumed that we as readers can scrutinize given examples and the characterizations of them and then compare such empirical facts with our own intuitions about how such practices work.

But how do we know the presentation of examples is not selectively biased to support any particular empirical claim? There are no clear-cut answers to this question, but it can be recommended that the analyst give evidence, or at least note, that (potential) counterexamples have been taken into account in formulating claims. In fact, the overall validity of this sort of research depends on 'the traditional warrants of qualitative research: the use of a large, comprehensive database of naturally occurring events, a detailed inspection of a representative sample of cases, and evidence of a search for fringe or deviant cases which may disconfirm an empirical claim (Jacobs 1988, 1990). As Jackson (1986) points out, it is not enough to follow the 'rules' of conversation analysis (transcribe well, use authentic data, etc.);

faithful adherence to these methodological practices allows us to have confidence in our reasoning about practices, and provides us with the necessary tools to generate our empirical claims.

In short:

* state empirical claims clearly,
* present evidence in the form of examples,
* account for exceptions.

Guidelines for presenting data

The first issue with respect to presenting data is: can, or should it be 'cleaned up'? P. Atkinson (1992: 23) observes that with ethnography, 'Informants cannot speak for themselves. ... Moreover, the more *comprehensible* and readable the reported speech, the less "authentic" it must be. The less the ethnographer intervenes, the more delicately he or she transcribes, the LESS readable becomes the reported speech.' This point applies equally to discourse analysis: the more precise the transcription, the less reader-friendly it becomes; the more it is cleaned up, the less it matches the actual production of the participants. Generally speaking, conversation analysts insist on presenting their data as transcribed, and publication outlets often need to be convinced to respect this choice.

A second issue is that publication outlets often do not permit full transcripts to be printed due to space limitations. This roadblock goes against CA orthodoxy: Psathas (1995) argues that CA research 'must include transcripts of the data that represent the phenomena analysed ... this is in contrast to field research reports of interactions and to descriptive or analytic reports based on codings of interaction ... in such studies the interactional phenomena have been modified and transformed into reported interactions, and we are left only with the possibility of discussing the reports, rather than examining the data on which the reports are based' (pp. 47–48).

Ochs, Schegloff, and Thompson (1996), in a similar vein, urge us to consider data in its totality. They point out that CA studies contain 'long stretches of data ... *It is key to the serious understanding of the vision informing the volume that readers engage the data citations in detail and with care* [italics in original], and familiarize themselves with the notational conventions' used (p. 18). Furthermore, they continue, 'The reader must stand shoulder to shoulder with [the authors], examine the data with them, understand what they are claiming about them and about the language structuring to be learned from them, and then assess those claims and their groundings in those data. No reading that detours around the data excerpts can properly support a reader's assessment of the result. On the other hand, if readers have taken the data seriously, they have at least partially engaged the project being prosecuted here, even if they find the author's take on it faulted. To find it faulted, the reader should (in principle, at least) undertake to wrest his/her understanding in engagement with the same recalcitrant reality of what is on the tape/transcript as challenged the author' (p. 18).

These issues, of presenting data as transcribed and in their entirety, present serious problems for those of us who attempt to publish in applied linguistics journals which may or may not understand the analytic relevance of having actual and complete transcripts to consult when reading CA research (see also Ford and Thompson 1996 on this point).

A. Mechanics

Once decisions have been made on how to present the transcribed data (in its original form or modified for readability), these steps should be followed.

A. Each fragment must be numbered, and the numbering should be consecutive throughout the paper. Note that fragments in this book are numbered within each chapter. Each fragment must also have an ID line which identifies the data source, the speakers, and the page and line numbers, if possible. Additional information may be included, as necessary (see Note 2).

B. Ideally, data fragments are presented in a different font, or a different font size, than the text of the paper. This aids readability. Also, be sure to use a mono-spaced font for the data, preferably Courier, so that overlaps align correctly.

C. Data fragments should be kept on one page. That is, if all the fragment cannot fit on one page and continues to the next, move all of it to the next page. If the segment is too long for one page, make sure the breaks occur at turn transition points and not in the middle of a turn or an overlap.

D. Line numbers greatly improve readability. They are a must if the fragment contains more than about five lines.

B. Organizing examples

A. Think through the presentation of the data. Which fragments and/or categories should come first? Why? How will fringe and deviant cases in the database be accounted for?

B. Be sure to draw explicit connections between categories, sub-categories, and data fragments. It is often useful to use a 'preview and summarize' strategy before moving on to the next fragment, sub-category, or category.

C. *Quality* of data analysis is more important than *quantity* of data presented. Do not overwhelm your reader with massive amounts of data, particularly if the analysis of them is skimpy. As a rule of thumb, two or three instances per feature is usually sufficient. Remember, examples are there to support empirical claims!

A research report format

Here is a set of proposed guidelines for reporting CA research in communication (adapted from Hopper *et al.* 1986: 183):

1. Include a review of relevant literature.

2. Recording

   a. Describe the sample on which the analysis is based – the number of hours of recording, relevant information on the participants, how samples were chosen for or excluded from study.

   b. Describe the recording circumstances: location set up, recording equipment used, procedures for data collection. Note if recordings or transcripts are available to others.

3. Transcribing

   a. Give credit to transcribers.

   b. Describe transcription procedures in detail.

   c. If possible, include transcripts with reports; urge editors to publish transcripts in their entirety.

4. Analysis

   a. Specify any research questions which drove or derived from the study.

   b. Specify the presumptions and procedures of analysis.

   c. Identify the source and location of all examples.

   d. State claims clearly; relate results back to the literature reviewed; separate rigorous results from speculative material.

The journal *Research on Language and Social Interaction* is a useful resource for information on formatting these reports.

Guidelines for evaluating other studies

Finally, here are some criteria that may be useful in judging other studies published in this analytic tradition. Jackson (1986) suggests that CA research should be subjected to critical questions such as:

- What alternative claims could the data support?
- What reason is there to prefer the claim as stated over its alternatives?
- What additional data would be required to rule out the alternatives?
- What effect could the selection of cases have had on the conclusion?
  TESOL Quarterly publishes qualitative research guidelines in every issue. While some of the criteria do not apply to discourse analytic studies, others are relevant (TESOL 1999: 175):

- *Look for studies that are 'credible, valid, and dependable rather than impressionistic and superficial'.*
- *Data collection (as well as analysis and reporting) should represent an emic perspective.*
- *Analysis: data should be subjected to 'comprehensive treatment' via the 'cyclical process of data collection, analysis ... creation of hypotheses, and testing' via more data collection.*
- *Reporting: 'provide "thick description" including the "theoretical or conceptual framework" guiding the study, a statement of research questions, a description of data collection methods, reports of patterns found in the data, with representative examples, grounded interpretations and conclusions'.*

Summary

The researcher must remember that the point of presenting examples is to support empirical claims. The examples should be comprehensive: they should illustrate, when possible, clear cases, fringe cases, and deviant cases. Additionally, data should be presented in their actual form and in their entirety. The actual form that the report takes, however, will depend on the requirements and conventions of any particular publication outlet.

Conclusion

This chapter has introduced the most important steps in undertaking a discourse analysis of some authentic, recorded data. A number of decisions that are made by the conversation analyst have been presented, but there is no dictum that each and every oral test validation project must follow these to the letter. Different research goals will always dictate different research procedures. However, engaging in unmotivated looking, employing the turn as the unit of analysis, analyzing single cases and collections, de-emphasizing sociological variables, and shunning the quantification and coding of data ensure that the analysis that ensues follows general CA principles.

Little has been said so far about how this analytic process can inform the test validation process: this is the topic of the next chapter. Perhaps it is encouraging to end this chapter with this reminder:

> *Analysis is a slow process of becoming increasingly aware of features of conduct and practices of action. It can and often does start with listening to your tape and transcribing it. In listening closely enough to transcribe something of what you hear, you will have thoughts about the conduct to explore further. As you continue to listen or watch your tape and make notes, your beginning analytic thoughts will gradually take on more shape. We know of no one, experienced conversation analysts included, who produces a finished analysis the first time around. This type of work lends itself to successive revision and refinement.*

> (Pomerantz and Fehr 1997: 87)

Notes

1. This transcript identification line was used by Lazaraton in her dissertation. This fragment is from Candidate MC's interview transcript, page 2, lines 29–42.

2. Here, the transcription identification line indicates the examination from which the data were drawn, the candidate number, the page number and the transcription lines from which the fragment was taken, an examiner identification symbol (not available for IELTS data), and the section of the examination where the discourse was produced. This format is used for all Cambridge examination data.

Practice problems

Guidance for approaching each of these problems can be found in Appendix 3.

1. Referring back to data fragments (1) and (2) earlier in the chapter, recall the comments that were made about the compliment/deprecation response patterns. Look at this data fragment from the ESL course placement interviews at UCLA (from Lazaraton 1991):

```
(12) RA     (3:43-4:32)    IN=Interviewer    CA=Candidate

 1 IN:  okay. .hhh (.2) i:f (.8) English thirty two: were not
 2      offered (1.0) would you take English thirty four?
 3      (2.0)
 4 CA:  thi:s quarte:r?
 5 IN:  yeah because (.) you kno:w that only one of them is gonna
 6      be offered. (.) not both.
 7 CA:  yeah sh- (.) sure. because I- I- I would like to- (1.0)
 8      to: develop my communication skill because right now
 9      I':m eh- (1.0) the president of one the union? in the
10      student government [n I have to: (.5) give them (in) a
11 IN:                     [mmhmm?
12 CA:  a speech n ta:lk (.8) about my: group?
13 IN:  ok(hh)[ay
14 CA:        [and(t)
15 IN:  what- what group are you presi(dent) o[f
16 CA:                                        [union of the student
17      with disability?
18 IN:  uh(hh) huh?
19      (.5)
20 CA:  and (.5) I (d a big want) I had experience very (1.0)
21      esc(hh)ary [hhh! when I went] to one of those retrea:ts (.)
22 IN:             [y(hh)ea:h hhh   ]
23 CA:  [they ask me to give a speech regarding our group and I
24 IN:  [uh huh
25 CA:  was (.8) feel- (.5) very: (.2) .hhh [(mezzed up)]
26 IN:                                     [ne:rvouz:  ] I spose
27 CA:  I was really very nervous because I didn't know how to:
28      .hhh (.) express myself
29      (1.2)
30 CA:  [when
31 IN:  [you sound pretty goo:d though
32      (.2)
33 IN:  huh? huh hah! [ .hhh ! huh!  huh! .huh!  ]
34 CA:               [I try(ed) my best (I mean) ] I did (.)
35 CA:  I did (.) I gave them (in) the speech but (.8) I didn't
36      it wasn't good as u- (.5) as I wanted.
```

There is a great deal of interesting talk here. Apply the five tools discussed in this chapter to a sequence of your choice. Be sure to justify your sequence boundaries.

2. Here is another narrative, produced by a German female, on Lazaraton and
   Riggenbach's tape-mediated oral test described earlier in the chapter:

(13)   **Lazaraton and Riggenbach speaking test**

```
 1  on the first picture you see two little boys, and a dog, and one
 2  of the boy eh found an old shoe, in a garbage eh tra- track...emm
 3  it's eh they are playing perhaps in a park? you c- can see the is
 4  ba-be-because on the right side there are eh trees,...and some
 5  plants, and on the eh...back- in the background you see two
 6  houses...and eh on the second picture you see that one of the boys
 7  throws the shoe away, and eh the dog eh...eh jumps behind the
 8  shoe. they ha- they play a little. on the third picture you
 9  see...eh the...dog coming with eh the shoe eh...out of the trees
10  and eh...on the eh eh fourth picture you see that eh t- eh that
11  the...dog didn't get the RIGHT shoe because there is a...nn man
12  coming out of these eh...trees with only one shoe, and you can see
13  that the dog has taken HIS shoe and not the old shoe which has eh
14  jumped away by the littl boy.
```

Review the criteria that Lazaraton and Riggenbach used to evaluate task
achievement of segment (3a). How does this student compare?

What are the benefits and drawbacks of this test method? If one were really
interested in assessing narrative production of these learners, what other test
methods might be more authentic and/or useful?

3. Here is a second film description produced by a Japanese female in the
   long turn monologue segment of CASE:

(14) **CASE – Candidate 59 (1:28-47) Examiner O Phase 2: Presentation**

```
 1  CA: %mmm% (.) eh::: the film's name is soo- Silence of the
 2      Lambs. (.) of- Silence of the Lambs. (.) and (.) this film
 3      was uh (.) (give many:::) (.) prize? (.) prize? of academy?
 4      (.) and .hhh (.) mm this film was (.) about psychological
 5      thriller. movie? and (.) and uh (.) mm (.) why I I enjoyed
 6      it because .hhh mmm (.) it is (.) so thrilling and uh:: .hhh
 7      (.) and uh:: quite hard for me but (.) ( . ) .hhh and
 8      (8.8)
 9  IN: can you tell us anything else about the movie?
10  CA: yeah. .hhh it (.) this film (.) is mmm (.) it happened that
11      .hhh one (.) mother (.) and uh .hhh (.) mmm (.) uh- (.)
12      one woman who FBI? (.) FBI police police uh called (.)
13      Clarise .hhh (.) an::d
14  IN: okay. (.5) we'll stop you there...
```

Recall the guidelines that were used to evaluate these film descriptions.
How does her film description compare with the description in fragment (4)
in the chapter?

4. Below are some data taken from the long turn monologue section of the revised FCE (from Lazaraton and Frantz 1997):

(15)   **FCE — Candidate 77 (6:305-325) Examiner 377, Part 2**

(Task: Summer and Winter: I'd like you to compare and
contrast these pictures saying when you think it would be
more pleasant to spend time there)

```
 1  OK they are: the same: place but (.) one is in w- (.) winter and
 2  the other one is s- spring .hhh so I think I would like to go
 3  there on spring because I I'm from I am from a very (.) warm place
 4  and I don't like .hhh snow and heh an this kind of things .hhh and
 5  it's good for skyi- (.) the: (.2) for skiing the: first (.2) the
 6  first photograph .hhh but I I'm not very fond of skiing because I
 7  haven't done it (.2) in my life .hhh so I I think I I won't be
 8  very good at doing it (.2) but it's good to: to try (.) once in
 9  your life perhaps .hhh so I will go there (.5) to: (.) in spring
10  (.) it's more hotter the: flowers very: (.) colorful .hhh and it's
11  more: (.2) interesting to:: (.) the views are very: (.8) very
12  beautiful .hhh and you can <u>climb</u> (.) with this weather but not
13  with (.) with snow it's (.) too cold for going out for a walk
14  .hhh and (.2) this m- I like <u>flowers</u> very much and gardering
15  .hhh and (.) it would be a quite (.2) eh: <u>quiet place</u> in:
16  <u>spring</u> (.2) there are small houses not very high buildings
17  .hhh and it's (.) eh: (.) in a <u>valley</u> (.5) and it's I think
18  it's (.) I prefer (.) the second one (.) going there in s-
19  (.) in spring=
```

Imagine that you were asked to determine the variety of speech functions that this candidate uses in this monologue turn. How would you go about this? What functions would you consider?

5. Here are some additional segments taken from IELTS, an examination that scores candidates at one of nine overall score bands (1–9) (from Lazaraton 1998). Imagine that you were interested in understanding the candidates' use of communication strategies. What do these data suggest to you?

(16)   **IELTS — Candidate 19 (3:56) Band 4**

C: so but when it was raining and and **I don't have I didn't
    have** any umbrella...

(17)   **IELTS — Candidate 19 (1:11—14) Band 4**

E: and have you been able to see much of Australia whilst
    you've been here?
C: **ah un a pardon?**
E: have you been able to visit many places?
C: yeah sure many place just beachies...

(18)   **IELTS — Candidate 15   (6:173—174) Band 5**

E: what type of education are you interested in? what level?
C: **um um da rebel what ah what does it mean?**

(19)   IELTS — Candidate 17 (2:41—46) Band 6

E: what does it look like? Is it a very old city?
C: yes. it is old city becau because it had ah a long long
   history. it is ah we have **I don't know how to use da
   word ah bicentenary...**

5 Some speaking test validation studies using this approach

- Test validity

- Background on Cambridge EFL examinations

  - Overview
  - The Cambridge approach

- Interlocutor behaviour in speaking tests

  - Research on CASE
  - Research on CAE
  - Research on KET
  - Comparative research on CAE–KET

- Candidate behaviour in speaking tests

  - Research on FCE
  - Research on IELTS

Previous chapters covered the theoretical and methodological underpinnings of qualitative discourse analysis, specifically conversation analysis. So far, we have not been concerned with the ways in which such an analysis can help us answer questions about the reliability and validity of speaking tests, only with the steps in the analytic process itself. Now that these steps have been introduced, explained, and practiced, it is time to look at how this approach has been applied to the process of speaking test validation in relation to a major exam board. After a brief review of the concept of validity as it relates to language testing and some background on Cambridge EFL examinations, this chapter summarizes a number of empirical studies carried out over the last decade that have employed these qualitative discourse analytic techniques to investigate various speaking test datasets with the express purpose of test validation. The first group of studies focused on the behaviour of the interlocutor in the testing process. The latter group represents a move towards characterizing features of candidate language, particularly how it reflects both the specifications on which the tests are built and the rating scales on which performance is evaluated.

The observant reader will note that these researchers came to some, but not all, of the same analytic decisions, discussed in the last chapter, that the conversation analyst generally makes. While all of the studies used real, recorded data, used the turn as the unit of analysis, and generally avoided appeal to sociological variables, in some cases explicit research questions were put forward, multiple cases were studied, and simple frequencies were tabulated. As much as possible, reasons for these differing choices are put forth.

Test validity

Validity has been and remains a, if not the, major concern in language testing (Stevenson 1981). In his view, 'the spirit of validation ... not only tries to prevent the willful and careless misuse of tests; it also tries to protect the test constructor from his or her own self-confidence. Moreover, and perhaps most importantly, it tries to protect the test constructor and any future examinees from the too willing acceptance of a measure by those test users who impatiently argue that their practical needs are of primary importance, and that test validation, while nice, is not' (p. 40).

Bachman (1990) distinguishes questions of reliability (what proportion of variance in test scores is reliable variance?) from questions of validity (what specific abilities account for the reliable variance in test scores?). Estimates of test reliability measure consistency across test characteristics: of scores across versions of a test or days a test is taken, of ratings across evaluators, and the like. It is generally agreed that, in the psychometric/positivist tradition at least, test reliability is a necessary but insufficient condition for test validity, so it is meaningless to speak of an unreliable but highly valid assessment measure. Yet, there are dissenting voices, most notably Moss (1994), who believes that hermeneutic approaches are potential alternatives to the assurance that evidence of test reliability (supposedly) provides.

Validity is increasingly seen, according to Bachman, as a unitary entity, evidence for which includes content relevance, criterion relatedness, and meaningfulness of the construct(s), among other 'general validity criteria' (Messick 1994). While demonstrating both content relevance and criterion relatedness are important aspects of the test validation process, they are insufficient alone, or even together. Content relevance can be shown if the test tasks are congruent with some prespecified content domain, but it fails to account for actual performance on the test. Evidence for criterion relatedness can be found in some sort of functional relationship (shown via correlations) between the test in question and another relevant measure of language ability; unfortunately, one cannot assume that the criterion measure is itself valid. As a result, a third type of evidence, which subsumes the first two, is sought through the process of construct validation. (Bachman 1990, Cumming 1996, Fulcher 1999, and Kunnan 1998b also consider this issue.)

Construct validation involves determining if test scores reflect underlying traits; that is, it empirically tests relationships between scores and abilities (Cohen 1994). But construct validity does not reside in a test; rather, it refers to the meaningfulness and the appropriateness of interpretations we make based on scores to a specific domain of generalization (Bachman and Palmer 1996; Fulcher 1999; Messick 1996). In other words, it informs us about the 'extent to which we can make inferences about hypothesized abilities on the basis of test performance' (Bachman 1990: 256). Construct validation involves, and requires, logical analysis to determine to what extent a given test is based on underlying theory, and empirical evidence, involving statistical procedures, such as correlation, factor analysis, and multitrait– multimethod techniques. (See Alderson, Clapham, and Wall 1995 on this point.)

In other words, validity, according to Messick (1996), 'is an overall evaluative judgment of the degree to which empirical evidence and theoretical rationales support the adequacy and appropriateness of interpretations and actions based on test scores or other modes of assessment' (p. 43). Messick's (1989) four-way 'progressive' matrix is the currently accepted way of looking at construct validation in language testing:

Figure 5.1

Messick's facets of validity

Sources of justification	Functions of outcome of testing	
	Test Interpretation	Test Use
Evidential basis	Construct validity	Construct validity + Relevance/Utility
Consequential basis	Construct validity Value implications	Construct validity + Relevance/Utility + Social consequences

(from Bachman 1990: 242)

Messick describes two threats to construct validity, both of which are in place in all assessments. The first is construct under-representation, where the test is designed too narrowly and overlooks important aspects of the relevant constructs; this threatens authenticity. Construct-irrelevant variance is a second threat, in which the assessment is too broad and contains variance that is irrelevant to the interpreted construct; this threatens directness.

Messick's theory of validity, which emphasizes the ongoing process of test validation to derive fair interpretations of test scores based on various kinds of evidence, is both strongly acknowledged and clearly embraced by language testers (e.g., Bachman and Palmer 1996). Yet, a broader view of language testing is emerging. For example 'test usefulness' is really *Validity* with a capital 'V' (Nick Saville, personal communication 1/18/00), and is a balance of four examination qualities: validity (construct, content, criterion), reliability, impact, and practicality. Principles of good practice underlie each of these qualities (Milanovic and Saville 1996a). There is also a growing awareness that we must look beyond the evidential bases of test interpretation and test by utilizing approaches from other research traditions to validate language tests, since the conventional means are powerful but limited (Bachman 1990; Cumming 1996; Hamp-Lyons and Lynch 1998; Kunnan 1998a). On these points, Cumming suggests that 'more thorough, systematic attention will need to be given in the future, not only to combining rigorous, multiple approaches to assess the evidential bases of test interpretation and test use, but more especially for evaluating the long-term consequential bases of test use on particular educational and societal systems' (p. 12). Kunnan echoes the same sentiment: 'Although validation of language (second and foreign language) assessment instruments is considered a necessary technical component of test design, development, maintenance, and research as well as a moral imperative for all stakeholders who include test developers, test-score users, test stockholders, and test-takers, only recently have language assessment researchers started using a wide variety of validation approaches and analytical and interpretive techniques' (p. ix).

More specifically, Bachman (1990) points out that psychometric procedures look only at test outcomes and ignore the test process itself; evidence of test usefulness should be both qualitative and quantitative (Bachman and Palmer 1996). This view is echoed by McNamara (1996: 7): 'The validity of second language performance assessments involves more than content- and criterion-related aspects of validity; the larger issue of construct validity has been insufficiently considered. In particular, empirical evidence in support of the claims concerning the validity of second language performance tests has in general been lacking.' More to the point, McNamara argues that current approaches to test validation put too much emphasis on the individual candidate. Since performance assessment is by nature interactional, he continues, we need to pay more attention to the 'co-constructed' nature of assessment. (See Jacoby and Ochs 1995 on co-construction.) 'In fact the study of language and interaction continues to flourish ... although it is too rarely cited by researchers in language testing, and almost not at all by those proposing general theories of performance in second language tests; this situation must change' (McNamara 1996: 85–86). Milanovic and Saville (1996) concur with this point of view. They see performance testing as encompassing many facets: 'in order to investigate these interactions between facets of performance testing [examiners, candidates, interlocutors, raters, task, etc.] a variety of research methods are required which can be both quantitative and qualitative in nature' (p. x).

Hamp-Lyons and Lynch (1998) see some reason for optimism on this point, based on their analysis of the perspectives on validity present in LTRC abstracts. Although they conclude that the LTRC conference is still 'positivist-psychometric dominated'[1], it 'has been able to allow, if not yet quite welcome, both new psychometric methods and alternative assessment methods, which has led to new ways of constructing and arguing about validity' (p. 272). Yet, they are clearly in agreement with Moss (1994: 10), who concludes that 'Current conceptions of reliability and validity in educational measurement constrain the kinds of assessment practices that are likely to find favor, and these in turn constrain educational opportunities for teachers and students. A more hermeneutic approach to assessment would lend theoretical support to new directions in assessment and accountability that honor the purposes and lived experiences of students and the professional, collaborative judgments of teachers. Exploring the dialectic between hermeneutics and psychometrics should provoke and inform a much needed debate among those who develop and use assessments about why particular methods of validity inquiry are privileged and what the effects of that privileging are on the community.' Such concerns about the explicit and implicit values, ethics, and impact inherent in language tests are shared by other language testers who contend that we must heed the policy and social contexts of language assessment and bear in mind that language testing 'is a social, value-laden, and intrinsically political activity' (McNamara 1998: 305; see also McNamara 1999; Shohamy 1999).

Undoubtedly, there is still much to be said on this contentious issue. Whatever approach to test validation is taken, we 'must not lose sight of what is important in any assessment situation: that decisions made on the basis of test scores are fair, because the inferences from scores are reliable and valid' (Fulcher 1999: 234). That is, 'the emphasis should always be upon the interpretability of test scores' (p. 226). In each study described below, the overriding aim was ensure confidence in just such interpretations based on the scores that the tests generated.

Background on Cambridge EFL examinations

Overview

Cambridge EFL examinations are taken by more than 900,000 people in around 150 countries yearly to improve their employment prospects, to seek further education, to prepare themselves to travel or live abroad, or because they want an internationally recognized certificate showing the level they have attained in the language (UCLES 1999c). The exams include a performance testing component, in the sense that they assess candidates' ability to communicate effectively in English by producing both a written and an oral sample; these components are integral parts of the examinations.

The examinations are linked to an international system of levels for assessing European languages established by the Association of Language Testers in Europe (ALTE):

Figure 5.2

The ALTE framework

Level 5 Upper advanced level

Fully operational command of the language at a high level in most situations, e.g. can argue a case confidently, justifying and making points persuasively.

Level 4 Lower advanced level

Good operational command of the language in a wide range of real world situations, e.g. can participate effectively in discussions and meetings.

Level 3 Upper intermediate level

Generally effective command of the language in a range of situations, e.g. can make a contribution to discussions on practical matters.

Level 2 Lower intermediate level

Limited but effective command of the language in familiar situations, e.g. can take part in a routine meeting on familiar topics, particularly in an exchange of simple factual information.

Level 1 Elementary level

Basic command of the language needed in a range of familiar situations, e.g. can understand and pass on simple messages.

Universities in Britain, North America and throughout the world accept the certificates awarded to successful candidates at Levels 4 and 5 as evidence of an adequate standard of English for admission to undergraduate and postgraduate degree courses.

(from UCLES 1999e: 3)

The 'Main Suite' Cambridge EFL Examinations test General English and include the Certificate of Proficiency in English (CPE, Level 5), the Certificate in Advanced English (CAE, Level 4), the First Certificate in English (FCE, Level 3), the Preliminary English Test (PET, Level 2), and the Key English Test (KET, Level 1). English for Academic Purposes is assessed by the International English Language Testing System (IELTS), jointly administered by UCLES, The British Council, and IDP Education Australia. IELTS provides proof of the language ability needed to study in English at degree level. Results are reported in nine bands, from Band 1 (Non-User) to Band 9 (Expert User). Band 6 is approximately equivalent to a good pass at Level 3 of the five-level ALTE scale above. Other Cambridge EFL examinations test Business English (BEC: Business English Certificates and BULATS: Business Language Testing Service) and English for Young Learners.

The Cambridge approach

The Cambridge approach to testing speaking acknowledges that complex interactions exist between the many test facets in the assessment process. One possible representation of these factors is shown in Figure 5.3 below:

Figure 5.3

Facets of performance assessment

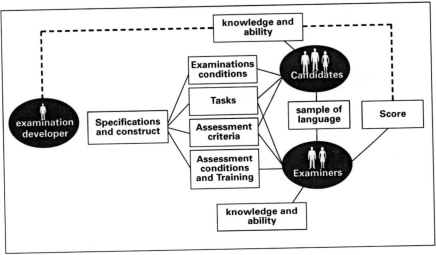

(from Milanovic and Saville 1996a: 6)

Obviously, the diagram suggests more than a lifetime's worth of potential research possibilities. The Cambridge speaking test validation research agenda has chosen to focus on some of these interactions with the research reported in this chapter. That is, Conversation Analysis offers unique insight into some of these facets, especially those relating to the examiner and to the interaction between the candidate and the examiner. Nevertheless, a multiplicity of other research perspectives is needed to understand the relationships between other factors, for example, between task, language output, and scores. Moreover, Cambridge would like to see the results of any such research feed back, whenever possible, into examiner training.

At the operational level of the speaking tests, attention to some of these facets is evident as well. The Speaking Tests require that an appropriate sample of spoken English be elicited, and that the sample be rated in terms of predetermined descriptions of performance. Therefore, valid and reliable materials and criterion rating scales, as well as a professional Oral Examiner cadre, are fundamental components in this enterprise. These concerns are addressed in the following ways:

1. a paired format is employed;
2. examiner roles are well defined;
3. test phases are predetermined;
4. a standardized format is used;
5. assessment criteria are based on a theoretical model of language ability and a common scale for speaking;
6. oral examiners are trained, standardized, and monitored.

Each of these features is now taken up in turn.

1. Paired format

The paired format, where two examiners evaluate two candidates (or three if the number of candidates in a session is uneven), was an optional format for FCE and CPE during the 1980s. It became obligatory for CAE in 1991, for KET in 1993, for PET 1995, and for FCE in 1996. In each case, various alternative formats were evaluated before the paired format was institutionalized, first, by asking test 'stakeholders' (examiners, teachers, students, and candidates) about the formats, as well as by conducting validation studies on them. The primary advantages of the paired format are, first, that two independent ratings from two examiners add fairness to the assessment process; that a greater variety of interaction patterns (candidate–candidate, candidate–candidate–interlocutor as well as candidate–interlocutor) is possible; that candidates are reassured and more relaxed in the presence of a partner; and that positive washback in the classroom will occur by encouraging more learner–learner interaction in the classroom.

The utility of the paired format has been questioned (for example, by Foot 1999) on the grounds that pairing of candidates may not allow for the best performance of one or both candidates and that assessments of ability will be compromised. This concern is being addressed in the Cambridge examinations by designing the test sections carefully, by training examiners thoroughly, and by requiring the use of an interlocutor frame to ensure both candidates are given equal opportunities for speech production.

It should be noted that the Speaking Test of IELTS does not employ a paired format for two reasons. First, because it is an on-demand test, there is no guarantee a second candidate will be available to form the pair. Secondly, each of the main suite examinations has a fairly well-defined candidature in terms of level, so that pairings do not involve wide disparities in ability. On IELTS, however, no preliminary gross assessment of ability can be made, and so there is no way to prevent this mismatch.

2. Well-defined examiner roles

The two examiners in the main suite examinations have well-defined roles and responsibilities in the Speaking Tests that are emphasized and evaluated during examiner training and monitoring. One examiner serves as the *Interlocutor*, in charge of eliciting the speech sample, managing the interaction, keeping time, and providing a global assessment of each candidate. The other is the *Assessor*, a passive observer who applies detailed, analytical criteria to the candidates' performance. Examiners exchange roles during test sessions to reduce fatigue and maintain a freshness of approach.

3. Pre-determined test phases

The Speaking Tests of the main suite examinations have distinct parts, eliciting different types of language and employing different interaction patterns. While PET, FCE, and CAE contain four sections, KET has only two and CPE, three (until its revision in 2002).

The first part of each puts the candidates on familiar ground by asking them to talk about themselves, their likes and dislikes, their family, etc. On some tests, the candidates are expected to respond to questions posed by the Interlocutor; in others, they may be asked to pose questions to each other.

FCE and CAE candidates then have an 'individual long turn' monologue of about a minute in the second part of the test (in PET, the long turn takes place in Part 3). Visual stimuli, such as color photographs, are designed to prompt description, comparison and contrast, and/or opinion from the test takers.

A third stage in each test is a collaborative task which involves making a decision (in PET, this is Part 2). The Interlocutor sets up the task, ensures the candidates know how to proceed, and then withdraws so the candidates can work towards completion of the task by exchanging ideas and opinions with each other.

The final part of PET, FCE, and CAE has the Interlocutor ask the candidates a question that continues the theme of the just-completed collaborative task, which they take up individually or together.

4. Standardized format

Interlocutor Frames are used in all UCLES Speaking Tests, which consist of scripts for the Interlocutor's role. The result is standardization of test administration, since all candidates are treated fairly and equally when the script is followed.

5. Theoretically-grounded assessment criteria as part of a common scale

The assessment criteria for Cambridge Speaking Tests are defined by and related to a model of Communicative Language Ability (CLA), based on work by Bachman (1990), among others, and illustrated in Figure 5.4 below:

Figure 5.4

Communicative language ability

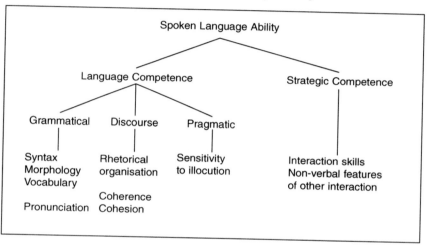

(from Saville 1996: 1)

Moreover, the specific assessment criteria for each main suite examination are contextualized in a Common Scale for Speaking, which provides norms to which specific criteria relate:

Figure 5.5

The UCLES Common Scale for Speaking

Cambridge Main Suite	Cambridge Common Scale for Speaking
	CAMBRIDGE LEVEL 5
CPE	**Fully operational command of the spoken language.** Able to handle communication in most situations, including unfamiliar or unexpected ones. Able to use accurate and appropriate linguistic resources to express complex ideas and concepts and produce extended discourse that is coherent and always easy to follow. Rarely produces inaccuracies and inappropriacies. Pronunciation is easily understood and prosodic features are used effectively; many features, including pausing and hesitation, are 'native-like'.
	CAMBRIDGE LEVEL 4
CAE	**Good operational command of the spoken language.** Able to handle communication in most situations. Able to use accurate and appropriate linguistic resources to express ideas and produce discourse that is generally coherent. Occasionally produces inaccuracies and inappropriacies. Maintains a flow of language with only natural hesitation resulting from considerations of appropriacy or expression. L1 accent may be evident but does not affect the clarity of the message.
	CAMBRIDGE LEVEL 3
FCE	**Generally effective command of the spoken language.** Able to handle communication in familiar situations. Able to organise extended discourse but occasionally produces utterances that lack coherence and some inaccuracies and inappropriate usage occur. Maintains a flow of language, although hesitation may occur whilst searching for language resources. Although pronunciation is easily understood, L1 features may be intrusive. Does not require major assistance or prompting by an interlocutor.
	CAMBRIDGE LEVEL 2 (Threshold)
PET	**Limited but effective command of the spoken language.** Able to handle communication in most familiar situations. Able to construct longer utterances but is not able to use complex language except in well-rehearsed utterances. Has problems searching for language resources to express ideas and concepts resulting in pauses and hesitation. Pronunciation is generally intelligle, but L1 features may put a strain on the listener. Has some ability to compensate for communication difficulties using repair strategies but may require prompting and assistance by an interlocutor.
	CAMBRIDGE LEVEL 1 (Waystage)
KET	**Basic command of the spoken language.** Able to convey basic meaning in very familiar or highly predictable situations. Produces utterances which tend to be very short - words or phrases - with frequent hesitations and pauses. Dependent on rehearsed or formulaic phrases with limited generative capacity. Only able to produce limited extended discourse. Pronunciation is heavily influenced by L1 features and may at times be difficult to understand. Requires prompting and assistance by an interlocutor to prevent communication from breaking down.
	Pre-Waystage Level
	Zero

(from UCLES 1999f: 53)

Each examination differs slightly in the criteria used. For example, in KET, both examiners apply the same holistic criteria and award two marks, each on a scale of 1–5. PET, FCE, and CAE examiners use five assessment criteria: one rating of global achievement by the Interlocutor (for overall effectiveness in tackling the specific tasks), then four analytic ratings by the Assessor for grammar and vocabulary (accuracy and appropriacy), discourse management (coherence, range, and extent of contribution), pronunciation (individual sounds and prosodic features), and interactive communication (initiating, responding, turntaking, amount of assistance required). Criteria are set out as grids with verbal descriptors for the main 'anchor' points of the scales.

6. Trained oral examiners

The network of professional Cambridge EFL oral examiners numbers nearly 11,000 worldwide. The network is hierarchical, as shown in Figure 5.6 below:

Figure 5.6

The Cambridge Oral Examiner network

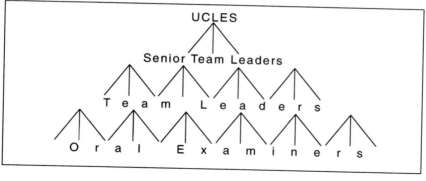

(from UCLES 1999b: 7)

The operational level consists of the Oral Examiners, the ones who administer the exams. At the next level are the Team Leaders, who supervise the Oral Examiners; Senior Team Leaders supervise the Team Leaders. Team Leaders and Senior Team Leaders are also practicing oral examiners.

Certain procedures regulate the activities at each of these three levels and are summarized by the acronym RITCME: Recruitment, Induction, Training, Co-ordination, Monitoring, and Evaluation. A list of Minimum Professional Requirements (MPRs: UCLES 1999b) defines the levels and sets out standards for each. Recruitment involves evaluating the background, experience, English language competence, professional and personal qualities, interpersonal skills, and administrative capability of potential Oral Examiners. Hired Oral Examiners are familiarized with the duties and principles of the Cambridge approach through Induction; the Training program allows the examiners to develop and practice the skills necessary to administer the Speaking Tests. Co-ordination is accomplished by requiring all examiners to attend a standardization meeting every 12 months. An extensive Monitoring process assures that all examiners continue to meet the Minimum Professional Requirements. Team Leaders evaluate examiners every two years using guidelines and an Oral Examiner Monitoring Checklist (UCLES 1999e). Finally, an Evaluation records the performance of examiners who meet the MPRs.

Interlocutor behaviour in speaking tests

Although several studies mentioned in Chapter 1 considered the role of the examiner in oral testing (e.g., Ross and Berwick 1992; Ross 1992; Ross n.d.), none of them did so with the explicit purpose of providing information that could be used in the test validation process. Even Lazaraton (1991) made no attempt to link her dissertation findings to questions about the integrity of the interview from which the data were taken. The studies summarized below all had as their goal to provide information about 'the examiner factor' in Cambridge EFL Speaking Tests to the test developers (UCLES).

Research on CASE

1. Background

The Cambridge Assessment of Spoken English (CASE) was[2] the prototype examination designed between 1990–1992 which has been influential in the development of the Cambridge Speaking Tests, such as FCE, IELTS, etc. CASE was a test of oral proficiency designed to assess both the linguistic and communicative skills necessary for oral communication between nonnative and other speakers of English in a wide variety of contexts. CASE sponsors included managers and employers, as well as educational institutions where English is an important or the main medium of communication. CASE provided an overall measure of spoken English language proficiency, as well as individual profile reports which described the candidates' spoken language proficiency in terms of specific areas of ability, including grammar, vocabulary, pronunciation, organization, communication strategies and interaction, and task achievement.

CASE was designed as a two-stage oral assessment, carried out by two trained examiners with groups of six candidates; the entire procedure with such a group took less than two hours. Its structure is shown in Figure 5.7:

Figure 5.7

The structure of CASE

5 mins.	5 mins.	1 min.	8 mins.	4 mins.
Stage One			Stage Two	
		Section One	Section Two	Section Three
Interview	Deciding on Timing	Warm up	Presentation	

(From Milanovic, Saville, Pollitt, and Cook 1996: 31)

In Stage 1, candidates were assessed individually by an Interlocutor and by a second assessor who observed, but did not take part in, the interaction. In this five-minute one to one interview, the emphasis was on drawing out the candidate to demonstrate his/her ability to speak English, so an initial impression check could be made. An Interlocutor Frame prescribed topics and questions to be dealt with, generally related to everyday life (work, studies, interests). In Stage 2, the candidates took part in a 13–15 minute task-based interaction where they were assessed on the basis of their interaction with a fellow candidate. The pairs, and the particular tasks in which they engaged, were based on a variety of factors, including overall ability, gender, etc. In the first part of Stage 2, the candidates took turns making one to two minute presentations to their partners; upon completion the listener asked questions of the presenter. Here, candidates were expected to organize their discourse, use appropriate speech functions, and respond to comments and questions. In the second part, the candidates worked together on a task which required three to four minutes of discussion and negotiation; the examiners listened but did not take part. Candidates were expected to negotiate meaning through turntaking, summarizing, and monitoring their performance.

Examiner training was designed to meet the needs of local testing centers and was delivered in three stages. The first was participation in two half-day intensive group training sessions. These training sessions were followed by standardization exercises, and then a certification tape and score grid. On rating the certification tape successfully, examiners were certified for a set period of one year. (Adapted from pp. 3. 16–17 of the CASE Manual: UCLES 1992.)

CASE assessments were rated using eight scales, each containing descriptions of language behaviour appropriate to it: six focused on specific elements of language performance: grammar, vocabulary, pronunciation, organization, communication strategies and interaction skills, and interlocutor support; one rated task achievement; the last was a six-point overall assessment scale of spoken language proficiency which ranged from 300–800, the range of the entire ALTE scale shown on p. 117.

2. Research goals

As part of a validation program for CASE (UCLES 1992), this study (Lazaraton 1993, 1996a) was the first commissioned by the University of Cambridge Local Examinations Syndicate to use qualitative discourse analysis to understand the speaking test process. For this reason, it was unclear at the outset what kind of information the data would provide, if it would be useful to the test developers, and in what format it might be presented to that group. As a result, no specific research questions guided the study, and no plans were made to make demographic variables such as gender, age, etc. the focus of analysis. Still, the techniques used in and the findings from her dissertation (as well as the results reported by Ross and Berwick (1992)) provided a starting point for coming to grips with the large dataset that was made available.

3. Method

The data for this project were collected in September 1992 at a language school in Tokyo, Japan. A total of 58 Japanese speakers (24 males and 34 females), all of whom were part-time English language school students, took part in the study. All 10 of the examiners were teachers who had TEFL/TESOL qualifications and experience with different levels; some had acted as examiners for other UCLES exams. All the data were audiotaped and videotaped (a standard examination procedure that participants were aware of beforehand), and the audiotapes were transcribed according to the conversation analysis conventions set out in Chapter 3.[3]

The task-sets which were used in this administration included four presentation cards covering eight topics for Stage 2 Presentation, where candidates make a short presentation to their partners, who then asked questions of the speaker. These topics included, for example, 'Describe a film you enjoyed' or 'Describe a recent book you read'. Two Stage 2 Discussion topics were used, both of which asked candidates to select a famous person (either a well-known athlete or one of three specified world leaders) and come up with interview questions to ask him/her.

4. Results

The 1993 Study

Because UCLES was primarily interested in the role of the examiner and the use of the Interlocutor Frame in the CASE exam, the first step was to establish how well the interlocutors followed the Stage 1 Interlocutor Frame, which prescribes 26 prompts requiring responses from the candidates. By working through the 58 transcripts, it was determined that adherence to the frame, as worded, ranged from about 40%–100% across interlocutors. One of the benefits of the turn-by-turn analysis was being able to pinpoint specific difficulties that arose in the interaction. For example, several of the prompts were quite problematic for the candidates. Prompt 1e, 'What would you prefer me to call you?' was misunderstood by many of them and required a great deal of negotiation to come to an understanding of what was being asked, if one was achieved at all. It was also determined that several prompts which required the use of hypothetical language and speculation were not used at all because the interviewers did not have enough time to get to them. It was suggested that this warranted attention if the ability to produce that sort of language distinguishes a higher level candidate. A report of prompt usage by each interlocutor was also prepared so that this information could be compared across and shared with examiners. Here is one such diagram that shows which of the 26 prompts (shown by + signs) Interlocutor W used in the six assessments he conducted. Notice that he used between 14 to 20 of the 26 prompts, which were particularly scanty in the fifth section:

Figure 5.8

CASE Stage 1 Prompt Usage – Interlocutor W

	PROMPTS						
Tape	1c d e f	2a b c d e f g	3a b c	4a b c d e	5a b c d e	6a b	Total
31	+ + + +	+ + +	+ + +	+ + + +		+ +	16
32	+ + + +	+ + + + +	+ + +	+ + + + + +		+ +	20
33	+ + + +	+ + + +	+ +	+ + +		+ +	15
34	+ + + +	+ + + + +	+ + + +	+ + +	+ + +	+	19
35	+ + + +	+ + + + +	+ +	+ + +	+ + +	+	18
36	+ + +	+ + + +	+ +	+ + +		+ +	14

A second set of findings dealt with specific interlocutor speech behaviors that were not prescribed by the interlocutor frame but which occurred anyway. This step required the analyst to return to each transcript repeatedly and to scrutinize each on a turn-by-turn basis to locate and to understand each of these behaviors. While the behaviors identified do not exhaust the possibilities (as later studies would show), they certainly form a group of observable actions which, once defined and identified, could be located in other transcripts, and in data from other examinations. These behaviors seemed particularly interesting in light of their similarity to the types of accommodative behaviour found in the SLA research (e.g., Freed 1980). More importantly, they seemed likely to introduce some sort of uncontrolled variability into the assessments, variability that might undermine the integrity of the test itself. The eight salient behaviors in which the interlocutors routinely engaged (the first six of which are illustrated on pp. 131–2) included:

- supplying vocabulary; completing responses
- rephrasing questions
- evaluating responses
- repeating or correcting responses
- stating questions
- drawing conclusions
- slowing rate
- fronting (in later studies called topic priming)

Finally, an analysis of interlocutor behaviour in the second and third sections of CASE revealed that Stage 2 Presentation was the least problematic, since the interlocutor merely provided directions and kept time. While not studied *per se*, the candidates had little trouble understanding the task, even if they had trouble completing it. Candidates did display difficulty with the Stage 2 Discussion task: only 8 of 25 pairs (32%) completed it successfully. On a positive note, the interlocutors were generally able to withdraw from the discussion and let candidates talk among themselves (a finding that was somewhat contradicted by results from a subsequent CASE study).

Since UCLES expressed an interest in being able to obtain information on behaviour of the interlocutors and to relay it to them on a routine basis, this work culminated in the development of a proposed CASE Examiner Evaluation Template (from Lazaraton 1993):

Figure 5.9

CASE Examiner Evaluation Template

Examiner Name:
Assessment #:

I   Interlocutor Frame Adherence

Stage 1 Prompts	*Used as is*	*Reworded as*	*Skipped*

1c Would you tell me your name please

•

•

•

6b Are there any new activities you
     would like to take up

Comments on adherence:

II. Speech Behaviors

Stage 1 Behaviors	*Rare*	*Occasional*	*Frequent*	*Excessive*

laughing
correcting responses
repeating responses
slowing rate/increasing pitch
completing responses
stating questions
rephrasing questions
evaluating responses
other:

Comments on speech behaviour in Stage 1:

Stage 2 Behaviors	*Rare*	*Occasional*	*Frequent*	*Excessive*

intervening to encourage talk
explaining vocabulary
explaining procedures
prompting a focus on task
asking questions
suggesting questions
other:

Comments on speech behaviour in Stage 2:

III. Rater Reliability

The template evaluates performance in three broad areas – Interlocutor Frame Adherence, Speech Behaviors, and Rater Reliability. The first section, Interlocutor Frame Adherence, could contain all 26 Stage 1 prompts or just those that were judged to be problematic in this study. A column is also included that allows UCLES to capture the rewordings interlocutors use. The second section, Speech Behaviors, would utilize a checklist of behaviors derived from this study. Rater Reliability was not a focus of this project, so no suggestions were made regarding its implementation. It was envisioned that CASE trainers would select tapes from each interlocutor and evaluate them using the template, which would constitute feedback to the interlocutor. By making interlocutors accountable for their ratings as well as their behaviour in the assessments, more reliable and valid interpretations of outcome ratings can be assured. In fact, further developments since 1993 have seen checklists for Oral Examiner monitoring being used as part of the Monitoring procedures for Cambridge examinations in general as part of RITCME (see UCLES 1999c).

The 1994 Study

As an extension of this discourse analytic research on CASE, Lazaraton and Saville (1994) reanalyzed the original dataset using a two-fold approach to investigate the features of interlocutor behaviour which emerged in conjunction with outcomes in terms of candidate behaviour and ratings assigned. First, major interactions between eight test method characteristics (Candidates (N=58), Raters (N=10), Gender (N=2), Ages (N=26), Tasks (N=18), Items (scales, N=11), Interlocutor Effect Stage 1 (N=5 interlocutors), and Interlocutor Effect Stage 2–4 (N=8 interlocutors)) were investigated statistically using the many-faceted Rasch model (FACETS version 2.7, Linacre 1989–94). Second, qualitative discourse analysis was used to document actual interlocutor behaviour in the transcripts of the assessments. In other words, we were interested in whether outcomes, as measured by ratings, would be influenced by variations in the assessment process, as operationalized by these same speech behaviors.

The results of the FACETS analysis have been reported elsewhere (Lazaraton and Saville 1994); of interest here are the results for Interlocutor Effect, since our goal was to gauge the effect of interlocutor behaviour on test outcomes. Essentially, no significant Stage 1 effect for interlocutor was detected, except for Interlocutor 2, who appeared to bring out candidates better. However, a significant effect for interlocutors in Stage 2 was clearly present, especially for Interlocutors 10, 9, 7, and 4, all of whom 'fit' very badly. We then asked whether these findings could be explored through and supported by a qualitative analysis of the transcript data. Since Lazaraton (1993) established that Interlocutor 2 consistently, and sometimes intrusively, supported the candidates in the assessments in which he acted as interlocutor, we chose his interviews as a possible evidential basis for the FACETS results. Here are some examples which demonstrate the range and kinds of support in which he engaged in Stage 1:

Supplying vocabulary

(1) CASE — Candidate 40 (2:14—18) Examiner 2

```
         IN: is there something you don't like (.) about your job?
         CA: psk .hhh ah. .hhh mm (.) yah. um nothing (.) %to— cr%
   --->  IN: nothing special.
         CA: nothing special.
```

Rephrasing questions

(2) CASE — Candidate 8 (3:2-18) Examiner 2

```
   ---> IN: and do you think you will stay in the same (.) um (.)
            area? in the same company?
            (.5)
   ---> IN: [in the future? (.) in your job.
5       CA: [same?
        CA: m-
            (.)
        CA: [same company?
   ---> IN: [in the f- (.) in the same company in the future.
10          (1.0)
        CA: uh: .hhh uh- (.) my company's eh (.) country?
   ---> IN: .hhh no .hhh in (.) in your future career?,=[will you stay
        CA:                                            =[hmm
   ---> IN: with (.) in the same area? in pharmaceuticals?
15 --->     or do you think you may change
        CA: oh: ah .hhh I want to stay (.) in the same (.) area.
```

Evaluating responses

(3) CASE — Candidate 37 (1:23-34) Examiner 2

```
         IN: what's your job
         CA: I'm working in an advertising agency ... our company manages
             psk all advertising plan? for our clients. .hhh and I'm a (.)
             media planner for radio there.
5        IN: media planner for [radio.
         CA:                   [yah.
   --->  IN: sounds interesting?
         CA: mmhmm.
```

Repeating and/or correcting responses

```
(4) CASE - Candidate 36 (2:7-10) Examiner 2
         IN: which country would you like to go to.
         CA: I: want to go: (.) in Spain.
   ---> IN: to Spain. [ah. (.) why? Spain.
         CA:          [yah
```

Stating questions that require only confirmation

```
(5) CASE - Candidate 9 (2:52-3:5) Examiner 2
         IN: okay? .hhh an: (.) and would you like to stay with
             Anderson  (.8) corporation? in the future?
             (.)
         CA: %mm I don't know%
  5 ---> IN: you don't know. [okay. .hhh um: (.) so English is
         CA:                 [mm
    ---> IN: important [to you career. .hhh would you like (.) some
         CA:          [%yeah%
         IN: higher responsibility?
```

Drawing conclusions for candidates

```
(6) CASE - Candidate 41 (2:37-42) Examiner 2
         IN: %oh. I see.% .hhh (.) and will you stay in the same (.)
             job? with the same company? in the future? (.) do you
             think?
         CA: hhh uh no:. .hhh hhh!
  5 ---> IN: you want to change again.
         CA: yes? [I .hhh I want to change (.) again.
         IN:     [hhh!
```

It did seem curious to us that only Interlocutor 2 seemed to have a statistical effect on ratings in Stage 1, where one might expect such an outcome in a one-on-one directed interaction and where the initial study reported frequent and consistent support for the candidate. On the other hand, in Stage 2, where the interlocutor is merely supposed to facilitate the interaction by giving instructional cues, 4 of the 8 interlocutors were shown to affect ratings significantly. Since all eight of the interlocutors, to a greater or lesser degree, engaged in behaviour that went above and beyond providing instructions to the candidates as suggested by the Interlocutor Frame, data from three discussions overseen by one of these 'problem' Interlocutors (as per the FACETS analysis; Interlocutor 7) are examined below. The fragments were chosen to show the scope and extent of Interlocutor 7's intervention, but it is important to reiterate that all of the interlocutors engaged in some sort of intervention after setting out the task in most, if not all, of the assessments they conducted.

The first fragment contains a discussion between a pair of candidates who were perhaps the weakest in the dataset (overall ratings of 3 (on a 3–8 point scale) and Stage 2 Discussion task achievement ratings of 4 (out of 4, 4 being the worst). It is intuitively appealing to assume that this would be the sort of situation (i.e., very low proficiency candidates) in which the interlocutor may be required to do more than just set out the task in order for any talk, much less a discussion, to occur at all.

```
(7) CASE — Candidates 56 and 58 (3:41-5:3) Examiner 7
Stage 2: Discussion

          IN: %okay.% (.2) alright. (.2) okay. this is the last session.
              (.2) and in this session. you must take part in a
              <discussion>. okay? .hhh so you should talk to <each other>.
              (.2) okay I will just listen. (.2) okay? .hhh now I'm going
     5        to give you a ca::rd (.) and I'm going to give you one.
              minute to read the card (.2) and then three minutes (.8) <to
              discuss it>.
          KT: oh
   ---> IN: okay? .hhh and I just want you to make sure (.) uh .hhh (.) .
  10---->    to to I want you to point to you (.) to the last two
   --->      sentences.= they are very important.
          KT: hhh!
          IN: okay?
              ((39 seconds reading))
     15   IN: okay so when you're ready?, (.5) you may wish to start (.8)
              talking about
          KT: oh[::
          IN:    [the task.
          KT: task? uh? eh huh huh
     20       (10.0)
          KT: %(    )%
          FO: %(yes)%
          KT: oh?
          FO: may I? (.) ask (you?) heh hhh! mm
     25       (.)
          KT: oh
   ---> IN: okay. so .hhh uh:: (.) you are going to you and your partner
   --->      can interview only one of the following people. (1.0) okay?
          KT: m
  30---> IN: Prime Minister? (.) (of) UK (.) President of the United
   --->      States  (.) Prime Minister of Canada. (.) ^which person (.)
   --->      would you choose to interview. (.8) [okay? and can you
          KT:                                    [oh oh oh
   --->      think of some questions
     35       (1.0)
   ---> IN: to ask that person.
              (1.0)
   ---> IN: okay?
              (3.8)
  40---> IN: Kitsu which person [[(.) would you choose
          KT:                   [which person uh (.) oh the President of
              the United States?,
          IN: %mmhmm?, mmhmm?,%
          KT: yeah? yeah? (1.0) %(   )% .hhh hhh!
```

```
45     FO:  %(    )%
       KT:  %yeah% hhh! hhh! hhh! [I don't-
---->IN:                          [and why.
       KT:  why?, oh (.) oh uh %( . )% the United States are President
            .hhh uh::: vote?, (.) with the .hhh (.) uh:: next uh
50          %(master)%
       FO:  %(    )%
       KT:  oh:: (.) uh
       FO:  %(    )%
            (.)
55     KT:  oh hn::h?,
            (4.0)
 ---> IN:  Fasiko? (.) who would you choose. which person.
       FO:  mmm I want to choose uh mmm the Prime Minister of the United
            Kingdom?, or the President of the United States?, .hhh
60          because (.) I don't know (.) the Prime Minister of Canada.
       IN:  mmhmm
            (.)
       KT:  oh
            (4.0)
65---> IN:  do you have [any questions [you can think of [to ask
       KT:              [oh           [oh               [oh
       KT:  oh ask?,
       IN:  mmhmm
       KT:  ask?
70---> IN:  to any:: uh:: (.) [uh: do you have any questions to ask the
       KT:                    [uh
 ---> IN:  President or the Prime Minister.
       KT:  oh oh yes. .hhh oh oh (.) what what do you think?, the (.)
            hhh! President (.) of the United States .hhh eh did uh:: is
75          uh (.) %( . )% mmmm
            ((laughter))
       FO:  mmm? mmm?
            (.8)
       IN:  okay. we're going to have to stop you there...
```

It is clear from reading this fragment carefully that these candidates are pretty much incapable of putting together a comprehensible utterance, much less discussing a fairly abstract topic. Note how the interlocutor gives special emphasis to the directions in lines 9–11, then goes on to re-explain the task in more explicit terms in lines 27–38 after an attempt for clarification by FO in line 24. When the candidates fail to respond after almost 4 seconds (line 39), the interlocutor asks one candidate directly 'Which person would you choose' in line 40, and when he responds, the interlocutor asks 'Why' in line 47. He then repeats the same procedure with the other candidate in lines 57 and 65–72. But by this point, they have run out of time. Clearly, this interlocutor works hard to draw out these candidates; just as obvious is the fact that there is no 'discussion' going on here at all, as the interaction deteriorates into an interlocutor question–candidate (attempt at) response situation not unlike the interview in Stage 1. The interlocutor's attempts to engender a discussion, however noteworthy, have failed.

In contrast, fragment (8) shows an instance where minimal interlocutor support was provided, perhaps to the candidates' detriment. These candidates, whose proficiency is fairly high (overall ability ratings of 6 out of 8 possible), were awarded disparate task achievement ratings by the interlocutor (1, the best rating) and the assessor, Rater 1, who found their performance lacking (rating of 3):

```
(8) CASE — Candidates 55 and 57 (3:38-4:32) Examiner 7
Stage 2: Discussion
           IN: okay. (.2) I'll stop you there. (.2) thank you. .hhh okay.
               can you have a look (.2) uhm this is the last session .hhh
               and you must take part (.) in a <discussion (.) together>.
               okay so you should talk to each other. .hhh okay?, .hhh
    5          please look at this card (.2) psk! I'm only going to listen
               (.8) psk! and (.8) you have one minute to read it and three
               minutes (.) to talk about it.
               ((23 seconds reading))
           IN: okay. so when you're ready (.8) you may like to start
   10          discussing
               (7.0)
           KS: who do you want huh huh to choose. .heh!
           MM: %(choose) President of the United States% [hah hah
           KS:                                           [ah yes
   15      MM: hah hah hah because [I don't ( . ) heh heh heh]
           KS:                     [heh.heh heh heh.heh      ] huh huh
           KS: (.) hhh .hhh then we choose?, (another) Pre- President of
               the United States.
           MM: %mmm%
   20      KS: ((clears throat)) uh who is the Presid(hhh)ent of the United
               States?,
           MM: uh the (.) [(%Bush%) ah that uh you know their .hhh
           KS:            [(    )
           MM: [(uh running)
   25      KS: [Mister George Bush?
           MM: mmhmm the Bush and the Clinton? is now the President
               [election,
           KS: [^uh huh.
               (.)
   30      KS: yes (.) the: election is coming
           MM: mmm (.) mmm
           KS: ah when when is the election.
           MM: mm[:
           KS:   [%do you know% (sorry) huh huh huh]
   35      MM:   [eh huh huh huh            ] %I think November%
           KS: November? [I'm not sure [heh heh
           MM:           [I'm not sure [heh heh
 ---> IN:                             [you may want to look at the last
 ---> IN: two sentences. (.8) this gives you an [idea of
   40      ??:                                   [((whispering)) %what
               (to do)%
 ---> IN: n what you need to %talk about%.
               (5.0)
           KS: %mm so% (.) %we have to prepare questions to ask%
   45      MM: ((clears throat))
           KS: %him%
               (.)
           KS: %maybe wha-%
               (.)
```

```
50    MM: %we'll interview% (.) %the President of the United States%
           ((7 seconds unintelligible whispering))
      IN: okay. (.) .hhh sorry I'm going to have to stop you there...
```

Although the candidates start off well by choosing the person in lines 12–18, they get sidetracked and go on to discuss the upcoming election rather than questions to ask the President. At this point, the interlocutor reminds them in lines 38–42 to stay on task, but in much less explicit terms than he did in the previous discussion. In fact, he refers them back to the task card to read the directions themselves, rather than just stating the directions to them. The candidates cannot seem to get going after this point, and it is likely that the examiners had difficulty hearing the subsequent talk (as the transcriber did). We do have to wonder why the raters came up with such different ratings for task achievement in this discussion. Looking at the transcript, we are inclined to agree more with the assessor's rating of 3 rather than the interlocutor's rating of 1. It is interesting to speculate about the impact of the interlocutor's impression of the candidates on his actual behaviour, and vice versa. Did he think they were doing so well that they didn't need more support or direction? Or did the fact that he didn't do more intervention persuade him that the candidates deserved ratings of 1? This analysis cannot answer this question, but it would be fruitful to pursue further.

The last discussion occurs between two candidates who were assigned overall ability ratings of 4 to 5, thus placing them above the first pair and below the second. Their task achievement ratings also differed by rater, with the interlocutor giving them a 2 and Rater 1 (the assessor) giving them a 3:

(9) CASE - Candidates 59 and 60 (3:1-4:10) Examiner 7

Stage 2: Discussion

```
         IN: okay? .hhh and this is the- this is the last session. .hhh
             uh: (.) you must take part in a discussion (.) together. (.)
             so you should <talk to each other>. (.5) psk okay?, and I
             will just listen. (.8) .hhh okay?, .hhh I want you to look
   5         at this ca::rd in a moment .hhh and I'll give you one minute
             (.) to read it (.) and three minutes (.) then to talk about
             it. (.8) okay?, .hhh and just pay attention to last pa:rt
             (.8) of the- of the uh (.5)the task. (.8) okay? psk
             ((41 seconds reading))
  10     IN: okay so when you're ready you may wish to (.) start (.)
             discussing.
             (9.0)
  ---> HU: whose s'pose choose one
  ---> IN: yes
  15     HU: question,
         ??: %question%
             (1.0)
  ---> IN: uh you may have different opinions (.) but you can talk.
  --->     about that.
  20     ??: %mmm%
             (5.0)
```

```
---> IN: who would you like to choose to interview. (.8) Hiromi.
     HU: uh:: yes I:'d like to: interview about (.) the President of
         the United States.
  25     (1.5)
---> IN: %mmhmm?% (.) %why%
     HU: .hhh mmmmmmmm .hhh uh because uh:: (.) the new:: President
         will be elected (.) this year?, so .hhh (.) %mmm% (.) I'd
         like to ask (.) mm Namiko's opinion of (.) the President of
  30     the United States.
         (.)
     NY: hm (.) and I think too I'd like to ask to the President of
         the United States
     HU: mmhmm? (.) okay
  35     (.)
---> IN: and do:: yeah
         (.)
     NY: [(     )
     HU: [an:d uh Namiko .hhh uh::m eh now the President is uh:: B-
  40     [Bu- Bu- Bush] Bush? uh::m what do you think about him.
     NY: [George Bush ]
         (.)
     NY: mmm (.) uh well he's (.) good President?, but .hh mmm (.)
         mmm (.) he has a little problem [(   )
  45 HU:                                 [what problems
     NY: psk (.) well:: (.) mm
     HU: %(for example)%
     NY: %(for example)% (.) he he thinks (.) he thinks the America
         hhh (.) is more big country,
  50 HU: than?
     NY: than (.) an ora- or- other (par-   )
     HU: (other) country
     NY: yeah (the) country
     HU:  %(   )%?
  55 NY: mmm .hhh so .hhh (sometime) he show the: .hhh (.) the other
         country (.) own (.) own country's power.
         (.)
     HU: (he's weak)
     NY: (weak).
  60 ??: %ah:::%
     NY: %(I think)%
     HU: oh really?
     NY: mm
     HU: to Japan (.) to Japan mm he also think so?,
  65     (.)
     NY: psk .hhh mmm maybe he think so too .hhh but (.) Japan and
         (.) America is (.) mmm (.) two countries should be more f-
         friendly?,
     HU: %mmm%
  70 IN: okay. (.) alright. we'll have to stop you there?,
```

In this discussion, the interlocutor allows the candidates to talk between themselves briefly and then reminds them in lines 18–19 that they can have different opinions. But when they fail to talk after 5 seconds, he uses the same strategy he did with the first pair of candidates, asking one of them directly who she would like to choose and why (lines 22 and 26). This seems to help, as the candidates agree on a person by line 34. After one more reminder in line 36, they are able to go and have a discussion, but not on the assigned task.

This may account for the assessor's mark of 3 for task achievement, the same mark she gave the last pair, who also had a discussion but not on the assigned task. The interlocutor's mark of 2 is lower than his mark of 1 for the second pair, and his intervention, in the form of direct questioning of one of the candidates, more resembled his behaviour with the first pair (lower proficiency) than with the second.

In summary, these three discussions show some interesting similarities and differences in terms of interlocutor behaviour. In each of them, the interlocutor felt the need to intervene and to provide varying amounts of assistance that was not suggested by the Interlocutor Frame for this section of the assessment. In the first discussion, extensive intervention was probably necessary with such low proficiency candidates, but no discussion resulted, even with the support. The second discussion between two more proficient candidates contained little interlocutor intervention, perhaps to the candidates' detriment. Their relatively low task achievement rating by the assessor suggests that more support early on by the interlocutor might have helped them to focus on the task and to achieve higher ratings. The fact that the interlocutor himself rated these candidates 1 out of 4 (1 being high) on task achievement raises an interesting possibility that interlocutor intervention, or lack thereof, affects his or her own ratings more than those of the assessor. The last pair of candidates were the recipients of direct interlocutor intervention early on in the discussion that focused their attention on the task. They were then able to attempt a discussion, on a related topic, and this may be why the interlocutor awarded them a 2. The assessor seemed to be unimpressed, though, and rewarded them both with 3s.

5. Implications

Only tentative conclusions were reached on the basis of these two studies. First, we attempted to exemplify an approach that could and should be conducted on other speaking test procedures. In fact, this study was only one part of the much larger Cambridge EFL examination validation program, just one aspect of which deals with candidate–examiner interaction in the oral assessment context. More specifically, we tried to portray both the possibility and the benefits of using qualitative and quantitative analyses in tandem to understand language test data (see also Pavlou 1997, whose statistical and qualitative analyses of the candidate language produced on COAST, the Cyprus Oral Academic Skills Test, led to incongruous results). Furthermore, we were again reminded of the complexity of language test data and of the relationships and interrelationships between factors that are part of them. While we could not definitively answer the validation questions we set out to address, we felt confident in saying that interlocutor language and behaviour must be standardized to some point, but it remains unclear to what extent it *should* be controlled, or to what extent it *can* be controlled. There does seem to be evidence, however, to suggest that the 'neutral' role of the interlocutor in Stage 2 of the CASE assessment cannot be assumed (Lazaraton 1996b). In fact, the results from both the statistical and the qualitative analyses suggest the opposite: that outcome ratings are affected by the interactional processes at work in the assessments themselves. Therefore, on a very practical level, it may be that Interlocutor Support, which is a bona fide rating subscale for Stage 1 of the CASE assessment, should be rated in Stage 2 as well. In any case, it was rewarding to be able to suggest a practical solution for an unexpected result that emerged from this particular research project.

More generally, these results also pointed to numerous possibilities for further research, as is evidenced by UCLES' long term program of validation to improve their operational speaking tests. Would these results obtain on different exams, with different candidates? How do candidates themselves behave? Questions like these prompted the subsequent studies reported below.

Research on CAE

1. Background

Once the CASE project was completed, UCLES commissioned a second study (Lazaraton 1994b), proposing similar goals and using the same methodology as the first, to analyze data from one of the main-suite examinations, the Certificate in Advanced English (CAE). This exam is at Cambridge Level Four within a five-level series and 'is designed to offer a high-level qualification in the language to those wishing to use English for professional or study purposes … CAE also falls within Level 4 of the ALTE framework' in which learners are termed Competent Users (UCLES 1999f: 7). That is, unlike CASE, which spanned the entire ALTE scale, CAE targets only Level 4 on the Cambridge Common Scale for Speaking. The rating criteria require the assessor to use detailed analytic scales for grammar and vocabulary (accuracy and appropriacy), discourse management, pronunciation (individual sounds and prosodic features), and interactive communication (turn-taking, initiating and responding), while the interlocutor uses a global scale.

The CAE Speaking Test consists of four parts, shown in Figure 5.10:

Figure 5.10

The structure of the CAE Speaking Test

Part	Task Type and Focus	Length of Parts	Task Format
1	Three-way conversation between the candidates and the Interlocutor Using general interactional and social language	3 minutes	The candidates are asked to respond to one another's questions about themselves, and respond to the Interlocutor's questions.
2	Two-way interaction between the candidates Using transactional language	3-4 minutes	Each candidate in turn is given visual prompts. They make comments on the prompts for about one minute; the second candidate responds as specified.
3	Two-way interaction between the candidates Negotiating and collaborating; reaching agreement or 'agreeing to disagree'	3-4 minutes	The candidates are given visual and/or written prompts to set up a problem-solving task, involving sequencing, ranking, comparing & contrasting, selecting, etc. Based on this output candidates are asked about their decisions.
4	Three-way conversation between the candidates and the Interlocutor Explaining, summarising, developing the discussion	3-4 minutes	The topic area from Part 3 is opened up by discussing wider issues.

(from UCLES 1999f: 49)

The 15-minute test is composed of four parts. In Part 1, the two candidates and the interlocutor engage in a three-way interaction. The candidates ask each other questions of a general nature about themselves, and the interlocutor may ask questions of them as well. Part 2 requires candidates to produce a long turn monologue of about one minute based on visual prompts (photographs, pictures) that elicit discourse of description, comparison-contrast, comment, speculation, and the like. The listener is expected to comment briefly on the speaker's turn. In Part 3, the candidates are given visual and/or written prompts to set up a problem-solving task, which they work on between themselves by negotiating, collaborating, and adjusting their language, as necessary. Finally, in Part 4, the interlocutor asks the candidates a question which continues and expands on the problem-solving topic from Part 3, which they respond to and discuss together.

2. Research goals

The previous CASE study suggested some broad guidelines for analyzing the CAE data. Specifically, these features were targeted:

- Interlocutor adherence to the CAE interlocutor frame,
- Interlocutor speech behaviors,
- elements to be included in a proposed CAE Oral Examiner evaluation template.

3. Method

For this study, audiotaped data were collected at four locations in Cambridge in December 1993. A total of 120 candidates were assessed in this test administration, although data from only 56 subjects, comprising 28 pairs, and 7 interlocutors and 3 additional assessors, were analyzed for this study. The data were again transcribed according to conversation analysis conventions.[4]

4. Results

The first set of results covered Part 1 of the test, where the two candidates and the interlocutor talk together. An analysis of the interlocutor input showed that only the first three of the nine prescribed prompts were used by the interlocutors; they used their own questions to round out this section.

A departure from the CASE study was a task-by-task analysis of behaviour by the interlocutors in Part 2 of CAE. A total of 20 visuals were used in this test administration; how the interlocutors handled each was ascertained. No consistent problems, either for the candidates or the interlocutors, were noted. Any discrepancies that did arise seemed to be matters of individual style, rather than a consistent across the board effect. Two suggestions were made based on analysis of this section: first, the use of paired tasks, where there are two related visuals but only one set of directions, seemed to work better than using two unrelated visuals.

A second recommendation was that the drawing tasks be deleted. In these tasks, one candidate must describe a visual in order for it to be drawn by the other. One example of this task was B4: Chairs, a segment of which is shown below. The interlocutor not only paraphrased the instructions, he gave some preliminary information about the task, gave his opinion of it, and then let the candidates interact with each other for over five minutes in order to complete the task. (In addition to one minute for the directions and one minute for the candidates to apologize to each other about how poorly they described or drew the chair, this section lasted almost six minutes.)

(10) CAE — Tape 33 (3:33-4:18) **Examiner M Part 2, Task B4**

```
         IN:  the next part is a little bit different.
              (1.0)
    ---> IN:  how good is your drawing.
              (1.0)
5   ---> IN:  'kay .hhh! ^okay. s:o:: uh:: (look) we'd like you to do some
    --->      drawing?
         ??:  %yeah%
    ---> IN:  %(so give me that.) there. it's alright% .hhh! now. this is
    --->      bit complicated?, .hhh! Antigone here are some
10            pictures of some chai:::rs.
              (1.0)
    ---> IN:  how interesting. [hmh ok(hah hah hah)ay? ri::ght?, and (.)
         AM:                   [^yeah:::
         IN:  now. I'd like you to choose one of those chairs. (.) okay one
15            that you like?, [.hhh!
    ---> AM:                  [(I'm not very good at drawing but)=
    ---> IN:  =no problem.
         AM:  heh heh
         IN:  okay and I'd like you to try to describe the chair (.) so
20            that Holly can (.) draw it.
              (.)
         AM:  o[kay
         IN:   [okay?,
              (.)
25       AM:  [okay
         IN:  [%alright% .hhh! you have about a minute for that=just- uh it
              doesn't matter about (arty) if you're English?, okay?, .hhh!
              I'd like you to imagine that she wants you to buy this chair.
              from I don't know Ikea?, or somewhere [like that?, (.) psk
30       HG:                                        [mmmhmm
         IN:  and (.) she's going to describe it so you can buy it.
         HG:  yep
         IN:  o^kay
         HG:  okay?
35            (.)
    ---> AM:  .hhh! uhm I mean can I change the: describing to her the (.)
    --->      my chair. can I change the position of the chair.
         IN:  su::re. whatever. but [uh just- don't mix them up.
         AM:                        [oh alright.
40            (.)
         AM:  %alright uhm% the chair I've chosen?, is uh black and uh it
              could be [(      )
    ---> HG:           [can I can I write?
         IN:  sure yes
45       AM:  it could be made uhm (.) of iron? %because (    )% is
              black...
```

The first salient observation is that the interlocutor may have inadvertently given the impression that this Part 2 task does require good drawing, by asking 'How good is your drawing?' and 'We'd like you to do some drawing' in lines 3–6. He then went on to comment that 'this is a little bit complicated' in lines 8–9, which probably did not encourage the candidates. Then, after giving the candidate the pictures of chairs, he sarcastically commented 'How interesting' in line 12; the candidate seemed to pick up on this attitude with her equally sarcastic reply '^yeah:::' in line 13.[5] In fact, the speaker (AM) states that she is not very good at drawing in line 16; the interlocutor missed an opportunity to remind them it is not a drawing test. Two clarification requests also occurred, both about the directions. The first in lines 36–37 shows the speaker asking about what she can do; the second in line 43 shows the listener (the drawer) when she can start writing. Also notice that nowhere in the directions does the interlocutor tell the listener not to ask questions during the speaker's turn.

The problem that becomes apparent in the subsequent chair description (not shown) is that the candidates interact during it, negotiating what is being drawn, instead of one candidate giving directions and the other simply drawing. It was somewhat surprising to see that the Interlocutor Frame for this drawing task did not direct the interlocutor to prohibit the candidates from discussing the task; even the CAE Oral Examiner Guidelines (UCLES 1993: 4) mention this. In fact, drawing tasks were used for seven pairs, and the only time that interaction between candidates did not take place was when the interlocutor specifically prohibited it. A second problem with these tasks, and one that stems from the first, is the length of time they take to complete. In those in which interaction (rather than a monologic description) took place, all lasted more than the recommended minute or so; two of them required almost six minutes just for the drawing task. Finally, the candidate responsible for producing the drawing indicated discomfort with the task unless the interlocutor said specifically it was not a test of drawing; again, this is mentioned in the Examiner Guidelines (UCLES 1993: 4). It was recommended that this reminder should be clearly spelled out in the Interlocutor Frame for these tasks.

The results of analyzing interlocutor behaviour in Parts 3 and 4 showed no gross violations from the interlocutor frame; however, the examiners sometimes used continuers ('mmhmm', 'right') during Part 3, when candidates should be talking with each other, and rarely used the prescribed Part 4 questions, instead making up their own.

Finally, an analysis of examiner behaviour with respect to speech modifications showed a great deal of consistency with the behaviors found in CASE (where no tallies were made), although a few differences did emerge. Modifications to the CASE list included splitting 'repeating and correcting responses' and 'evaluating responses' into separate categories in the CAE data. Also, Behaviour G (sarcasm) and K (assessing CAE tasks) that occurred in a few assessments did not occur (or were not noted to do so) in CASE. Table 5.1 below tallies the frequency of each behaviour across assessments; counts for individual interlocutors were also reported in the study.[6]

Table 5.1

Tally of speech behaviors across CAE assessments

A)	Drawing conclusions	22/28 interviews
B)	Assessing responses	18/28 interviews
C)	Rephrasing questions	16/28 interviews
D)	Evaluating performance	15/28 interviews
E)	Completing turns/ Supplying vocabulary	12/28 interviews
F)	Repeating responses	9/28 interviews
G)	Sarcasm	9/28 interviews
H)	Stating questions	5/28 interviews
I)	Priming topics	4/28 interviews
J)	Correcting responses	4/28 interviews
K)	Assessing CAE tasks	4/28 interviews
L)	Adjusting rate	2/28 interviews

5. Implications

Finally, an examiner evaluation template for CAE was proposed, much like the one for CASE given earlier, but reflecting some of the findings mentioned here. For example, a section on Test Administration was proposed to check that assessments are recorded in their entirety, that time is managed well, and that the examiners adhere to their test roles. Additionally, criteria for each part of the test were proposed for Interlocutor Frame Adherence to capture the different requirements in each stage. And, the Speech Behaviors section was modified to account for the behaviors found in the CAE data.

Research on KET

1. Background

One hypothesis that came out of these initial studies was that the behaviors noted probably vary with the proficiency of the candidate – that the lower the level of the candidate, the more prevalent the behaviors would become. As an initial step towards testing this idea, a study of the Speaking Test from the Key English Test (KET: UCLES 1998b) was commissioned to continue inquiry into the role of the interlocutor in the assessment process. KET, which represents Cambridge Level One (of five), 'offers a basic qualification in English' and 'falls within ALTE Level One – A Waystage User' (UCLES 1998b: 3–4). Both examiners give an impression mark (on a 1–5 point scale) for each of the two parts of the test by considering factors such as task achievement, communicative ability, appropriateness of interaction, linguistic resources, pronunciation, fluency, and independence of interlocutor.

The KET Speaking Test consists of two parts, lasting a total of 8–10 minutes. In Part 1, candidates relate personal factual information to the interlocutor, such as name, occupation, family, etc. In Part 2, the candidates use prompt cards to ask and give personal or non-personal information to each other. This information is shown in Figure 5.11:

Figure 5.11

The structure of the KET Speaking Test

Features				
	Task Format		Candidate Output	
Parts	Interaction Pattern	Input	Discourse Features	Functions
1 ocutor e ninutes	Interlocutor interviews candidate	Verbal questions from frame with 'follow-on' and 'back-up' questions	• responding to questions (including one extended response)	• giving factual information about self ('bio-data') • talking about present circumstances • expressing opinions • explaining and giving reasons • talking about future plans • talking about past experiances
2 pt Card ty ninutes	Interlocutor uses scripts to introduce candidate – candidate interaction	Interlocutor script visual and/or verbal prompts	• initiating and responding appropriately	• requesting/giving information of a personal or non-personal kind (This may include requesting/ giving informationon: - present circumstances - likes/dislikes - habits - past experiences - factual information dates/times/prices etc.)

(from UCLES 1999g: 24)

2. Research goals

With two studies already completed, UCLES proposed explicit goals for the KET study, based on the findings from CASE and CAE:

• an analysis of interlocutor frame adherence in Parts 1 and 2,
• an examination of interlocutor behaviour in Part 2 with respect to their use of the nine task cards for this section,
• a description of accommodative speech behaviors in the data, and,
• the development of a KET examiner evaluation template.

3. Method

The data for this study (Lazaraton 1995b), in the form of audiotaped recordings, were collected in late 1994 at five locations in England. There were 39 candidates, comprised of 15 pairs of two and 3 groups of 3. Eight examiners acted as either interlocutors or second assessors. Transcripts were prepared as in earlier studies.[7]

4. Results

The following results were notable. In Part 1, where the interlocutor speaks with each candidate separately, interlocutors tended to rephrase questions rather than to use the prescribed back-up questions. Also, the last prescribed question, which requires justification, was often skipped. Interlocutors also showed a marked preference for just four of the 11 topics. Part 2, which requires candidates to speak with each other to complete a task, was generally completed in the designated time frame of 3–4 minutes. And, topics were distributed equally and intrusive speech behaviors were minimal.

A second aspect of the analysis was to make sense of the interlocutor speech behaviors present in the data, both ones that were found in the CASE and CAE speaking tests, and ones that were not. Table 5.2 shows the tally across the assessments:

Table 5.2

Tally of speech behaviors across KET assessments

A)	Repeating responses	16/18 interviews
B)	Using feedback markers.	13/18 interviews
C)	Commenting on responses	10/18 interviews
D)	Drawing conclusions	8/18 interviews
E)	Rephrasing questions	8/18 interviews
F)	Adjusting rate	7/18 interviews
G)	Evaluating performance	5/18 interviews
H)	Completing/correcting responses	4/18 interviews
I)	Stating questions	1/18 interviews
J)	Priming topics	1/18 interviews
K)	Other behaviors	6/18 interviews

In these KET data, and unlike in the CAE study, the most common interlocutor behaviour was repetition of candidate responses. These repetitions function to show agreement, to ask for clarification, or to delay a response; here, they seemed to serve as confirmation checks, as in fragment (11) below:

```
(11) KET - Tape 18 (2:85-89) Examiner T Part 1

        IN: tell me Edgard. how long have you been here. in London.=
        CA: =yes three months.
  ---> IN  three months?=
        CA: =yes
```

The second most frequent behaviour (not noted in CASE or CAE) was the use of feedback markers showing attentive listening, such as the continuers 'mmhmm' or 'right,' response comments like 'really,' or conclusion statements:

```
(12) KET — Tape 16 (2:86-89)  Examiner T Part 1

        CA: but I like London because it's uh for me it's very good it's
            a big town and: interesting.
 ---> IN: mm really
        CA: psk! mmm

(13) KET — Tape 24 (2:105-111)  Examiner N Part 1

        IN: and- and how often do you play tennis.
        CA: at home? or in Cambridge.
        IN: uhm in Cambridge heh [heh
        CA:                       [Cambridge no
 ---> IN: you don't play.
        CA: I don't play tennis.
```

A third behaviour that was found much more frequently in the CASE and CAE data occurred far less on KET. Rephrased questions took several forms: they appeared as 'doubles' as in (14) or in awkward or ungrammatical form as in (15), without any (verbal) indication from the candidates that they needed such help:

```
(14) KET — Tape 19 (3:125-126)  Examiner Y Part 1

        IN: tell me something about your family. have you got any
            brothers or sisters?

(15) KET — Tape 20 (2:107)  Examiner E Part 1

        IN: you are from which country.
```

Sometimes responses were completed or corrected, but not nearly as often as on CAE:

```
(16) KET — Tape 17 (1:29-35)  Examiner Y Part 1

        IN: which town is it
        CA: uh it's called uh (Casaltdeshino).
        IN: is that a tourist place.
        CA: yes. (.2) many: ((sniff)) *uh::* (.2) mm much people come in
            for uh ho- spend=
 ---> IN: =%holiday%
        CA: (their) holidays.

(17) KET — Tape 18 (3:119-122)  Examiner T Part 1

        IN: hhh and so how often do you go to the cinema.
        CA: hhh the weekend.
 ---> IN: at the weekends.=
        CA: =%mmm%
```

It was suggested that UCLES personnel should continue to monitor interlocutor performance on the KET speaking test, but that the highly scripted interlocutor frame probably helped keep troubling behaviors to a minimum.

5. Implications

With these results on KET, a test representing the lowest level Cambridge candidates, and CAE, one representing much higher level learners, a logical next study would be to determine whether candidate proficiency level plays a role in the speech behaviour which interlocutors display. That is, do the same interlocutors behave differently with higher level CAE candidates than with lower level KET candidates?

Comparative research on CAE–KET

1. Background

KET and CAE were described in previous sections. Again KET (The Key English Test) represents Level 1 on the Cambridge Common Scale for Speaking, where candidates are expected to have a basic command of the spoken language. CAE (The Certificate in Advanced English) represents Level 4, candidates at which are expected to have a good operational command of the spoken language.

2. Research goals

In this final study on interlocutor behaviour (Lazaraton 1996c), UCLES wanted to establish whether intra-examiner variations in speaking test behaviour could be detected by analyzing data from both KET and CAE, where the same interlocutor administered at least one of each test.

3. Method

The data were collected during KET and CAE administrations in late 1995 at twelve locations in England. A total of 52 candidates were assessed, 25 KET candidates in 11 pairs and 1 group of 3, and 27 CAE candidates in 12 pairs and 1 group of 3. Eight interlocutors took part in the assessments, but data from one were unusable, as were a number of other tapes. As a result, a total of 8 KET and 9 CAE assessments, conducted by 7 different examiners (two of whom conducted 2 CAE tests and one of whom conducted 2 KET tests) were chosen for transcription.[8]

4. Results

Table 5.3 displays a rough breakdown of behaviors found across interlocutors and between examinations. For example, 6 of the 7 interlocutors reworded questions on KET while 5 of 7 did so on CAE:

Table 5.3

Speech behaviors by examination
all Interlocutors (*N*=7)

			KET	CAE
A)	Rewording questions/instructions		6/7	5/7
B)	Repeating responses		6/7	3/7
C)	Asking non-agenda questions		3/7	4/7
D)	Prompting candidate responses		2/7	4/7
E)	Drawing conclusions		3/7	1/7
F)	Varying the number of questions		4/7	0/7
G)	Commenting on responses		2/7	2/7
H)	Using feedback markers		0/7	3/7
I)	Joking with candidates		1/7	2/7
J)	Completing responses		0/7	2/7
K)	Evaluating with 'good'		2/7	0/7
L)	Correcting candidates		1/7	0/7

The most frequent interlocutor speech behaviour on both tests was rewording of questions and instructions. A behaviour not studied systematically in earlier speaking test data but found here (in three KET and four CAE tests) was the use of non-agenda questions:

```
(18) KET — Tape 85 (4:183-223) Examiner F Part 1

--->  IN1:    and what about the weather.
              (.2)
      CA1:    weather?
      IN1:    heh [huh (.2) hmh hmh hmh
 5    CA1:        [huh
      CA1:    the weather::::*uh:* (.) is: different! (1.0) uh: (.5) this
              ti:me (.2) in my country  (1.0) uh::: (.8) it uh::
              likes uh: (.2) cold, (.5) mainly very cold!
              (.2)
10--> IN1:    colder than here?
      CA1:    yes it (   ) (.5) there is: colder than here. (.5) maybe::
              (.8) I don't know!
              (.5)
      IN1:    hhh [hhh
15    CA1:        [at this moment uh
              (1.0)
      CA2:    about ten, (.2) [fifteen
      CA1:                    [suh- (.) twelve? (.8) maybe twelve, (.5)
              minus!
20    IN1:    minus::!=
      CA1:    =yes?!
              (.2)
      IN1:    TWELVE!
              (.5)
```

5 Some speaking test validation studies

```
25    CA1:    yes! [.hhh
      IN1:         [>ho ho< (oh! that's so cold!) heh [heh .hhh
      CA1:                                                [sometimes in the-
      CA1:    (.8) abou:t eh (.2) [twenty four? (.2) twenty (    )
      CA2:                        [twenty! (.) twenty five
30    CA1:    [five?, (.2) minus
      IN1:    [hhh::! (.5) dear!
              (.5)
      IN1:    so we are LUCKy here!
```

The question the interlocutor asks in line 1 is not prescribed by the agenda. While it generates some interesting candidate talk, it does lead the interview off track, and probably accounts for it lasting too long.

The discourse analysis also showed more repetition of responses with KET candidates than with CAEs in the first part of the tests. Since CAE interlocutors don't ask candidates questions directly (rather, candidates question each other), there is less opportunity to do these repetitions. Unlike on KET, where repetitions served as confirmation checks, on CAE they seemed to express surprise:

(19) CAE — Tape 80 (3:118-126) Examiner F Part 1

```
      CA1:    after in the winter (really) and in the summer (.8) used
              to: (.8) be a lifeguard (.5) on the beach.
              (.5)
      CA2:    mmhmm
              (.5)
--->  IN1:    a LIFEguard!
      ??:     %life[guard!%
      CA1:         [yeah: (.5) sounds good!
```

Two other behaviors that emerged which were not noticed in earlier projects include prompting responses and joking with candidates. In (20), Examiner F was quite aggressive in her KET exam, where she actually told one of the candidates to ask the 'next question':

(20) KET — Tape 85 (4:233-251) Examiner F Part 2

```
      CA1:    what (.) do you: (1.0) have (.5) for breakfast.
              (1.0)
      CA2:    uh:: (1.5) I have hhh (1.5) egg- uh:: (.) I have some eggs::
              (1.8) so:m::e (1.8) sandwich (2.5) (%and%) uh:: (.5) a cup.
5             of (1.0) %a cup of.% (.5) tea! (1.8) with milk, (3.8)
              usually::, (.5) I: have, (.5) a yogurt, (5.2) sometimes::
              uh::*::* I have (.2) *uh:* (1.0) some juice
              (.5
--->IN1:      psk! okay:! (.2) NEXT question.
10            (1.8)
      CA1:    what sort (.2) of (eat) (.5) you li:ke (.5) best.
              (6.0)
      ??:     (mm:)
              (1.0)
```

```
15      CA2:  I: (1.2) I preFER (.8) vegetables!
              (.2)
--->    IN1:  psk alri:ght! (.) ^next question.
              (1.0)
        CA1:  psk (3.5) what do you: (.5) cook, (4.0) %tsk% (1.5) do you
              cook
```

Joking was a behaviour that was prevalent by certain interlocutors in previous research, but was fortunately infrequent in these data. Two of the seven interlocutors joked with candidates:

(21) KET — Tape 35 (5:226-231) Examiner L Part 1

```
        IN1:  um! (.5) ^what do you do: (.2) in your free ti:me. (.5) in
              London.
              (.5)
5       CA:   %uh% (2.0) (I) study English,
              (1.0)
--->    IN1:  >in your heh free TIME!< ((laughing)) (.2) alright!
```

(22) CAE — Tape 31 (3:111-120) Examiner L Part 1

```
        IN:   tsk! .hhh Pete you can also find OUT um:, (.2) about Hiromi
        CA1:  CAN I!
              (.2)
--->    IN1:  YES!=
5       CA2:  =[hhh! heh! heh! [heh! huh!
        CA1:  =[heh heh huh huh
--->    IN1:                   [you:r allowed! heh heh heh
--->    IN1:  [heh .hhh::::! hhh!
        CA1:  [yeah well
```

5. Implications

Although no clear-cut differences across the two examinations were detected, interlocutor behaviour seems to be more a matter of individual 'style' (or lack thereof) than of candidate proficiency level. However, since only one or two samples of each test were available for each of the seven interlocutors, it is impossible to determine if the behaviors found occur in other tests with these same interlocutors or with the same frequency — that is, whether these data point to sources of random or systematic error (or both). Inevitably, we can only anticipate outcomes of the long and laborious research process on how these and other interlocutors behave on these and other EFL speaking tests.

Summary

This series of studies is clear on at least one point: the interlocutor cannot be considered a neutral factor in these assessments. Variability in behaviour is frequent, and the FACETS results on CASE suggest this to be a problem. Using an interlocutor frame, monitoring interlocutor behaviour, and training examiners thoroughly are all ways to reduce, or at least control, this variability. It is unlikely, however, that it would be possible, or even desirable, to eradicate the behaviour entirely, since 'the examiner factor' is the most important characteristic that distinguishes face-to-face speaking tests from their tape-mediated counterparts. Yet, we should be concerned if that factor decreases test reliability, even if it appears to increase the face validity of the assessment procedure. Further research in this area is most certainly warranted.

Candidate behaviour in speaking tests

The previous studies of examiner behaviour on CASE, CAE, and KET employed a conversation analytic approach to understand the role of the interlocutor in the assessment process. This approach to understanding speaking test data has become more widely used in recent years but has yet to be deployed much to focus on candidate behaviour on Cambridge (and other) EFL Speaking Tests. Two preliminary studies, however, suggested that discourse analysis is a viable approach to understanding candidate language within the context of an oral examination.

Lazaraton and Wagner (1996) undertook a functional analysis of the Revised Test of Spoken English (ETS 1999) to complement the quantitative research (e.g., Henning, Schedl, and Suomi 1995) that described the revised test's psychometric qualities in comparison with the original test version. Lazaraton and Wagner analyzed data from native and non-native speakers separately and comparatively. Native speakers, for the most part, used the speech functions that the test specifications predicted. When this same procedure was repeated with the non-native speaker data, few differences were noted, especially at the higher band levels; non-native speaker performance at Band 60 (the highest awarded score) was essentially the same as that of the native speakers in the sample.

A pilot study on candidate language output on CAE (Wagner 1994b) analyzed four paired assessments of 8 NNS from the 1994 CAE Standardization Videotape by examining the language produced in Part 2 (the long turn monologue) by means of the visual materials provided to each candidate. A total of 16 tasks (each of the eight candidates was required to produce a monologue based on pictures and a response to their partner's monologue and pictures, thus there were 2 tasks per candidate) were analyzed individually for functional genre, lexical items, and other linguistic content, and then comparatively across tasks. Her results showed that a total of seven functions were present in the data: description, speculation, opinion, support for opinion, support for speculation, comparison, and contrast. The description language was consistent across tasks (adjectives, presentatives, and present or present continuous verb usage), as was the language of opinion (prefaced by 'I think' or 'I like'). Both types of support were marked with 'because'. Wagner found speculation the most complex of the seven functions identified: candidates speculated about what was actually in the visual materials, the nature of the ideas or feelings of people shown in the materials, and the reasons why people were doing what they were in the materials.

Research on FCE

1. Background

With these studies serving as a guide for a larger project on candidate performance, Lazaraton (1997b) and Lazaraton and Frantz (1997) looked at a previously unstudied speaking test, the First Certificate in English (FCE: UCLES 1998a). FCE is the most widely taken Cambridge EFL examination and represents Cambridge Level Three (of five) as well as ALTE Level Three, an Independent User. The Speaking Test of FCE also employs a paired format and contains four parts lasting about fourteen minutes. In Part 1, the interlocutor interviews the candidates separately, asking them questions about themselves, their present circumstances, past experiences, and future plans. Candidates produce a 'long turn' of about a minute in Part 2, based on some visual material, which might be structured as comparison–contrast, description, etc., depending on the visual stimuli and the instructions of the interlocutor. In Part 3, candidates engage in a collaborative task, also based on visual stimuli, which requires negotiation and appropriate turn-taking. This topic is then discussed and expanded on in Part 4 in a discussion that the interlocutor leads with both candidates. This is illustrated in Figure 5.12:

Figure 5.12

The structure of the FCE Speaking Test

Parts	Task Format		Candidate Output	
	Interaction Pattern	Input	Discourse Features	Functions
Part 1 Interview three minutes	Interlocutor interviews candidates	Verbal questions	• responding to questions • expanding on responses	• giving personal information • talking about present circumstances • talking about past experience • talking about future plans
Part 2 Individual long turn four minutes	Interlocutor delegates an individual task to each candidate	Visual stimuli, with verbal rubrics	• sustaining a long turn • managing discourse: - coherence - organisation of language & ideas - appropriacy of vocabulary - clarity of message	• giving information • expressing opinions through comparing & contrasting
Part 3 Two-way collaborative task three minutes	Interlocutor delegates a collaborative task to the pair of candidates	Visual stimuli, with verbal rubrics	• turn-taking (initiating & responding appropriately) • negotiating	• exchanging information & opinions • expressing & justifying opinions • agreeing and/or disagreeing • suggesting • speculating
Part 4 Three-way discussion four minutes	Interlocutor leads a discussion with the two candidates	verbal prompts	• responding appropriately • developing topics	• exchanging information & opinions • expressing & justifying opinions • agreeing and/or disagreeing

(from UCLES 1998a: 45)

2. Research goals

These two studies on FCE were part of a larger FCE Speaking Test Revision Project which took place during the five years preceding the implementation of the new version in 1996. Generally, according to Taylor (1999), revisions of Cambridge EFL tests aim to account for the current target use of the candidates/learners, as well as developments in applied linguistics and description of language, in models of language learning abilities and in pedagogy, and in test design and measurement. The process typically begins with research, involving specially commissioned investigations, market surveys, and routine test analyses, which look at performance in the 5 skill areas, task types, corpus use, and candidate demographics. With FCE, a survey of 25,000 students, 5,000 teachers, 1200 oral examiners, and 120 institutions asked respondents about their perspectives on the proposed revisions. This work is followed by an iterative cycle of test draft, trialling, and revision.

As a result, UCLES had a specific research question in mind for the FCE studies, which the researchers used to guide their analyses:

What is the relationship between the task features in the four parts of the revised FCE Speaking Test and the candidate output in terms of speech production?

The rationale for this question was to establish that the features of speech which are purported to be evaluated by the rating criteria are in fact produced by the candidates. The goal of the first study, which looked at data from the 1996 FCE Standardization Video, was, first, to provide supplementary information to the standardization video materials, where appropriate, and second, to provide a framework for examining candidate output in a dataset of live FCE Speaking Tests that formed the basis of the second study.

Once the Standardization Video study was completed, Lazaraton and Frantz (1997) proceeded to examine a corpus of live data from November–December 1996 FCE test administrations. The rationale for this second project, again, was to establish that the features of speech which are predicted as output and which are to be evaluated by the rating criteria are actually produced by the candidates, and then to make recommendations, if necessary, about how the descriptions of the test may be amended to make the descriptions fit the likely speech output from the candidates.

3. Method

The 1996 Standardization Video study (Lazaraton 1997b), used transcribed assessments (five pairs and one group of three), from 13 nonnative speaker subjects (9 females and 4 males), representing a variety of native languages (Spanish, Swedish, German, Russian, Italian, and French). Four interlocutors (one female and three males) took part in the assessments. The data were previously transcribed according to conversation analysis conventions.[9]

In the second study of live assessments, 14 audiotaped Speaking Tests from the November-December 1996 FCE examinations were transcribed and analyzed.[10] The dataset included 28 nonnative speaker subjects and 5 interlocutors. A wide range of native languages was represented (Spanish, French, Chinese, Japanese, Korean, Thai, Swedish, Italian, Greek, and Czech), but it should be noted that only one of the 28 candidates and only one of the 5 interlocutors were males; it is unclear whether our findings are generalizable to other male candidates who take or examiners who administer this examination, or if gender is a factor at all.

4. Results

The Standardization Video

Each of the six transcripts from the Standardization Video was then analyzed for the speech functions employed by the candidates in each part of the examination. This was accomplished by dividing each transcript into four parts and labeling candidate speech functions present in each section. The hypothesized speech functions that are described in the FCE materials (UCLES 1996: 26–7; see Figure 5.14 on p.158) were used as a starting point and were modified or supplemented as the results from the data analysis progressed.

The analysis indicated that candidates, for the most part, did employ the speech functions that are hypothesized in the printed FCE materials. This was particularly true for Parts 3 and 4, and mostly so for Part 1. Part 2 showed the most deviation from the expected output. Here, the candidates did not always explicitly compare and contrast as they were directed, but they did employ a number of other speech functions in this section, including description, justification, narration, and speculation, as the task instructions directed.

Not all candidates in Part 1 (where the interlocutor interviews the candidates) of the examination were given the opportunity, via interviewer questions, to engage in all of the suggested speech functions. With the exception of giving personal information, which candidates in the first five assessments were all asked to do, it seemed rather hit or miss as to whether they would be asked to talk about present circumstances, past experiences, *and* future plans. Figure 5.13 below shows which of the 13 candidates were asked to talk about past, present, and future in Part 1:

Figure 5.13

Questions Asked of Candidates in Part 1 of FCE

Speech Function	Candidates												
	1H	1P	2M	2C	2R	3A	3S	4E	4C	5E	5N	6M	6F
Personal Information	*	*	*	*	*	*	*	*	*	*	*		
Present Circumstances	*	*	*		*			*	**		*		
Past Experiences				*		*	*		*	*			
Future Plans	*	*	*		*	*	**	*	*	*	*	**	*

First, it should be clear that no candidate was given the opportunity to engage in all four of the hypothesized speech functions. Candidates 2C and Pair 6 seemed to be shortchanged in this respect. Also, notice that three candidates were able to use a speech function in response to other questions (indicated by double asterisks). That is, candidates could and did use speech functions that were not asked for, or ones that were different from the question called for.

One suggestion to FCE test developers and administrators was to decide how important it is for candidates to get the opportunity talk about different time frames, via the use of a variety of verb tenses, in this part of the test, and how any changes in this direction could be accomplished.

Candidate output in Part 2 (where each candidate has a long turn) deviated most noticeably from the speech functions expected for this section of the examination in that a larger variety of functions was found than anticipated. In addition, although every one of the prompts used asked the candidates to compare and contrast, fewer than half did so in a way that was evident. On the other hand, each candidate was required to either express a preference/opinion or relate a personal experience, and all did so. In addition, candidates engaged in description, justification, and speculation to enhance their monologues.

One line of inquiry that was proposed in relation to Part 2 would be to collect some native speaker baseline data to determine which functions are critical for 'success' in this part and which are enhancing functions. Since no ratings for 'task achievement' were available for these candidates (it doesn't appear that there are rating criteria for such a feature in FCE), it is impossible to evaluate the products other than impressionistically based on transcript data.

Candidate talk in Part 3 (where candidates engage in a collaborative task) of the examination matched fairly well what is laid out in the FCE materials. Likewise in Part 4 (the interlocutor-led discussion on the Part 3 topic): candidate speech functions matched what was expected. The most notable finding from this last section was the highly collaborative nature of responses to interviewer questions. In other words, a sense of 'task achievement' was hard to evaluate for one candidate without taking into account the contributions of the other. This was particularly true for the two female candidates, both of whom were from Columbia, in Pair 1. While this may not be so important for evaluating linguistic skills like pronunciation, it seems critical for any sort of explicit evaluation of discourse management and interactive communication and any implicit judgments about task completion.

The Live Assessments

Each of the 14 transcripts was studied for the speech functions employed by the candidates in each part of the examination. The preliminary framework developed in the earlier Standardization Video study was used as a starting point for examining candidate output in this dataset. Again, labeling candidate speech functions in each part was carried out, using the hypothesized speech functions that are described in the FCE materials (UCLES 1997c: 35–6) and the findings from the Standardization Video study.

A total of 15 speech functions were identified in the transcripts, a number of which were ones that UCLES had identified as predicted candidate output functions. Some, however, were components of the expected functions which were thought to be too broad, too vague, or which showed too much overlap with another function. That is, then, some of the expected functions were divided into more specific functions. Finally, a few of the 15 identified functions were ones which were not predicted in the FCE materials, either directly or as part of a broader function. The general framework that emerged is presented in Figure 5.14:

Figure 5.14

Expected and Actual FCE Speech Functions

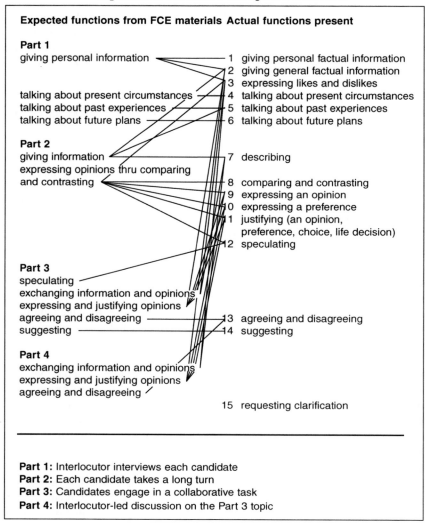

Expected functions from FCE materials Actual functions present

Part 1
giving personal information
       1 giving personal factual information
       2 giving general factual information
       3 expressing likes and dislikes
talking about present circumstances 4 talking about present circumstances
talking about past experiences 5 talking about past experiences
talking about future plans 6 talking about future plans

Part 2
giving information 7 describing
expressing opinions thru comparing
and contrasting 8 comparing and contrasting
       9 expressing an opinion
      10 expressing a preference
      11 justifying (an opinion, preference, choice, life decision)
      12 speculating

Part 3
speculating
exchanging information and opinions
expressing and justifying opinions
agreeing and disagreeing 13 agreeing and disagreeing
suggesting 14 suggesting

Part 4
exchanging information and opinions
expressing and justifying opinions
agreeing and disagreeing

      15 requesting clarification

Part 1: Interlocutor interviews each candidate
Part 2: Each candidate takes a long turn
Part 3: Candidates engage in a collaborative task
Part 4: Interlocutor-led discussion on the Part 3 topic

The expected list gives the impression that certain functions will be found in or restricted to a particular part of the test. While each part of the test did elicit a predominance of certain functions, there was a good deal of overlap between the four test parts and some functions. Using a list of more specific function names shows this more clearly. For example, the functions 'expressing likes and dislikes' and 'giving general factual information' are used by candidates in all four parts of the FCE examination. Lazaraton and Frantz felt that their proposed list of speech functions present in these FCE Speaking test data is both a more accurate and a more comprehensive framework with which to judge candidate language output. Figure 5.15 below presents a schematic of these findings:

Figure 5.15

Summary of speech functions in the four parts of FCE

Speech Function	Part 1	Part 2	Part 3	Part 4
1. Giving personal factual information	**		*	*
2. Giving general factual information	**	*	*	*
3. Expressing likes and dislikes	**	*	**	*
4. Talking about present circumstances	**	*	*	
5. Talking about past experiences	**	*	*	*
6. Talking about future plans	**			
7. Describing		***		*
8. Comparing and contrasting	**	**		*
9. Expressing an opinion	*	**	***	**
10. Expressing a preference	*	**	***	**
11. Justifying (an opinion)	*	*	***	**
12. Speculating	***		***	*
13. Agreeing and disagreeing	*		***	*
14. Suggesting			**	
15. Requesting clarification	**		*	

	= blank indicates it does not occur[11]
*	= infrequent
**	= common
***	= frequent

Part 1: Interlocutor interviews each candidate
Part 2: Each candidate takes a long turn
Part 3: Candidates engage in a collaborative task
Part 4: Interlocutor-led discussion on the Part 3 topic

Part 1 of the examination (where the interlocutor interviews each candidate) elicits the widest range of speech functions, including all but description, speculation, and suggestion. The results showed that candidates were given multiple opportunities to engage in these speech functions through direct elicitation. This is an improvement over the assessments on the Standardization Video, where some candidates were shortchanged with questions regarding present circumstances and past experiences.

Part 2 (where each candidate takes a long turn) elicits a rather narrow range of speech functions, with description and speculation the most prevalent and comparison–contrast, opinion, and preference also common. As with the Standardization Video, the range of functions is much greater than the original list of expected functions suggests. Also, more candidates seemed to engage in actual comparison and contrast than did those on the Standardization Video.

A range of speech functions was also present in **Part 3** (where candidates engage in a collaborative task), with opinion, preference, justification, speculation, and agreement/disagreement all being quite common.

Part 4 (the interlocutor-led discussion on the Part 3 topic) exhibited the most restricted range of speech functions, none of which was very frequent. Since candidate output in this section of the examination is heavily dependent on the quantity and type of interlocutor questions that are asked, output in this section could probably be modified by requiring or eliminating any of the scripted follow-up questions.

As for the speech functions themselves, most seem to be present in all parts of the examination, but to greater or lesser degrees. For example, the first five functions occur, although not with great frequency, throughout the examination. Other functions, such as talking about future plans, description, and suggestion, seem to be limited to certain parts of the examination. Still others, such as expressing opinions, expressing preferences, justification, and speculation, occur very frequently in some parts and less so in others.

5. Implications

In short, it was hoped that the results of this study would be useful to FCE test developers and trainers in making more accurate assessments of candidate output in the examination. Although there is no explicit task achievement rating scheme for FCE, the list of 15 speech functions generated from these data may prove helpful in developing one. Additionally, the list may be useful for analyzing candidate output in other Cambridge speaking tests, although it remains an empirical question whether the same functions, with the same distribution, would appear at a range of candidate ability levels. This question seems like fertile territory for further research.

Research on IELTS

1. Background

The last study to date (Lazaraton 1998) shifted gears somewhat; first, although it continued a focus on candidate language, data from another examination, the IELTS Speaking Test (UCLES 1999a) was analyzed. Secondly, since the purpose was to analyze specific features of candidate language produced on the test, rather than interlocutor–candidate interaction, conversation analysis could not be used. Rather, a more general type of discourse analysis, discussed in Chapter 4 (see p. 99) was applied.

The International English Language Testing System (IELTS) is an EFL examination, jointly managed by UCLES, the British Council, and the International Development Program Education Australia (IDPEA), which is 'recognized as an entrance requirement by British, Australian, New Zealand, American, and Canadian universities and for secondary, vocational and training programmes' (UCLES 1998c: 19). The test consists of listening, reading, writing and speaking modules, equally weighed, with scores reported on a 9-band scale of ability (from Non User to Expert User). The Speaking module uses an interview format that emphasizes general speaking skills in five sections, lasting from 10–15 minutes. The first section, the introduction, has candidates talk briefly about themselves, their homes, and their interests. The second section asks the candidate to produce some extended discourse on a familiar topic involving explanation, description, or narration. In the third part, the candidate must elicit some information from the interlocutor via a task card. Finally, the candidates are encouraged to speculate and discuss their future plans. Unlike the other Cambridge EFL examinations, IELTS candidates are tested alone, rather than in pairs (see p. 119).

2. Research goals

Like the work on FCE, the work on IELTS should also be seen in a larger context of the IELTS Speaking Test Revision Project, currently underway, which involves clarifying task specifications to reflect input and expected candidate output, introducing an interlocutor frame to encourage standardization of test delivery, and revising the rating scales to reflect actual candidate output (UCLES 1999d). Much of this work is supported by research commissioned by UCLES (such as this study), by IELTS Australia (e.g., Brown and Hill 1998), and jointly by the British Council and IELTS Australia.

Specifically, this study looked at live examination performance at different levels in order to identify features of language which distinguish different band scores. This required looking at linguistic features, such as grammar, vocabulary, and pronunciation, as well as discourse and conversational features in order to, potentially, provide information for the revision of the ratings scales for IELTS Speaking. Given that there has been very little published work on the empirical relationship between candidate speech output and assigned ratings (but see Douglas 1994, Fulcher 1996a, and Young 1995b), there was little guidance on how to approach this task.

3. Method

This project analyzed 20 IELTS Speaking Tests which were recorded under live examination conditions. These recordings were collected by LTC Australia as part of a collaborative UCLES/IELTS Australia Research Project. These recordings were selected as being typical of candidate ability at different bands. The 20 subjects for the study were distributed as follows: 2 males at Band 3, 3 females and 1 male at Band 4, 6 females and 1 male at Band 5, 3 males and 3 females at Band 6, and 1 male at Band 7. Native languages represented included Thai, Indonesian, Chinese, Japanese, Korean, French, Vietnamese, Burmese, Italian, Serbian, Portuguese, and German. No information was made available that allowed for identification of different examiners.

The recordings were transcribed very roughly, using standard orthography, by someone unknown to the researcher. Unfortunately, the quality of transcription precluded analysis of certain features of test talk and interaction. For one, the transcripts were often inaccurate and so it was not clear what was said by the candidates in a number of places. More important is the fact that two features of turntaking, namely overlaps in talk and pauses between turns, were not transcribed, so that an analysis of candidate responsiveness was not possible. In addition, since pauses within candidate turns were not transcribed, descriptions of fluency could only be impressionistic since they cannot be illustrated with the data. The fact that the analyses were carried out anyway should not be misinterpreted as condoning the preparation or use of rough and/or sloppy transcripts.

4. Results

Table 5.4 provides an overall summary of the features found by level for this group of IELTS candidates. The tally shows the number of assessments in which the feature occurred at each band score:[12]

Table 5.4

Tabulation of features by score band on IELTS
(*N*=20)

	B	A	N	D
FEATURE	3	4	5	6	7
Communication Strategies					
repair initiation	2/2	4/4	4/7	2/6	1/1
repeating Ex. talk	2/2	3/4	1/7	---	---
self-correction	1/2	3/4	3/7	3/6	1/1
Coherence					
coordinators					
(and, but)	2/2	4/4	7/7	6/6	1/1
subordinators					
(so, because)	2/2	4/4	7/7	6/6	1/1
lists	1/2	1/4	---	---	---
listing words					
(1st, 2nd)	---	3/4	5/7	4/6	1/1
other items					
(especially,					
actually, etc.)	---	1/4	3/7	3/6	1/1
Speculation					
maybe	2/2	3/4	2/7	5/6	1/1
will	---	2/4	4/7	5/6	1/1
would like to	---	3/4	1/7	4/6	---
want to	1/2	3/4	4/7	---	1/1
have to	---	---	1/7	3/6	---
intend to	---	---	---	1/6	1/6
I'm going to	1/2	---	1/7	1/6	---
Grammatical Structures					
topic-comment	2/2	1/4	2/7	1/6	---
missing subject	2/2	2/4	4/7	---	---
missing verb	2/2	1/4	1/7	---	---
double negative	---	---	---	3/6	---
relative clause	---	---	2/7	2/6	1/1
conditional	---	3/4	5/7	6/7	1/1
passive	---	---	2/7	1/6	1/1
Section 3 – Questioning					
taking initiative	---	1/4	6/7	6/6	1/1
Conversational Language					
you know	---	2/4	4/7	1/6	---
I mean	---	---	1/7	1/6	---
(a) lot(s) of	---	1/4	1/7	3/6	1/1
sort of	---	---	---	1/6	---

Communication Strategies: the tally in the first category shows that repair initiations on and repetitions of interlocutor talk become less frequent towards the upper bands, while self-correction remains fairly constant. For example, the Band 4 candidate in (23) and (24) is able to self-correct and to initiate repair:

(23) IELTS — Candidate 19 (3:56) Band 4

    C: so but when it was raining and and **I don't have I didn't have any umbrella**...

(24) IELTS — Candidate 19 (1:11-14) Band 4

    E: and have you been able to see much of Australia whilst you've been here?
    C: **ah un a pardon?**
    E: have you been able to visit many places?
    C: yeah sure many place just beachies...

By Band 5, the candidates exhibit ability to target problematic items more precisely in the discourse in their repair initiations:

(25) IELTS - Candidate 15   (6:173-174) Band 5

    E: what type of education are you interested in? what level?
    C: **um um da rebel what ah what does it mean?**

And at Band 6, circumlocution is used as a communication strategy:

(26) IELTS — Candidate 17 (2:41-46) Band 6

    E: what does it look like? Is it a very old city?
    C: yes. it is old city becau because it had ah a long long history. it is ah we have **I don't know how to use da word ah bicentenary**...

Coherence: all candidates at all band scores were able to use the most frequent coordinators and subordinators, but other signals, such as 'first', 'the most important', and 'especially', are more apparent at higher levels. Listing as a strategy was only used at Bands 3/4. Some data supporting these findings were presented in Chapter 4 (Examples 6–11, pp. 99–100).

Speculation: the ability to speculate was achieved by all candidates using 'maybe', but at higher levels, a broader range of expressions expressing future plans or hypothetical reality.

At Band 3, only two speculation strategies were used – 'want to' and 'maybe':

(27) IELTS – Candidate 2 (6:148-150) Band 3

    C: I **want to** improve my country because my country is many
       pollution

Candidate 9, however, had only one strategy for talking about future plans, and that was by using 'maybe':

(28) IELTS – Candidate 9 (6:169-172) Band 3

    E: and then after high school what are you going to do?
    C: mm **maybe** university.
    E: mmhmm. and what would you like to study at university?
       computers?
    C: mm. **maybe** mm computer and business together.

By Band 4, candidates still employ 'maybe' as a speculative marker but also attempt to use other grammatical structures to express speculation, such as conditionals:

(29) IELTS – Candidate 6 (6:155-156) Band 4

    E: and when you're maybe doing this for ten years would you
       like to own many hotels or just make one big hotel?
    C: oh the first is da one big hotel but **if the business is**
       successful maybe continue with da several hotel.

(30) IELTS – Candidate 11 (7:219-220) Band 4

    E: why did you choose hotel management?
    C: because my father's job and a dis a little **if** I ah **if I**
       get um **if I enter dis colle college and den graduate**
       my father can help me get job.

By Band 5, candidates also reveal a greater ability to talk about the hypothetical future, especially using conditional expressions (which are not always structurally accurate):

(31) IELTS - candidate 13 (11:283-288) Band 5

    E: so you two will be a good combination you and your
       brother will be a good combination.
    C: yeah I sink so
    E: yeah yeah
    C: but dat but it depen I sink it depen on me **if I a don't**
       fi a a good course and I don't study hard is
       not a good combination.

```
(32) IELTS — Candidate 8 (4:81-82) Band 5
```

> E: and does that mean that you would start you say a
>   bachelor degree you'd start with you you'd start architecture
>   again?
> C: yes because um I study graduate university ah in Vietnam
>   so I think **if I am pass IALT test ah I I think I**
>   **will stay at university ah in a second years at**
>   **post years yeah maybe.**

The one candidate at Band 7 was able to speculate about the future using a wide range of expressions, such as 'intend to', 'will', 'maybe', a conditional, and various time markers:

```
(33) IELTS — Candidate 20 (7:166-172) Band 7
```

> C: **in one week I leave** ah Australia but I **intend to stay**
>   in Australia in Jinuree. So I will um I applied a for
>   um to to participate ah in a course...here at the
>   university and um if **I get in into it into this course**
>   **I will come back** but **at first I have to** return to
>   Switzerland to to join the army.

Grammatical Structures: grammatical errors were more prevalent at the lower Bands, and complex structures, such as relative clauses, conditionals, and passives, appeared at the higher Bands.

Section 3 – Questioning: one clear finding was that taking the initiative by contextualizing Section 3 questions and responding appropriately to interlocutor answers becomes a regular feature of candidate talk as Band score increases.

At Band 3, candidates were limited to reading expressions off the task sheets with 'what' in initial position to form questions:

```
(34) IELTS — Candidate 9 (5:142) Band 3
```

> C: what **is reason for taking course?**

```
(35) IELTS — Candidate 9 (6:150) Band 3
```

> C: **what lent of course?**

Band 4 testees constructed questions that sometimes lacked wh-words or inversion:

```
(36) IELTS — Candidate 6 (5:120) Band 4
```

> C: **the leng of time it took to get better?**

In contrast, look at a section of the Band 7 candidate's interaction with the tester. His request 'but maybe I can take it' was not a scripted question; notice also how he 'acts' the role by claiming that he won first prize in the competition the interlocutor is talking about:

(37) IELTS — Candidate 20 (6:145-148) Band 7

> E: so although I won th the this prize and ah I'm sure the
>   menu would be very good if it has this recipe that I
>   wrote I don't think I want to take it.
> C: **but um maybe I can take it? Because uh**
> E: Would you like it?
> C: **Yeah. very much. ah in fact I I won da first prize.**

Conversational Language: the use of conversational discourse appears at Band 4 and becomes more regular at higher proficiency levels. Note also the informal expressions used here by Band 6 candidates:

(38) IELTS — Candidate 12 (9:287-288) Band 6

> E: and if you don't get residency what are your plans?
> C: **I'm dying.** If I don't ah I must come back in Europe....

(39) IELTS — Candidate 4 (7:178-180) Band 6

> C: so I I I need to learn Mandarin and yes I have **sort of**
>   um alot of difficulties in Taiwan...

A number of recommendations were made based on these findings. First, there wasn't always consistency in the features mentioned across bands. For example, Fluency is mentioned at Bands 3 and 8; Pronunciation is mentioned at the ends of the scale (Bands 2, 3, 8, 9).

Second, it was suggested that some of the terms used in the rating scale should be operationally defined. For example, what counts as a 'modifier'? Only adjectives? Are prepositional phrases, adverbs, and relative clauses to be considered modifiers too? Similarly, 'connectives' and 'cohesive features' are mentioned, but it is unclear how broad this category is: does it include conjunctions? subordinators? logical connectives? Anything else?

Third, detecting errors that 'impede communication' was not always straightforward. There were many instances where it was difficult to determine what was being said, but the interlocutors indicated no trouble. Conversely, there were places where the interlocutors initiated repair on items that seemed clear. And is there a difference between 'interfere with' (Band 4) and 'impede' communication (Band 3)? Related to this is the question of what is meant by 'effective communication' (Band 6 and up).

Similarly, what is meant by 'circumlocution'? This fits into the category of 'communication strategies', where it was found that candidates engaged in self-correction and initiated repair. Is self-correction a form of circumlocution? What else is covered by this term?

As in earlier studies, a number of language functions were predicted, but not always employed. The rating scale mentions description and attitude expression (Band 4), extended argument, speculation, and narration (Band 5), and variations of these at the higher levels. Obviously, not all candidates were given opportunities to show all of these skills. For example, one candidate at Band 6 was never really asked about her future plans. It might also be worth considering further how speculation is accomplished. Table 5.4 (p.163) indicates that there is a broadening of speculative strategies at higher levels; even though the same expression 'maybe' is used at all levels, it is essentially the only expression used at Band 3.

Finally, a mention of the use of conversational language (i.e., discourse markers and fillers) should be considered, since this language appears to be part of the communicative repertoire of candidates at higher levels.

5. Implications

These findings are useful, but limited in several ways. First, judgments about fluency and turntaking were not possible since the transcripts were not prepared in such a way as to show these features accurately. It was suggested that if further work is planned for this dataset, the transcripts would need to be redone. Secondly, the distribution of candidates across bands was unequal, and was particularly problematic at the ends: there were only two Band 3 candidates, one Band 7 candidate, and none higher than that. Not only would a wider distribution be beneficial, but more equal numbers at each Band would allow for more confidence in the claims drawn about those underrepresented levels. Finally, although a native speaker 'norm' is presumably not assumed on the IELTS test, it might be interesting to collect some data from a group of native speakers of equivalent age, background, etc. to see how they deal with the tasks with which they are confronted. Clearly, we shouldn't expect a performance from IELTS candidates that we would not expect from a group of comparable native speakers.

In short, these findings suggest a number of modifications to the rating scales, which should not only increase the reliability of the assessment (e.g., so that all raters are clear on what 'cohesive features' are), but lead to rating scales which more accurately reflect facts about language in use. Thus, confidence in score interpretations, the fundamental goal of construct validation, can undoubtedly be increased.

Summary

Clearly, these studies have only dealt with isolated aspects of candidate behaviour; there remains much to be done. While both the FCE and the IELTS studies had as their goals informing rating scale development and refinement, this sort of effort probably needs to be made for all rating scale criteria in a more systematic fashion, across examinations.

Conclusion

These studies on various Cambridge EFL Speaking Tests represent an extension of the discourse-based work on oral assessment mentioned in Chapter 1. We now know more about how interlocutors and candidates behave during the test, and how this behaviour approximates to conversation. The IELTS study attempted to compare features of the discourse produced with assigned band scores, and along with the FCE studies, made some headway on informing rating scale construction and validation. The unique contribution of all these studies to the field of language testing, though, is their demonstration of both the applicability and the suitability of conversation/discourse analysis for understanding the process of oral assessment via an examination of the discourse produced in this context. Some further thoughts on these issues are the subject of the next, and final, chapter.

Notes

1. This observation is supported by the fact that in the edited collections by Cumming and Berwick (1996) and Kunnan (1998c), only one of the 20 empirical test validation studies published in the books can be considered 'qualitative'; see also Lazaraton (2000) on similar trends in applied linguistics journal articles.

2. CASE is no longer available as a speaking test; it has been superseded by the optional speaking test in BULATS (Business Language Testing Service).

3. These data were transcribed in 1993 by Gina Fuller and Sharon Wilkinson, graduate students at the Pennsylvania State University, under the supervision and direction of the researcher, using a Dictaphone transcriber. All transcripts were checked carefully, and corrected where necessary, by the researcher. Subsequent credits for transcription will only name the transcriber and the year the transcripts were produced, since all were completed under the same conditions.

4. Transcribed by Sharon Wilkinson in 1994.

5. This characterization of sarcasm is based on hearing how the examiner and the candidate deliver these turns. Unfortunately, the reader cannot hear this intonation and thus cannot evaluate this conclusion.

6. The data were tallied in this manner so as to avoid skewing the frequencies in the cases where one examiner contributed most instances of the behaviour. For example, the behaviour 'evaluating performance' occurred in 15 of the 28 interviews; however, fully 9 of those instances (60%) were the work of just one interlocutor. The point of these tallies (also present in Tables 5.2 and 5.3) was to suggest the scope of the phenomenon in the dataset. In no cases were counts made of behaviors in each individual assessment (in line with Schegloff's numerator and denominator problems discussed in Chapter 4).

7. Transcribed by Amy Bargfrede in 1995.

8. Transcribed by Erin Chervenak in 1996.

9. Transcribed by Stacie Wagner in 1997.

10. Transcribed by Roger Frantz in 1998.

11. These characterizations of frequency were arrived at impressionistically, in line with CA orthodoxy.

12. Consistent with the procedure described in Note 6 above, these figures show frequencies across band scores, not the number of times a feature occurred in a single interview or across interviews at one band score.

6 Summary and future directions

The preceding chapters have endeavored to put forth a detailed description of the methodology of conversation analysis and a rationale for employing it in oral language test validation. Examples have been provided to illustrate the different steps in the analytic process and to explore a range of issues, both theoretical and practical, that may arise at each stage.

It has been argued that conversation analysis provides a uniquely suited vehicle for understanding the interaction, and the discourse produced, in face-to-face oral assessment procedures. With its focus on real, recorded data that are carefully transcribed, CA allows us to move beyond mere intuitions about face-to-face test interaction and the discourse produced in it to empirically grounded findings that carry weight. While CA does not provide much guidance for dealing with monologic data, some of its principles, in terms of unmotivated looking, comprehensive single case analysis, and a general avoidance of quantifying data and of isolating sociological variables, have much to offer us in understanding a range of oral language examinations.

Chapter 1 began with an overview of the field of language testing, especially its ongoing interest in the assessment of the speaking ability of second and foreign language learners. It was noted that there is now a substantial body of work on well-known oral tests, such as the ACTFL OPI; some of this research was reviewed here. Yet, it was argued that many of these past outcome-based studies have been both inconclusive and limited in scope; there is now a clear impetus for engaging in other sorts of work on these tests. Specifically, there is a growing interest in the benefits of engaging in qualitative research on oral language assessment. The remainder of the chapter highlighted a number of recent discourse-based research studies with which this book aligns but also extends.

Chapter 2 described the historical roots and current work in conversation analysis, the sociological approach to talk-in-interaction advocated in this book, which can explain so much about oral communication. It was assumed that most readers would be unfamiliar with the history, empirical findings, and prevailing interests of CA, so the chapter offered succinct explanations of these matters as well copious references for those interested in learning more about CA. This portion of the book situated conversation analysis in the wider body of discourse analytic work and traced its historical roots from

Garfinkel's ethnomethodology and Goffman's interaction analysis to one of its current concerns, institutional talk. The major organizational systems of conversation, including turntaking, repair, sequence structure, preference organization, and topic organization were detailed with respect to the empirical findings that have emerged about these systems. It was remarked that the role of nonverbal behaviour in conversation has not received as much attention as it perhaps merits, mostly due to the difficulties of collecting, transcribing, and making sense of gestures, gaze, and the like. Following an evaluation of conversation analysis as an analytic approach, the parameters of institutional talk, especially interviews, were delineated. I contended that this growing body of work on news and survey interviews, medical encounters, and standardized testing situations is directly relevant to work in language testing in terms of understanding the oral interview process.

Chapter 3 introduced the first steps in the conversation analytic process, collecting and transcribing data. Practical suggestions were put forward for collecting data in both audiotaped and videotaped formats, and for selecting data for analysis. A number of philosophical issues regarding transcription were then raised, noting that transcription is always a selective, interested process that attempts to represent speech in written form. Suggestions were put forward about learning the CA transcription system as well as training others to use it. The actual conventions of CA were then introduced with numerous examples, with descriptions noting the different decisions that transcribers must reach in the process. The chapter concluded by discussing techniques for transcribing and presenting languages other than English and nonverbal behaviour.

Chapter 4 continued with an explanation of the analytic process by first elucidating some of the philosophical issues underlying the CA approach, such as insisting on the use of real, recorded data, approaching data in an unmotivated way, parsing the discourse into turns, comprehensively analyzing single cases, de-emphasizing sociological variables, and eschewing the coding and counting of data. Actual conversation analysis was then demonstrated on two oral interview segments following a series of steps proposed by Pomerantz and Fehr (1997), which they refer to as 'analytic tools' that guide the researcher in identifying sequential boundaries, characterizing the turn-by-turn actions in the sequence, relating turntaking, packaging of actions, and timing of turns to certain understandings, and relating these understandings to participant roles, relationships and identities. Because CA cannot be appropriately applied to monologic data, three methods for analyzing the speech of a single speaker were illustrated: a rhetorical analysis of narratives and descriptions, a functional analysis of speech acts, and a structural analysis of linguistic features; further practice with both interactive and monologic data was provided by end-of-chapter exercises. The chapter concluded with a discussion of and justification for 'argument from example', the method by which conversation analysts report their findings. This method requires the analyst to state empirical claims clearly, present evidence in the form of examples, and account for exceptions. Guidelines were put forward for selecting data to report, presenting data in a report, and critiquing other studies that use the same methodology.

Chapter 5 opened with a review of the current thinking on test validity by focusing on Messick's theory of construct validation and its potential shortcomings, as noted by a number of language testers who have called for broader, more comprehensive approaches to construct validation, especially those that stem from qualitative research traditions. As background to the empirical studies that follow, the Cambridge approach to speaking tests was then detailed. Therewith, a series of actual speaking test validation studies which analyzed data from five UCLES EFL Speaking Tests (CASE, CAE, KET, FCE, IELTS) and which employed conversation/discourse analysis were summarized. Some of the unique findings that emerged from these studies were highlighted, especially those that were unexpected, intuited but as yet unverified by data, or beyond the reach of traditional psychometric procedures. The studies on interlocutor behaviour point to one unambiguous conclusion: that the interlocutor in oral assessment is not a neutral factor and must be accounted for in test validation. The two studies on candidate behaviour merely scratched the surface of the crucial question of whether/how rating scale components are accurate reflections of actual candidate performance, since they did not focus on the role that other test method factors play in candidate performance (for example, the test materials used (visuals, discussion tasks), or the grouping of the candidates into pairs or threes). Yet, all of these studies furnished the test developers with concrete ideas for monitoring examiner behaviour, and revising and refining rating scales, both of which represent just one part of a long-term program of test validation that is currently being applied to other Cambridge EFL examinations.

It is as well to keep in mind the shortcomings of the conversation analysis approach, though. Aside from the theoretical and conceptual objections mentioned in Chapter 2, we have seen that CA is not helpful for analyzing monologic data, where there is an absence of interaction; for the same reason, CA cannot be applied to the modality of writing. Equally troubling is the fact that CA is difficult, if not impossible, to learn without the benefit of tutelage under a trained analyst and/or with others. As a result, the number of researchers who feel comfortable with and driven to use the methodology will undoubtedly remain small. It is hoped that language testers employed at universities would encourage their students (or be encouraged themselves) to seek out such training. A third obstacle is that this sort of work, which results in copious amounts of transcribed talk but no 'hard' statistical data, has generally had a difficult time finding a home in professional dissemination outlets, such as conferences and journals. Until the results of this research can be more widely circulated, argued, and replicated, the approach itself may retain its marginal status in language testing.

Do these facts imply that CA will be of no use to the language testing community in the long run? One would hope not; the fact that discourse analyses of oral test data have become more prevalent, as professional conference presentations and as published work, suggests that discourse analysts can move beyond an interest in discourse *per se* to questions about the uses to which the oral examinations and the scores derived from them are put. Will this approach or other qualitative research techniques ever achieve respectability in language testing? Perhaps, but like the larger field of applied linguistics, which, for the most part, aspires to the rigor of traditional social science, language testers will undoubtedly view qualitative methodologies as, at best, complements to more 'powerful' quantitative techniques.

On the other hand, it bears repeating that conversation analysis has much to recommend it as a means of validating oral language tests (and as a tool in language pedagogy; see Riggenbach 1999). For example, along with more traditional quantitative measures of test, subtest, or item integrity, the process of pretesting, testing, and revising can be strengthened by using discourse analysis to look at the language produced in addition to the ratings assigned. While we would, rightfully, be surprised to discover that each candidate in a test of writing was given slightly different instructions, the fact that oral examiners routinely modify any set of instructions to deal with the turn-by-turn interactional contingencies in the assessment process has only recently been questioned, empirically verified, and, to some extent, remedied through examiner training and standardization; discourse analysis of oral test data is directly responsible for these achievements. It seems to me, though, that perhaps the most important contribution that CA can make to language testing is in the accessibility of its data and the claims based on them. That is, for many of us, the highly sophisticated statistical analyses of language test datasets are comprehensible only to those versed in those analytic procedures; this group rarely includes the examiners themselves, or administrators and ESL/EFL teachers who are stakeholders in the test and its outcomes. The results of conversation analysis are patently observable, even if one does not agree with the conclusions at which an analyst may arrive. As such, language testers who engage in conversation analyses of test data have the potential to reach a much larger, and less exclusive readership.

Finally, I would be remiss if I didn't mention other qualitative approaches to test validation that show great promise. Banerjee and Luoma (1997) overview many of these approaches, which they see as providing valuable information on test content, the properties of testing tasks, and the processes involved in taking tests and assessing test output. That is, qualitative validation techniques help to clarify the nature of performance that scores are based on, rather than to detail the psychometric properties of tests and items, as quantitative techniques are designed to do. Much of their chapter is devoted to explaining the utility of verbal reports, a topic which has received book-length coverage recently by Alison Green (1998) and is currently finding its way into empirical studies on language tests (e.g., Meiron 1999). Banerjee and Luoma also note that observations (of item writing meetings, rating sessions), questionnaires and interviews (as in Hill's 1998 study of test-taker impressions of **access:**), and analyses of test language (the topic of this book) are just a few means by which test validation can be achieved qualitatively; they believe that we can go even further in this direction, by using, for example, learner/rater diaries and qualitative software analysis programs, and by applying these techniques to look into the interpretations and uses of test scores by teachers and administrators, stakeholders whose voices often remain unheard in the validation process (Moss 1994; Hamp-Lyons and Lynch 1998).

In sum, the field of language testing is in the midst of important changes in perspective and practice. As it matures, I am optimistic that we can welcome those whose interests and expertise lie outside the conventional psychometric tradition: qualitative researchers like myself, of course, but also those who take what Kunnan (1998b) refers to as 'postmodern' and 'radical' approaches to language assessment research. Furthermore, I would also hope, along with Moss, Hamp-Lyons, and Lynch, that the stakeholders in assessment, those who use the tests that we validate, would have a greater voice in the assessment process in order to ensure that our use of test scores is, first and foremost, responsible use. I hope you share my eagerness in awaiting these exciting, and long overdue, developments.

References

Alderson, J. C., Clapham, C., and Wall, D. 1995. *Language Test Construction and Evaluation*. Cambridge: Cambridge University Press.

American Council on the Teaching of Foreign Languages. 1986. *ACTFL/ETS Proficiency Guidelines*. Hastings-on-Hudson, NY: Author.

Anderson, J. A. (ed.) 1988. *Communication Yearbook 11*. Newbury Park, CA: Sage.

Atkinson, J. M. 1982. Understanding formality: The categorization and production of 'formal' interaction. *The British Journal of Sociology* 33: 86–117.

Atkinson, J. M. 1992. Displaying neutrality: Formal aspects of informal court proceedings. In P. Drew and J. Heritage (eds.), *Talk at Work: Interaction in Institutional Settings*. Cambridge: Cambridge University Press, pp. 199–211.

Atkinson, J. M. and Drew, P. 1979. *Order in the Court*. London: Macmillan.

Atkinson, J. M. and Heritage, J. C. (eds.) 1984. *Structures of Social Action: Studies in Conversation Analysis*. Cambridge: Cambridge University Press.

Atkinson, P. 1992. *Understanding Ethnographic Texts*. Newbury Park, CA: Sage.

Austin, J. L. 1962. *How to Do Things With Words*. Cambridge, MA: Harvard University Press.

Bachman, L. F. 1988. Problems in examining the validity of the oral proficiency interview. *Studies in Second Language Acquisition* 10: 149–64.

Bachman, L. F. 1989. Language testing – SLA research interfaces. *Annual Review of Applied Linguistics* 9: 193–209.

Bachman, L. F. 1990. *Fundamental Considerations in Language Testing*. Oxford: Oxford University Press.

Bachman, L. F. 1991. What does language testing have to offer? *TESOL Quarterly* 25: 671–704.

Bachman, L. F. and Eignor, D. R. 1997. Recent advances in quantitative test analysis. In C. Clapham and D. Corson (eds.), *Language Testing and Assessment*. Encyclopedia of Language and Education Volume 7. Dordrecht: Kluwer Academic Publishers, pp. 227– 42.

Bachman, L. F., Lynch, B. K., and Mason, M. 1995. Investigating variability in tasks and rater judgments in a performance test of foreign language speaking. *Language Testing* 12: 238–57.

Bachman, L. F. and Palmer, A. S. 1981. The construct validation of the FSI oral interview. *Language Learning* 31: 167–86.

Bachman, L. F. and Palmer, A. S. 1982. The construct validation of some components of communicative proficiency. *TESOL Quarterly* 16: 449–65.

Bachman, L. F. and Palmer, A. S. 1996. *Language Testing in Practice*. Oxford: Oxford University Press.

Bachman, L. F. and Savignon, S. 1986. The evaluation of communicative language proficiency: A critique of the ACTFL oral interview. *Modern Language Journal* 70: 380–90.

Banerjee, J. and Luoma, S. 1997. Qualitative approaches to test validation. In C. Clapham and D. Corson (eds.), *Language Testing and Assessment*. Encyclopedia of Language and Education Volume 7. Dordrecht: Kluwer Academic Publishers, pp. 275–87.

Bargfrede, A. 1996. *Don't Hang Up Yet: NNS Negotiation of Telephone Closings*. Unpublished Master's Paper, The Pennsylvania State University, PA.

Barnwell, D. 1989. 'Naive' native speakers and judgments of oral proficiency in Spanish. *Language Testing* 6: 152–63.

Bennett, A. and Slaughter, H. 1983. A sociolinguistic/discourse approach to the description of the communicative competence of linguistic minority children. In C. Rivera (ed.), *An Ethnographic/Sociolinguistic Approach to Language Proficiency Assessment*. Clevedon: Multilingual Matters Ltd., pp. 2–26.

Benson, D. and Hughes, J. A. 1991. Method: evidence and inference – evidence and inference for ethnomethodology. In G. Button (ed.), *Ethnomethodology and the Human Sciences*. Cambridge: Cambridge University Press, pp. 109–36.

Berwick, R. and Ross, S. 1996. Cross-cultural pragmatics in oral proficiency interview strategies. In M. Milanovic and N. Saville (eds.), *Studies in Language Testing 3: Performance Testing, Cognition, and Assessment: Selected Papers from the 15th Language Testing Research Colloquium, Cambridge and Arnhem*. Cambridge: Cambridge University Press, pp. 34–54.

Birdwhistell, R. L. 1972. A kinesic-linguistic exercise: The cigarette scene. In J. J. Gumperz and D. Hymes (eds.), *Directions in Sociolinguistics: The Ethnography of Communication*. Oxford: Basil Blackwell, pp. 381–404.

Briggs, C. L. 1986. *Learning How To Ask: A Sociolinguistic Appraisal of the Role of the Interview in Social Science Research*. New York, NY: Cambridge University Press.

Brown, A. 1995. The effect of rater variables in the development of an occupation-specific language performance test. *Language Testing* 12: 1–15.

Brown, A. and Hill, K. 1998. Interviewer style and candidate performance in the IELTS oral interview. *IELTS Research Reports 1998 Volume 1*. Sydney: IELTS Australia, pp. 1–19.

Brown, G. and Yule, G. 1983. *Discourse Analysis*. Cambridge: Cambridge University Press.

Brown, J. D. 1997. Computers in language testing: Present research and some future directions. *Language Learning and Technology* 1: 44–59.

Button, G. 1987. Answers as interactional products: Two sequential practices used in interviews. *Social Psychology Quarterly* 50: 160–71.

Button, G. 1992. Answers as interactional products: Two sequential practices used in interviews. In P. Drew and J. Heritage (eds.), *Talk at Work: Interaction in Institutional Settings*. Cambridge: Cambridge University Press, pp. 212–31.

Button, G. and Casey, N. 1984. Generating topic: The use of topic initial elicitors. In J. M. Atkinson and J. Heritage (eds.), *Structures of Social Action: Studies in Conversation Analysis*. Cambridge: Cambridge University Press, pp. 167–90.

Byrnes, H. 1987. Features of pragmatic and sociolinguistic competence in the oral proficiency interview. In A. Valdman (ed.), *Proceedings of the Symposium on the Evaluation of Foreign Language Proficiency*. Bloomington, IN: Indiana University, pp. 167–77.

Campbell, C. 1990. Writing with others' words: Using background reading text in academic composition. In B. Kroll (ed.), *Second Language Writing: Research Insights for the Classroom*. Cambridge: Cambridge University Press, pp. 211–30.

Canale, M. and Swain, M. 1980. Theoretical bases of communicative approaches to second language teaching and testing. *Applied Linguistics* 1: 1–47.

Celce-Murcia, M. (1998). Preface. In R. Young and A. W. He (eds.), *Talking and Testing: Discourse Approaches to the Assessment of Oral Proficiency*. Philadelphia: John Benjamins, pp. vii–viii.

Chalhoub-Deville, M. 1995. Deriving oral assessment scales across different tests and rater groups. *Language Testing* 12: 16–33.

Chervenak, C. E. 1996. *Rater Perceptions of International Teaching Assistant Narrative Speech*. Unpublished Master's Paper, The Pennsylvania State University, PA.

Clapham, C. and Corson, G. (eds.) 1997. *Language Testing and Assessment*. Encyclopedia of Language and Education Volume 7. Dordrecht: Kluwer Academic Publishers.

Clark, J. L. D. 1979. Direct vs. semi-direct tests of speaking ability. In E. J. Briere and F. B. Hinofotis (eds.), *Concepts in Language Testing: Some Recent Studies*. Washington, DC: TESOL, pp. 35–49.

Clark, J. L. D. 1980. Towards a common measure of speaking proficiency. In J. L. Frith (ed.), *Measuring Spoken Language Proficiency*. Washington, DC: Georgetown University Press, pp. 15–26.

Clark, J. L. D. 1988. Validation of a tape-mediated ACTFL/ILR-scale based test of Chinese speaking proficiency. *Language Testing* 5: 187–205.

Clark, J. L. D. and Hooshmand, D. 1992. 'Screen-to-screen' testing: An exploratory study of oral proficiency interviewing using video teleconferencing. *SYSTEM* 20: 293–304.

Clark, J. L. D. and Lett, J. 1988. A research agenda. In P. Lowe, Jr. and C. W. Stansfield (eds.), *Second Language Proficiency Assessment: Current Issues*. Englewood Cliffs, NJ: Prentice Hall, pp. 53–82.

Clayman, S. E. 1988. Displaying neutrality in television news interviews. *Social Problems* 35: 474–92.

Clayman, S. E. 1989. The production of punctuality: Social interaction, temporal organization, and social structure. *American Journal of Sociology* 95: 659–91.

Clayman, S. E. 1992. Footing in the achievement of neutrality: The case of news interview discourse. In P. Drew and J. Heritage (eds.), *Talk at Work: Interaction in Institutional Settings*. Cambridge: Cambridge University Press, pp. 163–98.

Clayman, S. 1995. The dialectic of ethnomethodology. *Semiotica* 107: 105–23.

Clayman, S. E. and Maynard, D. W. 1995. Ethnomethodology and conversation analysis. In P. Ten Have and G. Psathas (eds.), *Situated Order: Studies in the Social Organization of Talk and Embodied Activities*. Washington, DC: International Institute for Ethnomethodology and Conversation Analysis & University Press of America, pp. 1–30.

Cohen, A. 1984. On taking tests: What the students report. *Language Testing* 1: 70–81.

Cohen, A. D. 1994. *Assessing Language Ability in the Classroom,* 2nd Edition. Boston, MA: Heinle and Heinle.

Conlan, C. J., Bardsley, W. N. and Martinson, S. H. 1994. *A study of intra-rater reliability of assessments of live versus audio-recorded interviews in the IELTS Speaking component.* Report of study commissioned by the International Editing Committee of IELTS.

Cortazzi, M. 1993. *Narrative Analysis*. London: Falmer Press.

Crookes, G. 1990. The utterance, and other basic units for second language discourse analysis. *Applied Linguistics* 11: 183–99.

Cumming, A. 1996. Introduction: The concept of validation in language testing. In A. Cumming and R. Berwick (eds.), *Validation in Language Testing*. Clevedon: Multilingual Matters Ltd, pp. 1–14.

Cumming, A. and Berwick, R. (eds.) 1996. *Validation in Language Testing*. Clevedon, Avon: Multilingual Matters Ltd.

Dandonoli, P. and Henning, G. 1990. An investigation of the construct validity of the ACTFL Proficiency Guidelines and oral interview procedure. *Foreign Language Annals* 23: 11–22.

Davis, K. A. 1992. Validity and reliability in qualitative research on second language acquisition and teaching. *TESOL Quarterly* 26: 605–8.

Davis, K. A. 1995. Qualitative theory and methods in applied linguistics research. *TESOL Quarterly* 29: 427–53.

Derek, R. and Bull, P. (eds.) 1989. Conversation: *An interdisciplinary Perspective.* Clevedon, Avon: Multilingual Matters Ltd.

Dore, J. and Dorval, B. 1990. The politics of intimacy: A dialogic analysis of 'Being Intimate' in a psychology experiment. In B. Dorval (ed.), *Conversational Organization and its Development.* Norwood, NJ: Ablex, pp. 78–98.

Dorval, B. (ed.) 1990. *Conversational Organization and its Development.* Norwood, NJ: Ablex.

Douglas, D. 1994. Quantity and quality in speaking test performance. *Language Testing* 11: 125–44.

Douglas, D. and Selinker, L. 1992. Analyzing oral proficiency test performance in general and specific purpose contexts. *SYSTEM* 20: 317–28.

Drew, P. 1992. Contested evidence in courtroom cross-examination: The case of a trial for rape. In P. Drew and J. Heritage (eds.), *Talk at Work: Interaction in Institutional Settings.* Cambridge: Cambridge University Press, pp. 470–520.

Drew, P. and Heritage, J. C. 1992a. Analysing talk at work: An introduction. In P. Drew and J. Heritage (eds.), *Talk at Work: Interaction in Institutional Settings.* Cambridge: Cambridge University Press, pp. 3–65.

Drew, P. and Heritage, J. C. (eds.) 1992b. *Talk at Work: Interaction in Institutional Settings.* Cambridge: Cambridge University Press.

Drew, P. and Wootton, A. (eds.) 1988. *Erving Goffman: Exploring the Interaction Order.* Boston, MA: Northeastern University Press.

Dubois, J. 1991. Transcription design principles for spoken discourse research. *Pragmatics* 1: 71–106.

Duff, P. A. 1986. Another look at interlanguage talk: Taking task to task. In R. R. Day (ed.), *Talking to Learn: Conversation in Second Language Acquisition.* Rowley, MA: Newbury House, pp. 147–81.

Duncan, S. 1972. Some signals and rules for taking speaking turns in conversation. *Journal of Personality and Social Psychology* 23: 283–92.

Edge, J. and Richards, K. 1998. May I see your warrant, please?: Justifying outcomes in qualitative research. *Applied Linguistics* 19: 334–56.

Educational Testing Service 1999. *The Test of Spoken English.* Princeton, NJ

Edwards, J. A. 1993. Principles and contrasting systems of discourse transcription. In J. A. Edwards and M.D. Lambert (eds.), *Talking Data: Transcription and Coding in Discourse Research.* Hillsdale, NJ: Lawrence Erlbaum, pp. 3–31.

Edwards, J. A. and Lambert, M. D. (eds.) 1993. *Talking Data: Transcription and Coding in Discourse Research*. Hillsdale, NJ: Lawrence Erlbaum.

Egbert, M. M. 1997. Schisming: The collaborative transformation from a single conversation to multiple conversations. *Research on Language and Social Interaction* 30: 1–51.

Egbert, M. M. 1998. Miscommunication in language proficiency interviews of first-year German students: A comparison with natural conversation. In R. Young and A. W. He (eds.), *Talking and Testing: Discourse Approaches to the Assessment of Oral Proficiency*. Philadelphia: John Benjamins, pp. 149–72.

Eggins, S. and Slade, D. 1997. *Analyzing Casual Conversation*. London: Cassell.

Ellis, D. G. and Donohue, W. A. (eds.) 1986. *Contemporary Issues in Language and Discourse Processes*. Hillsdale, NJ: Lawrence Erlbaum Associates, Publishers.

Erickson, F. and Schultz, J. 1982. *The Counselor as Gatekeeper: Social Interaction in Interviews*. New York, NY: Academic Press.

Fairclough, N. 1992. Discourse and text: Linguistic and intertextual analysis within discourse analysis. *Discourse and Society* 3: 193–217.

Fisher, S. and Todd, A. D. (eds.) 1983. *The Social Organization of Doctor–Patient Interaction*. Washington, DC: Center for Applied Linguistics.

Fiksdal, S. 1990. *The Right Time and Pace: A Microanalysis of Cross-cultural Gatekeeping Interviews*. Norwood, NJ: Ablex.

Foot, M. C. 1999. Relaxing in pairs. *ELT Journal* 53: 36–41.

Ford, C. E. and Thompson, S. A. 1996. Interactional units in conversation: Syntactic, intonational, and pragmatic resources for the management of turns. In E. Ochs, E. A. Schegloff, and S. A. Thompson (eds.), *Interaction and Grammar*. Cambridge: Cambridge University Press, pp. 134–84.

Fox, B. A., Hayashi, M. and Jasperson, R. 1996. Resources and repair: A cross-linguistic study of syntax and repair. In E. Ochs, E. A. Schegloff, and S. A. Thompson (eds.), *Interaction and Grammar*. Cambridge: Cambridge University Press, pp. 185–237.

Frankel, R. M. 1983. The laying of hands: Aspects of the organization of gaze, touch, and talk in a medical encounter. In S. Fisher and A. D. Todd (eds.), *The Social Organization of Doctor–Patient Interaction*. Washington, DC: Center for Applied Linguistics, pp. 19–54.

Frankel, R. M. 1990. Talking in interviews: A dispreference for patient-initiated questions in physician–patient encounters. In G. Psathas and R. Frankel (eds.), *Interaction Competence*. Washington, DC: International Institute for Ethnomethodology and Conversation Analysis & University Press of America, pp. 231–62.

Freed, B. F. 1980. Talking to foreigners versus talking to children: Similarities and differences. In R. C. Scarcella and S. D. Krashen (eds.), *Research in Second Language Acquisition*. Rowley, MA: Newbury House, pp. 19–27.

Fulcher, G. 1987. Tests of oral performance: The need for data-based criteria. *ELT Journal* 41: 287–91.

Fulcher, G. 1996a. Does thick description lead to smart tests? A data-based approach to rating scale construction. *Language Testing* 13: 208–38.

Fulcher, G. 1996b. Testing tasks: Issues in task design and the group oral. *Language Testing* 13: 23–51.

Fulcher, G. 1997. The testing of speaking in a second language. In C. Clapham and D. Corson (eds.), *Language Testing and Assessment*. Encyclopedia of Language and Education Volume 7. Dordrecht: Kluwer Academic Publishers, pp. 75–85.

Fulcher, G. 1999. Assessment in English for Academic Purposes: Putting content validity in its place. *Applied Linguistics* 20: 221–36.

Fuller, G. 1993. *Non-native English Speakers in Telephone Openings.* Unpublished Master's Paper, The Pennsylvania State University, PA.

Garfinkel, J. 1967. *Studies in Ethnomethodology.* Englewood Cliffs, NJ: Prentice-Hall.

Gaskill, W. H. 1980. Correction in NS–NNS conversation. In D. Larsen-Freeman (ed.), *Discourse Analysis in Second Language Research.* Rowley, MA: Newbury House, pp. 125–37.

Goffman, E. 1981. *Forms of Talk.* Philadelphia, PA: University of Pennsylvania Press.

Good, C. 1979. Language as social activity: Negotiating conversation. *Journal of Pragmatics* 3: 151–67.

Goodwin, C. 1981. *Conversational Organization: Interaction Between Speakers and Hearers.* New York, NY: Academic Press.

Goodwin, C. 1984. Notes on story structure and the organization of participation. In J. M. Atkinson and J. Heritage (eds.), *Structures of Social Action: Studies in Conversation Analysis.* Cambridge: Cambridge University Press, pp. 225–46.

Goodwin, C. 1994. Professional vision. *American Anthropologist* 96: 606–33.

Goodwin, C. and Heritage, J. C. 1990. Conversation analysis. *Annual Review of Anthropology* 19: 283–307.

Greatbatch, D. 1988. A turn-taking system for British news interviews. *Language in Society* 17: 401–30.

Greatbatch, D. 1992. On the management of disagreements between news interviewees. In P. Drew and J. Heritage (eds.), *Talk at Work: Interaction in Institutional Settings.* Cambridge: Cambridge University Press, pp. 268–301.

Green, A. 1998. *Verbal Protocol Analysis in Language Testing Research: A Handbook.* Cambridge: Cambridge University Press and University of Cambridge Local Examinations Syndicate.

Green, J., Franquiz, M., and Dixon, C. 1997. The myth of the objective transcript: Transcribing as a situated act. *TESOL Quarterly* 31: 172–6.

Grice, H. P. 1975. Logic and conversation. In P. Cole and J. Morgan (eds.), *Syntax and Semantics, Vol. 3: Speech Acts.* New York, NY: Academic Press, pp. 41–58.

Grotjahn, R. 1986. Test validation and cognitive psychology: Some methodological considerations. *Language Testing* 3: 159–85.

Gumperz, J. J. 1982a. *Discourse Strategies.* Cambridge: Cambridge University Press.

Gumperz, J. J. (ed.) 1982b. *Language and Social Identity.* Cambridge: Cambridge University Press.

Gumperz, J. J. 1992a. Interviewing in intercultural situations. In P. Drew and J. Heritage (eds.), *Talk at Work: Interaction in Institutional Settings.* Cambridge: Cambridge University Press, pp. 302–27.

Gumperz, J. J. 1992b. Contextualization and understanding. In A. Duranti and C. Goodwin (eds.), *Rethinking Context: Language as an Interactive Phenomenon.* Cambridge: Cambridge University Press, pp. 229–52.

Gumperz, J. J. and Berentz, N. 1993. Transcribing conversational exchanges. In J. A. Edwards and M. D. Lambert (eds.), *Talking Data: Transcription and Coding in Discourse Research.* Hillsdale, NJ: Lawrence Erlbaum, pp. 91–121.

Haarman, L. 1998. *Transcribing data.* Paper presented at the Research Methodology in Applied Linguistics: Tradition and Innovation Conference, Verona, Italy: May.

Hadley, A. O. 1993. *Teaching Language in Context,* 2nd Edition. Boston, MA: Heinle and Heinle.

Halberstam, S. 1978. Interviewing in sociology: A brief review. In L. Churchill (ed.), *Questioning Strategies in Sociolinguistics.* New York, NY: Newbury House, pp. 5–18.

Halliday, M. A. K. and Hasan, R. 1976. *Cohesion in English.* London: Longman.

Hamp-Lyons, L. and Lynch, B. K. 1998. Perspectives on validity: A historical analysis of language testing conference abstracts. In A. Kunnan (ed.), *Validation in Language Assessment: Selected Papers from the 17th Language Testing Research Colloquium, Long Beach.* Mahwah, NJ: Lawrence Erlbaum Associates Publishers, pp. 253–76.

Hatch, E. 1992. *Discourse and Language Education.* New York: Cambridge University Press.

He, A. W. 1998. Answering questions in LPIs: A case study. In R. Young and A. W. He (eds.), *Talking and Testing: Discourse Approaches to the Assessment of Oral Proficiency.* Philadelphia: John Benjamins, pp. 101–16.

He, A. W. and Young, R. 1998. Language proficiency interviews: A discourse approach. In R. Young and A. W. He (eds.), *Talking and Testing: Discourse Approaches to the Assessment of Oral Proficiency.* Philadelphia: John Benjamins, pp. 1–26.

Heath, C. 1984. Talk and recipiency: Sequential organization in speech and body movement. In J. M. Atkinson and J. Heritage (eds.), *Structures of Social Action: Studies in Conversation Analysis.* Cambridge: Cambridge University Press, pp. 247–65.

Heath, C. 1986. *Body Movement and Speech in Medical Interaction.* Cambridge: Cambridge University Press.

Heath, C. 1989. Pain talk: The expression of suffering in the medical consultation. *Social Psychology Quarterly* 52: 113–25.

Heath, C. 1992. The delivery and reception of diagnosis in the general-practice consultation. In P. Drew and J. Heritage (eds.), *Talk at Work: Interaction in Institutional Settings.* Cambridge: Cambridge University Press, pp. 235–67.

Henning, G. 1983. Oral proficiency testing: Comparative validities of interview, imitation, and completion methods. *Language Learning* 33: 315–32.

Henning, G. 1986. Quantitative methods in language acquisition research. *TESOL Quarterly* 20: 701–8.

Henning, G. 1992. The ACTFL oral proficiency interview: Validity evidence. *SYSTEM* 20: 365–72.

Henning, G. and Cascallar, E. 1992. *A Preliminary Study of the Nature of Communicative Competence.* TOEFL Research Report 36. Princeton, NJ: Educational Testing Service.

Henning, G. Schedl, M., and Suomi, B. K. 1995. *Analysis of Proposed Revisions of the Test of Spoken English.* TOEFL Research Report RR48. Princeton, NJ: Education Testing Service.

Heritage, J. C. 1984. A change of state token and aspects of sequential placement. In J. M. Atkinson and J. Heritage (eds.), *Structures of Social Action: Studies in Conversation Analysis.* Cambridge: Cambridge University Press, pp. 299–345.

Heritage, J. C. 1985. Analyzing news interviews: Aspects of the production of talk for an overhearing audience. In T. van Dijk (ed.), *Handbook of Discourse Analysis, Volume. 3: Discourse and Dialogue.* London: Academic Press, pp. 95–117.

Heritage, J. C. 1995. Conversation analysis: Methodological aspects. In U. M. Quasthoff (ed.), *Aspects of Oral Communication.* Berlin: Walter de Gruyter, pp. 391–418.

Heritage, J. C. 1999. Conversation analysis at century's end: Practices of talk-in-interaction, their distributions, and their outcomes. *Research on Language and Social Interaction:* 32: 69–76.

Heritage, J. C. and Greatbatch, D. 1989. On the institutional character of institutional talk: The case of news interviews. In P. A. Forstorp (ed.), *Discourse in Professional and Everyday Culture.* Linkoping studies in communication. Linkoping: University of Linkoping, pp. 47–98.

Heritage, J. C. and Roth, A. L. 1995. Grammar and institution: Questions and questioning in the broadcast news interview. *Research on Language and Social Interaction* 28: 1–60.

Heritage, J. C. and Sefi, S. 1992. Dilemmas of advice: Aspects of the delivery and reception of advice in interactions between health visitors and first time mothers. In P. Drew and J. Heritage (eds.), *Talk at Work: Interaction in Institutional Settings.* Cambridge: Cambridge University Press, pp. 359–417.

Heritage, J. C. and Sorjonen, M.-L. 1994. Constituting and maintaining activities across sequences: And-prefacing as a feature of question design. *Language in Society* 23: 1–29.

Hill, K. 1998. The effect of test-taker characteristics on reactions to and performance on an oral English proficiency test. In A. Kunnan (ed.), *Validation in Language Assessment: Selected Papers from the 17th Language Testing Research Colloquium, Long Beach.* Mahwah, NJ: Lawrence Erlbaum Associates Publishers, pp. 209–29.

Hobbs, J. 1990. Topic drift. In B. Dorval (ed.), *Conversational Organization and its Development.* Norwood, NJ: Ablex, pp. 3–22.

Hoekje, B. and Linnell, K. 1994. 'Authenticity' in language testing: Evaluating spoken language tests for international teaching assistants. *TESOL Quarterly* 28: 103–26.

Hopper, R., Koch, S. and Mandelbaum, J. 1986. Conversation analysis methods. In D. G. Ellis and W.A. Donohue (eds.), *Contemporary Issues in Language and Discourse Processes.* Hillsdale, NJ: Lawrence Erlbaum Associates Publishers, pp. 169–86.

Hymes, D. 1974. *Foundations in Sociolinguistics: An Ethnographic Approach.* Philadelphia, PA: University of Pennsylvania Press.

Hymes, D. 1982. What is ethnography? In P. Gilmore and A. A. Glatthorn (eds.), *Children In and Out of School: Ethnography and Education.* Washington, DC: Center for Applied Linguistics, pp. 21–32.

Jackson, S. 1986. Building a case for claims about discourse structure. In D. G. Ellis and W. A. Donohue (eds.), *Contemporary Issues in Language and Discourse Processes.* Hillsdale, NJ: Lawrence Erlbaum Associates Publishers, pp. 129–47.

Jacobs, S. 1986. How to make an argument from example in discourse analysis. In D. G. Ellis and W. A. Donohue (eds.), *Contemporary Issues in Language and Discourse Processes*. Hillsdale, NJ: Lawrence Erlbaum Associates Publishers, pp. 149–67.

Jacobs, S. 1988. Evidence and inference in conversation analysis. In J.A. Anderson (ed.), *Communication Yearbook* 11. Newbury Park, CA: Sage, pp. 433–43.

Jacobs, S. 1990. On the especially nice fit between qualitative analysis and the known properties of conversation. *Communication Monographs* 57: 243–49.

Jacoby, S. and Ochs, E. 1995. Co-construction: An introduction. *Research on Language and Social Interaction* 28: 171–83.

Jefferson, G. 1972. Side sequences. In D. Sudnow (ed.), *Studies in Social Interaction*. New York: Free Press, pp. 294–338.

Jefferson, G. 1984. On stepwise transition from talk about a trouble to inappropriately next-position matters. In J. M. Atkinson and J. Heritage (eds.), *Structures of Social Action: Studies in Conversation Analysis*. Cambridge: Cambridge University Press, pp. 191–222.

Jefferson, G. 1985. An exercise in the transcription and analysis of laughter. In T. van Dijk (ed.), *Handbook of Discourse Analysis, Volume 3: Discourse and Dialogue*. London: Academic Press, pp. 25–34.

Jefferson, G. 1989. Preliminary notes on a possible metric which provides for a 'standard maximum' silence of approximately one second in conversation. In R. Derek and P. Bull (eds.), *Conversation: An Interdisciplinary Perspective*. Clevedon, UK: Multilingual Matters, pp. 166–96.

Johnson, D. M. and Saville-Troike, M. 1992. Validity and reliability in qualitative research on second language acquisition and teaching. *TESOL Quarterly* 26: 602–5.

Johnson, M. and Tyler, A. 1998. Re-analyzing the OPI: How much does it look like natural conversation? In R. Young and A. W. He (eds.), *Talking and Testing: Discourse Approaches to the Assessment of Oral Proficiency*. Philadelphia: John Benjamins, pp. 27–52.

Jones, R. L. 1978. Interview techniques and scoring criteria at the higher proficiency levels. In J. L. D. Clark (ed.), *Direct Tests of Speaking Proficiency: Theory and Application*. Princeton, NJ: Educational Testing Service, pp. 89–102.

Katona, L. 1998. Meaning negotiation in the Hungarian oral proficiency interview. In R. Young and A. W. He (eds.), *Talking and Testing: Discourse Approaches to the Assessment of Oral Proficiency*. Philadelphia: John Benjamins, pp. 243–72.

Kendon, A. 1979. Some theoretical and methodological considerations of the use of film in the study of social interaction. In G.P. Ginsberg (ed.), *Emerging Strategies in Social Psychological Research*. New York, NY: John Wiley, pp. 67–91.

Kendon, A. 1985. Some uses of gesture. In D. Tannen and M. Saville-Troike (eds.), *Perspectives on Silence*. Norwood, NJ: Ablex, pp. 215–34.

Kendon, A. 1988. Goffman's approach to face-to-face interaction. In P. Drew and A. Wootton (eds.), *Erving Goffman: Exploring the Interaction Order*. Boston: Northeastern University Press, pp. 14–40.

Kendon, A. 1994. Do gestures communicate?: A review. *Research on Language and Social Interaction* 27: 175–200.

Kim, K. and Suh, K. 1998. Confirmation sequences as interactional resources in Korean language proficiency interviews. In R. Young and A. W. He (eds.), *Talking and Testing: Discourse Approaches to the Assessment of Oral Proficiency*. Philadelphia: John Benjamins, pp. 299–336.

Koike, D. A. 1998. What happens when there's no one to talk to? Spanish foreign language discourse in simulated oral proficiency interviews. In R. Young and A. W. He (eds.), *Talking and Testing: Discourse Approaches to the Assessment of Oral Proficiency*. Philadelphia: John Benjamins, pp. 69–100.

Kormos, J. 1999. Simulating conversations in oral-proficiency assessment: A conversation analysis of role plays and non-scripted interviews in language exams. *Language Testing* 16: 163–88.

Kramsch, C. 1986. From language proficiency to interactional competence. *Modern Language Journal* 70: 366–72.

Kunnan, A. 1998a. Preface. In A. Kunnan (ed.), *Validation in Language Assessment: Selected Papers from the 17th Language Testing Research Colloquium, Long Beach*. Mahwah, NJ: Lawrence Erlbaum Associates Publishers, pp. ix–x.

Kunnan, A. 1998b. Approaches to validation in language assessment. In A. Kunnan (ed.), *Validation in Language Assessment: Selected Papers from the 17th Language Testing Research Colloquium, Long Beach*. Mahwah, NJ: Lawrence Erlbaum Associates, pp. 1–16.

Kunnan, A. (ed.) 1998c. *Validation in Language Assessment: Selected Papers from the 17th Language Testing Research Colloquium, Long Beach*. Mahwah, NJ: Lawrence Erlbaum Associates Publishers.

Labov, W. 1972. *Sociolinguistic Patterns*. Philadelphia, PA: University of Pennsylvania Press.

Labov, W. and Fanshel, D. 1977. *Therapeutic Discourse*. New York, NY: Academic Press.

Labov, W. and Waletsky, J. 1967. Narrative analysis. In J. Helm (ed.), *Essays on the Verbal and Visual Arts*. Seattle, WA: University of Washington Press, pp. 12–44.

Lantolf, J. P. and Frawley, W. 1985. Oral-proficiency testing: A critical analysis. *Modern Language Journal* 69: 337–45.

Lantolf, J. P. and Frawley, W. 1988. Proficiency: Understanding the construct. *Studies in Second Language Acquisition* 10: 181–95.

Lazaraton, A. 1991. *A Conversation Analysis of Structure and Interaction in the Language Interview.* Unpublished Ph.D. dissertation, University of California at Los Angeles, CA.

Lazaraton, A. 1992. The structural organization of a language interview: A conversation analytic perspective. *SYSTEM* 20: 373–86.

Lazaraton, A. 1993. *The development of a quality control template based on the analysis of CASE transcriptions.* Report prepared for the EFL Division, University of Cambridge Local Examinations Syndicate, Cambridge, UK.

Lazaraton, A. 1994a. *Question turn modification in oral proficiency interviews.* Paper presented at the Colloquium on Discourse Issues in Oral Proficiency Assessment, American Association for Applied Linguistics (AAAL) Annual Conference, Baltimore, MD: March.

Lazaraton, A. 1994b. *An analysis of examiner behaviour in CAE Paper 5, based on audiotaped transcriptions.* Report prepared for the EFL Division, University of Cambridge Local Examinations Syndicate, Cambridge, UK.

Lazaraton, A. 1995a. Qualitative research in TESOL: A progress report. *TESOL Quarterly* 29: 455–72.

Lazaraton, A. 1995b. *An analysis of examiner behaviour in the KET Speaking Component, based on audiotaped transcriptions.* Report prepared for the EFL Division, University of Cambridge Local Examinations Syndicate, Cambridge, UK.

Lazaraton, A. 1996a. A qualitative approach to monitoring examiner conduct in CASE. In M. Milanovic and N. Saville (eds.), *Studies in Language Testing 3: Performance Testing, Cognition, and Assessment: Selected Papers from the 15th Language Testing Research Colloquium, Cambridge and Arnhem.* Cambridge: Cambridge University Press, pp. 18–33.

Lazaraton, A. 1996b. Interlocutor support in oral proficiency interviews: The case of CASE. *Language Testing* 13: 151–72.

Lazaraton, A. 1996c. *A comparative analysis of examiner behaviour in CAE Paper 5 and the KET Speaking Component, based on audiotaped transcriptions.* Report prepared for the EFL Division, University of Cambridge Local Examinations Syndicate, Cambridge, UK.

Lazaraton, A. 1997a. Preference organization in oral proficiency interviews: The case of language ability assessments. *Research on Language and Social Interaction* 30: 53–72.

Lazaraton, A. 1997b. *An analysis of the relationship between task features and candidate output for the Revised FCE Speaking Examination: 1996 Standardization Video.* Report prepared for the EFL Division, University of Cambridge Local Examinations Syndicate, Cambridge, UK.

Lazaraton, A. 1998. *An analysis of differences in linguistic features of candidates at different levels of the IELTS Speaking Test.* Report prepared for the EFL Division, University of Cambridge Local Examinations Syndicate, Cambridge, UK.

Lazaraton, A. 2000. Current trends in research methodology and statistics in applied linguistics. *TESOL Quarterly* 34: 175–81

Lazaraton, A. and Frantz, R. 1997. *An analysis of the relationship between task features and candidate output for the Revised FCE Speaking Examination.* Report prepared for the EFL Division, University of Cambridge Local Examinations Syndicate, Cambridge, UK.

Lazaraton, A. and Riggenbach, H. 1990. Oral skills testing: A rhetorical task approach. *Issues in Applied Linguistics* 1: 196–217.

Lazaraton, A. and Saville, N. 1994. *Process and outcomes in oral assessment.* Paper presented at the 16th Language Testing Research Colloquium, Washington, DC: February.

Lazaraton, A. and Wagner, S. 1996. The revised Test of Spoken English (TSE): Analysis of native speaker and nonnative speaker data. *TOEFL Monograph Series* MS-7. Princeton, NJ: Educational Testing Service.

Levinson, S. C. 1983. *Pragmatics.* Cambridge: Cambridge University Press.

Linacre, J. M. 1989–94. *FACETS, Version 2.7.* Chicago, IL: Mesa Press.

Linnell, P. and Markova, I. 1993. Acts in discourse: From monologic speech acts to dialogical inter-acts. *Journal for the Theory of Social Behaviour* 23: 173–95.

Lowe, P. Jnr. 1981. Structure of the oral interview and content validity. In A. S. Palmer, P. J. M. Groot, and G. A. Trosper (eds.), *The Construct Validation of Tests of Communicative Competence.* Washington, DC: TESOL, pp. 71–80.

Lowe, P. Jnr. 1982. *ILR Handbook of Oral Interview Testing.* Washington, DC: DLI/LS Oral Interview Testing Project.

Madsen, H. S. and Jones, R. L. 1981. Classification of oral proficiency tests. In A. S. Palmer, P. J. M. Groot, and G.A. Trosper (eds.), *The Construct Validation of Tests of Communicative Competence.* Washington, DC: TESOL, pp. 15–30.

Magnan, S. S. 1988. Grammar and the ACTFL oral proficiency interview: Discussion and data. *Modern Language Journal* 72: 266–76.

Markee, N. 2000. *Conversation Analysis*, Mahwah, NJ: Laurence Erlbaum.

Marlaire, C. L. 1990. On questions, communication, and bias: Educational testing as 'invisible' collaboration. *Perspectives on Social Problems* 2: 232–58.

Marlaire, C. L. and Maynard, P. W. 1990. Standardized testing as an interactional phenomenon. *Sociology of Education* 63: 83–101.

Maynard, D. W. 1992. On clinicians co-implicating recipients' perspective in the delivery of diagnostic news. In P. Drew and J. Heritage (eds.), *Talk at Work: Interaction in Institutional Settings.* Cambridge: Cambridge University Press, pp. 331–58.

Maynard, D. W. and Marlaire, C. L. 1992. Good reasons for bad testing performance: The interactional substrate of educational exams. *Qualitative Sociology* 15: 177–202.

McHoul, A. W. 1978. The organization of turns at formal talk in the classroom. *Language in Society* 7: 183–213.

McHoul, A. W. 1990. The organization of repair in classroom talk. *Language in Society* 19: 349–77.

McIlvenny, P. 1995. Seeing conversations: Analyzing sign language talk. In P. Ten Have and G. Psathas (eds.), *Situated Order: Studies in the Social Organization of Talk and Embodied Activities.* Washington, DC: International Institute for Ethnomethodology and Conversation Analysis & University Press of America, pp. 129–50.

McNamara, T. F. 1996. *Measuring Second Language Performance.* London: Longman.

McNamara, T. F. 1997. 'Interaction' in second language performance assessment: Whose performance?. *Applied Linguistics* 18: 446–66.

McNamara, T. F. 1998. Policy and social considerations in language assessment. *Annual Review of Applied Linguistics* 18: 304–19.

McNamara, T. F. 1999. Validity in language testing: The challenge of Sam Messick's legacy. Messick Memorial Lecture, Language Testing Research Colloquium, Tsukuba: July.

McNamara, T. F. and Lumley, T. 1997. The effect of interlocutor and assessment mode variables in overseas assessments of speaking skills in occupational settings. *Language Testing* 14: 140–56.

Mehan, H. 1979. *Learning Lessons.* Cambridge, MA: Harvard University Press.

Mehan, H. 1985. The structure of classroom discourse. In T. van Dijk (ed.), *Handbook of Discourse Analysis, Volume 3: Discourse and Dialogue.* London: Academic Press, pp. 119–31.

Mehan, H. 1993. Beneath the skin and between the ears: A case study in the politics of representation. In S. Chaiklin and J. Lave (eds.), *Understanding Practice: Perspectives on Activity and Context.* Cambridge: Cambridge University Press, pp. 241–68.

Meiron, B. E. 1999. *Inside raters' heads: An exploratory triangulated study of oral proficiency raters' thought processes.* Paper presented at the 33rd Annual TESOL Convention, New York, NY: March.

Merrylees, B. and McDowell, C. 1998. An investigation of speaking test reliability with particular reference to examiner attitude to the speaking test format and candidate/examiner discourse produced. *IELTS Research Reports 1998 Volume 2.* Sydney: IELTS Australia, pp. 1–35.

Messick, S. 1989. Validity. In R. L. Linn (ed.), *Educational Measurement,* 3rd edition. New York, NY: MacMillan, pp. 13–103.

Messick, S. 1994. The interplay of evidence and consequences in the validation of performance assessments. *Educational Researcher* 23, 2: 13–23.

Messick, S. 1996. Validity and washback in language testing. *Language Testing* 13: 241–56.

Milanovic, M. and Saville, N. 1992. *Principles of Good Practice for UCLES Examinations: A Discussion Paper.* Unpublished manuscript.

Milanovic, M. and Saville, N. 1996a. Introduction. In Milanovic, M. and Saville, N. (eds.), *Studies in Language Testing 3: Performance Testing, Cognition, and Assessment: Selected Papers from the 15th Language Testing Research Colloquium, Cambridge and Arnhem.* Cambridge: Cambridge University Press.

Milanovic, M., Saville, N., Pollitt, A., and Cook, A. 1996. Developing rating scales for CASE: Theoretical concerns and analyses. In A. Cumming and R. Berwick (eds.), *Validation in Language Testing.* Clevedon: Multilingual Matters, pp. 15–38.

Moder, C. L. and Halleck, G. B. 1998. Framing the language proficiency interview as a speech event: Native and nonnative speakers' questions. In R. Young and A. W. He (eds.), *Talking and Testing: Discourse Approaches to the Assessment of Oral Proficiency.* Philadelphia: John Benjamins, pp. 117–48.

Morton, J., Wigglesworth, G., and Williams, D. 1997. Approaches to the evaluation of interviewer behaviour in oral tests. In G. Brindley and G. Wigglesworth (eds.), ***access: Issues in language test design and delivery.*** Sydney: NCELTR, pp. 175–95.

Moss, P.A. 1994. Can there be validity without reliability? *Educational Researcher* 23, 2: 5–12.

Neu, J. 1990. Assessing the role of nonverbal communication in the acquisition of communicative competence in L2. In R. C. Scarcella, E. S. Andersen, and S. D. Krashen (eds.), *Developing Communicative Competence in a Second Language.* New York, NY: Newbury House, pp. 121–38.

Ochs, E. 1979. Transcription as theory. In E. Ochs and B. Schieffelin (eds.), *Developmental Pragmatics.* New York, NY: Academic Press, pp. 43–72.

Ochs, E., Gonzales, P., and Jacoby, S. 1996. 'When I come down I'm in the domain state': Grammar and graphic representation in the interpretive activity of physicists. In E. Ochs, E. A. Schegloff, and S. A. Thompson (eds.), *Interaction and Grammar*. Cambridge: Cambridge University Press, pp. 328–69.

Ochs, E., Schegloff, E. A. and Thompson, S. A. (eds.) 1996. *Interaction and Grammar.* Cambridge: Cambridge University Press.

Oller, J. W. 1979. *Language Tests at School.* London: Longman.

O'Loughlin, K. 1995. Lexical density in candidate output on direct and semi-direct versions of an oral proficiency test. *Language Testing* 12: 217–37.

Oreström, B. 1983. *Turn-taking in English Conversation.* Lund Studies in English 66. CWK Gleerup.

Palmer, A. S., Groot, P. J. M., and Trosper, G. A. (eds.) 1981. *The Construct Validation of Tests of Communicative Competence.* Washington, DC: TESOL.

Pavlou, P. 1997. Do different speech interactions in an oral proficiency test yield different kinds of language? In A. Huhta and S. Luoma (eds.), *Current Developments and Alternatives in Language Assessment: Selected Papers from the 18th Language Testing Research Colloquium.* Jyvaskyla: University of Jyvaskyla and University of Tampere, pp. 185–201.

Phillips, S. U. 1983. An ethnographic approach to bilingual language proficiency assessment. In C. Rivera (ed.), *An Ethnographic/Sociolinguistic Approach to Language Proficiency Assessment.* Clevedon: Multilingual Matters Ltd., pp. 88–106.

Pittenger, R. E., Hockett, C. F., and Danehy, J. J. 1960. *The First Five Minutes.* Ithaca, NY: Paul Martineau.

Pomerantz, A. 1984. Agreeing and disagreeing with assessments: Some features of preferred/dispreferred turn shape. In J.M. Atkinson and J. Heritage (eds.), *Structures of Social Action: Studies in Conversation Analysis.* Cambridge: Cambridge University Press, pp. 57–101.

Pomerantz, A. 1990. Chautauqua: On the validity and generalizability of conversational analysis methods: Conversation analytic claims. *Communication Monographs* 57: 231–5.

Pomerantz, A. and Fehr, B. J. 1997. Conversation analysis: An approach to the study of social action as sense making practices. In T. A. van Dijk (ed.), *Discourse as Social Action, Discourse Studies: A Multidisciplinary Introduction Volume 2.* London: Sage Publications, pp. 64–91.

Psathas, G. 1995. *Conversation Analysis: The Study of Talk-in-Interaction.* Thousand Oaks, CA: Sage.

Psathas, G. and Anderson, T. 1990. The 'practices' of transcription in conversation analysis. *Semiotica* 78: 75–99.

Raffaldini, T. 1988. The use of situation tests as measures of communicative ability. *Studies in Second Language Acquisition* 10: 197–216.

Reed, D. J. 1992. The relationship between criterion-based levels of oral proficiency and norm-referenced scores of general proficiency in English as a second language. *SYSTEM* 20: 329–45.

Reichman, R. 1990. Communication and mutual engagement. In B. Dorval (ed.), *Conversational Organization and its Development.* Norwood, NJ: Ablex, pp. 23–48.

Richards, J. C. and Schmidt, R. W. 1983. Conversational analysis. In J. C. Richards and R. W. Schmidt (eds.), *Language and Communication.* London: Longman, pp. 117–53.

Riggenbach, H. 1999. *Discourse Analysis in the Language Classroom. Volume 1. The Spoken Language.* Ann Arbor, MI: The University of Michigan Press.

Rivera, C. (ed.) 1983. *An Ethnographic/Sociolinguistic Approach to Language Proficiency Assessment.* Clevedon, Avon: Multilingual Matters Ltd.

Roberts, C. 1997. Transcribing talk: Issues of representation. *TESOL Quarterly* 31: 167–72.

Ross, S. no date. *Formulae and inter-interviewer variation in oral proficiency interview discourse.* Unpublished manuscript.

Ross, S. 1992. Accommodative questions in oral proficiency interviews. *Language Testing* 9: 173–86.

Ross, S. and Berwick, R. 1992. The discourse of accommodation in oral proficiency examinations. *Studies in Second Language Acquisition* 14: 159–76.

Roth, D. R. 1974. Intelligence testing as a social activity. In A. V. Cicourel, K. H. Jennings, S. H. M. Jennings, K. C. W. Leiter, R. MacKay, H. Mehan, and D. R. Roth (eds.), *Language Use and School Performance.* New York, NY: Academic Press, pp. 143–217.

Sacks, H. 1984. Notes on methodology. In J. M. Atkinson and J. Heritage (eds.), *Structures of Social Action: Studies in Conversation Analysis.* Cambridge: Cambridge University Press, pp. 21–7.

Sacks, H. 1987 [1973]. On the preferences for agreement and contiguity in sequences in conversation. In G. Button and J. R. E. Lee (eds.), *Talk and Social Organization.* Clevedon, Avon: Multilingual Matters Ltd, pp. 54–69.

Sacks, H. 1992. *Lectures on Conversation* (2 volumes). Oxford: Basil Blackwell.

Sacks, H., Schegloff, E. A. and Jefferson, G. 1974. A simplest systematics for the organization of turntaking in conversation. *Language* 50: 696–735.

Savignon, S. 1985. Evaluation of communicative competence: The ACTFL provisional proficiency guidelines. *Modern Language Journal* 6: 129–34.

Saville, N. 1996. *The Cambridge Approach to the Assessment of Speaking: Criteria, Tasks and Scales.* Paper presented at the Regional STL/TL Conference, Bangkok, Thailand: October.

Schegloff, E. A. 1968. Sequencing in conversational openings. *American Anthropologist* 70: 1075–95.

Schegloff, E. A. 1972. Notes on conversational practice: Formulating place. In D. Sudnow (ed.), *Studies in Social Interaction.* New York: Free Press, pp. 74–119.

Schegloff, E. A. 1979a. The relevance of repair for a syntax-for-conversation. In T. Givon (ed.), *Syntax and Semantics Volume 12: Discourse and Syntax.* New York, NY: Academic Press, pp. 261–86.

Schegloff, E. A. 1979b. Identification and recognition in telephone conversation openings. In G. Psathas (ed.), *Everyday Language: Studies in Ethnomethodology.* New York, NY: Irvington, pp. 23–78.

Schegloff, E. A. 1980. Preliminaries to preliminaries: 'Can I ask you a question?' *Sociological Inquiry* 50: 104–52.

Schegloff, E. A. 1984a. On some gestures related to talk. In J. M. Atkinson and J. Heritage (eds.), *Structures of Social Action: Studies in Conversation Analysis.* Cambridge: Cambridge University Press, pp. 266–96.

Schegloff, E. A. 1984b. On some questions and ambiguities in conversation. In J. M. Atkinson and J. Heritage (eds.), *Structures of Social Action: Studies in Conversation Analysis.* Cambridge: Cambridge University Press pp. 28–52.

Schegloff, E. A. 1988. Goffman and the analysis of conversation. In P. Drew and A. Wootton (eds.), *Erving Goffman: Exploring the Interaction Order.* Boston: Northeastern University Press, pp. 89–135.

Schegloff, E. A. 1989. From interview to confrontation: Observations of the Bush/Rather encounter. *Research on Language and Social Interaction* 22: 215–40.

Schegloff, E. A. 1990. On the organization of sequences as a source of 'coherence' in talk-in-interaction. In B. Dorval (ed.), *Conversational Organization and Its Development.* Norwood, NJ: Ablex, pp. 51–77.

Schegloff, E. A. 1992. Repair after next turn: The last structurally provided defense of intersubjectivity in conversation. *American Journal of Sociology* 97: 1295–345.

Schegloff, E. A. 1993. Reflections on quantification in the study of conversation. *Research on Language and Social Interaction* 26: 99–128.

Schegloff, E. A. 1996. Turn organization: One intersection of grammar and interaction. In E. Ochs, E. A. Schegloff, and S. A. Thompson (eds.), *Interaction and Grammar.* Cambridge: Cambridge University Press, pp. 52–133.

Schegloff, E. A. 1998. Reply to Wetherell. *Discourse and Society* 9: 413–16.

Schegloff, E. A. 1999. What next?: Language and social interaction study at the century's turn. *Research on Language and Social Interaction* 32: 141–8.

Schegloff, E. A., Jefferson, G., and Sacks, H. 1977. The preference for self-correction in the organization of repair in conversation. *Language* 53: 361–82.

Schegloff, E. A. and Sacks, H. 1973. Opening up closings. *Semiotica* 7: 289–327.

Schiffrin, D. 1987. *Discourse Markers.* Cambridge: Cambridge University Press.

Schiffrin, D. 1994. *Approaches to Discourse.* Oxford: Basil Blackwell.

Searle, J. R. 1969. *Speech Acts: An Essay in the Philosophy of Language.* Cambridge: Cambridge University Press.

Shohamy, E. 1983. The stability of oral proficiency assessment on the oral interview testing procedures. *Language Learning* 33: 527–40.

Shohamy, E. 1988. A proposed framework for testing the oral language of second/foreign language learners. *Studies in Second Language Acquisition* 10: 165–79.

Shohamy, E. 1991. Discourse analysis in language testing. *Annual Review of Applied Linguistics* 11: 115–31.

Shohamy, E. 1994a. The role of language tests in the construction and validation of second-language acquisition theories. In E. Tarone, S. M. Gass, and A. D. Cohen (eds.), *Research Methodology in Second Language Acquisition*. Hillsdale, NJ: Lawrence Erlbaum Associates Publishers, pp. 133–42.

Shohamy, E. 1994b. The validity of direct versus semi-direct oral tests. *Language Testing* 11: 99–123.

Shohamy, E. 1999. Language testing: Impact. In B. Spolsky (ed.), *Concise Encyclopedia of Educational Linguistics*. Oxford: Elsevier Science Ltd, pp. 711–14.

Sorjonen, M-L. 1996. On repeats and responses in Finnish conversations. In E. Ochs, E. A. Schegloff, and S. A. Thompson (eds.), *Interaction and Grammar*. Cambridge: Cambridge University Press, pp. 277–327.

Spolsky, B. 1990. Oral examinations: An historical note. *Language Testing* 7: 158–73.

Spolsky, B. 1995. Introduction: A not-too-special relationship. In L. F. Bachman, F. Davidson, K. Ryan, and I. Choi, *An Investigation into the Comparability of Two Tests of English as a Foreign Language*. Cambridge: Cambridge University Press.

Stansfield, C. W. and Kenyon, D. M. 1992. Research on the comparability of the oral proficiency interview and the simulated oral proficiency interview. *SYSTEM* 20: 347–64.

Stevenson, D. K. 1981. Beyond faith and face validity: The multitrait–multimethod matrix and the convergent and discriminant validity of oral proficiency tests. In A. S. Palmer, P. J. M. Groot, and G. A. Trosper (eds.), *The Construct Validation of Tests of Communicative Competence*. Washington, DC: TESOL, pp. 37–61.

References

Streeck, J. 1994. Gesture as communication II: The audience as co-author. *Research on Language and Social Interaction* 27: 239–67.

Styles, P. 1993. *Inter- and intra- rater reliability of assessments of 'live' versus audio- and video-recorded interviews in the IELTS Speaking Test.* UCLES Research Report, Cambridge.

Suchman, L. and Jordan, B. 1990. Interactional trouble in face-to-face survey interviews. *Journal of the American Statistical Association* 85: 232–53.

Sudnov, D. (ed.) 1972. *Studies in Social Interaction.* New York, NY: Free Press.

Swain, M. 1993. Second language testing and second language acquisition: Is there a conflict with traditional psychometrics? *Language Testing* 10: 193–207.

Tannen, D. 1985. Silence: Anything but. In M. Saville-Troike and D. Tannen (eds.), *Perspectives on Silence.* Norwood, NJ: Ablex, pp. 93–111.

Tannen, D. 1990. Gender differences in conversational coherence: Physical alignment and topical cohesion. In B. Dorval (ed.), *Conversational Organization and its Development.* Norwood, NJ: Ablex, pp. 167–206.

Tannen, D. and Saville-Troike, M. (eds.). 1985. *Perspectives on Silence.* Norwood, NJ: Ablex.

Taylor, L. 1999. *Constituency matters: Responsibilities and relationships in our test community.* Paper presented at the Language Testing Forum, Edinburgh, Scotland: November.

Teachers of English to Speakers of Other Languages. 1999. Qualitative research guidelines. *TESOL Quarterly* 33: 175–6.

Ten Have, P. and Psathas, G. (eds.) 1995. *Situated Order: Studies in the Social Organization of Talk and Embodied Activities.* Washington, DC: International Institute for Ethnomethodology and Conversation Analysis & University Press of America.

Thompson, I. 1995. A study of interrater reliability of the ACTFL oral proficiency interview in five European languages: Data from ESL, French, German, Russian, and Spanish. *Foreign Language Annals* 28: 407–22.

Todd, A. D. 1983. A diagnosis of doctor–patient discourse in the prescription of contraception. In S. Fisher and A. D. Todd (eds.), *The Social Organization of Doctor–Patient Interaction.* Washington, DC: Center for Applied Linguistics, pp. 159–87.

Turner, J. 1998. Assessing speaking. *Annual Review of Applied Linguistics* 18: 192–207.

Underhill, N. 1987. *Testing Spoken Language: A Handbook of Oral Testing Techniques.* Cambridge: Cambridge University Press.

University of Cambridge Local Examinations Syndicate. 1992. *Cambridge Assessment of Spoken English: CASE.* Cambridge.

University of Cambridge Local Examinations Syndicate. 1993. *CAE: Instructions to Oral Examiners* 11/93–6/94. Cambridge.

University of Cambridge Local Examinations Syndicate. 1996. *Notes to Accompany the 1996 FCE Standardization Video*. Cambridge.

University of Cambridge Local Examinations Syndicate. 1997a. *Key English Test: Instructions to Oral Examiners March 1997–December 1997*. Cambridge.

University of Cambridge Local Examinations Syndicate. 1997b. *Certificate of Advanced English: Handbook*. Cambridge.

University of Cambridge Local Examinations Syndicate. 1997c. *FCE: Instructions to Oral Examiners*. Cambridge.

University of Cambridge Local Examinations Syndicate. 1998a. *FCE: Handbook*. Cambridge.

University of Cambridge Local Examinations Syndicate. 1998b. *KET: Handbook*. Cambridge.

University of Cambridge Local Examinations Syndicate. 1998c. *EFL Examinations & ELT Schemes 1998/99*. Cambridge.

University of Cambridge Local Examinations Syndicate. 1999a. *The IELTS Handbook 1999*. Cambridge.

University of Cambridge Local Examinations Syndicate. 1999b. *MPRs: Minimum Professional Requirements for Cambridge EFL Speaking Tests. Guidelines for those involved in the supervision and deployment of oral examiners*. Cambridge.

University of Cambridge Local Examinations Syndicate. 1999c. *Guidelines to accompany the EFL Oral Examiner Monitoring Checklist*. Cambridge.

University of Cambridge Local Examinations Syndicate. 1999d. *IELTS: Annual Review 1998/9*. Cambridge.

University of Cambridge Local Examinations Syndicate. 1999e. *English for Life: An Introduction to the Cambridge EFL Examinations*. Cambridge.

University of Cambridge Local Examinations Syndicate. 1999f. *CAE: Certificate in Advanced English Handbook*. Cambridge.

University of Cambridge Local Examinations Syndicate. 1999g. *KET and PET: Instructions to Oral Examiners 1999*. Cambridge.

Upshur, J. A. and Turner, C. E. 1999. Systematic effects in the rating of second-language speaking ability: Test method and learner discourse. *Language Testing* 16: 82–111.

Valdman, A. 1988. Introduction. *Studies in Second Language Acquisition* 10: 121–8.

van Dijk, T. A. (ed.) 1985. *Handbook of Discourse Analysis, Volume 3: Discourse and Dialogue*. London: Academic Press.

van Lier, L. 1989. Reeling, writhing, drawling, stretching, and fainting in coils: Oral proficiency interviews as conversation. *TESOL Quarterly* 23: 489–508.

Wagner, S. 1994a. *Discourse Markers in the Oral Presentations of Ten Chinese Speaking Teaching Assistants.* Unpublished Master's paper, The Pennsylvania State University, PA.

Wagner, S. 1994b. *An analysis of candidate language by task type in Phase B of CAE Paper 5, based on audiotaped transcription of the standardization video.* Report prepared for the EFL Division, University of Cambridge Local Examinations Syndicate, Cambridge, UK.

West, C. 1983. 'Ask me no questions' …: An analysis of queries and replies in physician–patient dialogue. In S. Fisher and A. D. Todd (eds.), *The Social Organization of Doctor Patient Interaction.* Washington, DC: Center for Applied Linguistics, pp. 75–106.

West, C. and Zimmerman, D. 1983. Small insults: A study of interruptions in cross-sex conversations with unacquainted persons. In B. Thorne, C. Kramarae, and N. Henley (eds.), *Language, Gender, and Society.* Rowley, MA: Newbury House, pp. 102–17.

Wetherell, M. 1998. Positioning and interpretive repertoires: Conversation analysis and post-structuralism in dialogue. *Discourse and Society* 9: 387–412.

Wieder, D. L. 1993. On the compound questions raised by attempts to quantify conversation analysis' phenomena, Part 2: The issue of incommensurability. *Research on Language and Social Interaction* 26: 213–26.

Wigglesworth, G. 1993. Exploring bias analysis as a tool for improving rater consistency in assessing oral interaction. *Language Testing* 10: 305–35.

Wigglesworth, G. 1997. An investigation of planning time and proficiency level on oral test discourse. *Language Testing* 14: 85–106.

Wilkinson, S. 1994. *Topic nomination strategies in NNS–NNS interaction: A case study.* Paper presented at the American Association of Applied Linguistics Conference, Baltimore, MD: March.

Wolfson, N. 1989. *Perspectives: Sociolinguistics and TESOL.* New York, NY: Newbury House.

Wootton, A. J. 1989. Remarks on the methodology of conversation analysis. In R. Derek and P. Bull (eds.), *Conversation: An Interdisciplinary Perspective.* Clevedon, UK: Multilingual Matters, pp. 238–58.

Wylie, E. 1993. *Report to the international editing committee of IELTS on a study of the inter-rater reliability of the IELTS Speaking Test.* UCLES Research Report, Cambridge.

Yoshida-Morise, Y. 1998. The use of communication strategies in language proficiency interviews. In R. Young and A. W. He (eds.), *Talking and Testing: Discourse Approaches to the Assessment of Oral Proficiency*. Philadelphia: John Benjamins, pp. 207–42.

Young, R. 1995a. Conversational styles in language proficiency interviews. *Language Learning* 45: 3–42.

Young, R. 1995b. Discontinuous language development and its implications for oral proficiency rating scales. *Applied Language Learning* 6: 13–26.

Young, R. and Halleck, G. B. 1998. 'Let them eat cake!': Or how to avoid losing your head in cross-cultural conversations. In R. Young and A. W. He (eds.), *Talking and Testing: Discourse Approaches to the Assessment of Oral Proficiency*. Philadelphia: John Benjamins, pp. 359–88.

Young, R. and He, A. W. (eds.) 1998. *Talking and Testing: Discourse Approaches to the Assessment of Oral Proficiency*. Philadelphia, PA: John Benjamins.

Young, R. and Milanovic, M. 1992. Discourse variation in oral proficiency interviews. *Studies in Second Language Acquisition* 14: 403–24.

Zimmerman, D. H. 1988. On conversation: The conversation analytic perspective. In J. A. Anderson (ed.), *Communication Yearbook 11*. Newbury Park, CA: Sage, pp. 406–32.

Appendix 1

Glossary of CA Terms

action. The basic unit of analysis in CA; actions are orderly and meaningful for their producers and recipients and have a natural organization that can be specified in terms of machinery, rules and structure.

adjacency pair. Paired utterances such as question–answer and compliment–response, where the two parts are adjacent, produced by different speakers, and ordered as first and second. The first part requires a special, conditionally relevant second part.

closings. The actions which shut down an interaction, composed of at least one adjacency pair, such as 'bye-bye' (see Schegloff and Sacks 1973).

FPP. A first-pair-part, the first action in an adjacency pair, such as a request.

gap. The silence that occurs after a possible turn completion. It is noticeable and indicative of various interactional meanings, such as disagreement.

latched turn. A turn that begins with no interval between it and the end of the prior turn. It is shown by an equal sign =.

NTRI. A next turn repair initiation, done by a listener which invites repair on the speaker's previous turn in the speaker's next turn. Common NTRIs include 'huh?', 'what?', 'pardon?' (see Schegloff, Jefferson, and Sacks 1977).

openings. The actions which begin an interaction; they differ on the telephone and in person (see Schegloff 1979b).

overlap. A point at which two speakers talk simultaneously. It is shown by brackets [ ].

packaging. The form and delivery of actions.

pause. The silence that occurs within a turn constructional unit.

preclosing. A form of presequence that signals the shutting down of an interaction. Usually, one person initiates the preclosing, and the other can agree to the shutdown or not. Preclosings often take the form of paired 'okay's, 'alright's and the like (see Schegloff and Sacks 1973).

preference. A theory of social action that is somewhat like linguistic 'markedness'. It is not a theory of desires or psychological states, but one that elucidates why, when confronted with two choices in interaction (e.g., agree or disagree), one is felt to be more natural, normal, or unspecific.

pre-sequence. A type of sequence in which a set of turns occurs before the actual target sequence and which checks for listener compliance. For example, a pre-request prefaces a request and allows for collaboration in the action, or information that will head off the request and subsequent denial of it.

repair. The sequentially organized system for clearing up problems of hearing and understanding, even if no such problem seems to exist. Repair initiation, where a trouble source is targeted, is distinct from correction, where the actual repair takes place. There is a strong preference for self-repair (see Schegloff, Jefferson, and Sacks 1977).

sequence. A spate of talk, composed of at least two turns, with identifiable boundaries of action.

silence. The general term for periods when no talk takes place; it can refer to either gaps or pauses.

SPP. A second-pair-part, the second, conditionally relevant action in an adjacency pair that responds to a specific first-pair-part.

TCU. A turn-constructional-unit, the minimal units of talk from which turns are constructed. Speakers are usually allotted only one TCU, but they can make these quite long through various interactional devices. TCUs have syntactic, intonational, semantic and/or pragmatic status as complete; through these criteria they 'project' their upcoming completion, which would-be speakers can exploit to get a turn (see Sacks, Schegloff and Jefferson 1974).

transition space. 'The beat that potentially follows the possible completion point of a turn' (Sacks, Schegloff, and Jefferson 1974: 366).

TRP. A transition-relevance-place, which occurs at the end of a turn-constructional-unit and where speaker change can (but need not) occur.

turn. One person's allocation of talk; turns are composed of at least one turn-constructional-unit.

turntaking. The organizational system of talk where one person speaks, stops, another starts, stops, and so on, with all kinds of variations for the number of speakers, the type of speech event taking place, etc. (see Sacks, Schegloff, and Jefferson 1974).

Appendix 2

Transcription notation symbols

(from Atkinson and Heritage 1984)

1. **unfilled pauses or gaps** – periods of silence, timed in tenths of a second by counting 'beats' of elapsed time. Micropauses, those of less than .2 seconds, are symbolized (.); longer pauses appear as a time within parentheses: (.5) is five tenths of a second.

2. **colon (:)** – a lengthened sound or syllable; more colons prolong the stretch.

3. **dash (–)** – a cut-off, usually a glottal stop.

4. **.hhh** – an inbreath; **.hhh!** – strong inhalation.

5. **hhh** – exhalation; **hhh!** – strong exhalation.

6. **hah, huh, heh, hnh** – all represent laughter, depending on the sounds produced. All can be followed by an (!), signifying stronger laughter.

7. **(hhh)** – breathiness within a word.

8. **punctuation:** markers of intonation rather than clausal structure; a period (.) is falling intonation, a question mark (?) is rising intonation, a comma (,) is continuing intonation. A question mark followed by a comma (?,) represents rising intonation, but is weaker than a (?). An exclamation mark (!) is animated intonation.

9. **equal sign (=)** – a latched utterance, no interval between utterances.

10. **brackets ([ ])** – overlapping talk, where utterances start and/or end simultaneously.

11. **percent signs (% %)** – quiet talk.

12. **asterisks (*   *)** – creaky voice.

13. **carat (^)** – a marked rising shift in pitch.

14. **arrows (>   <)** – the talk speeds up; **arrows (<   >)** – the talk slows down.

15. **psk** – a lip smack; **tch** – a tongue click.

16. **underlining or CAPS** – a word or SOund is emphasized.

17. **arrow (--->)** – a feature of interest to the analyst.

18. **empty parentheses (   )** – transcription doubt, uncertainty; words within parentheses are uncertain.

19. **double parentheses ((   ))** – non-vocal action, details of scene.

Appendix 3

Guidelines for Chapter 4 practice problems

1. The interviewer's turn at line 31 'you sound pretty goo:d though' interested me, in light of the patterns of self-deprecation discussed in the chapter. Here is an interviewer compliment: what can be made of it?

1. Select a sequence of interest by looking for identifiable boundaries.

If line 31 is targeted, it makes sense to go back to and start at the candidate's turn at line 20, where he tells the interviewer about an 'escary' experience he had, because line 20 is the beginning of an 'account' for why the oral skills course is needed. The account concludes in lines 27–28 with the CA saying he felt very nervous because he couldn't express himself. The compliment follows. The sequence ends at the point where the interviewer initiates his first pre-closing move (not shown).

2. Characterize the actions in the sequence by answering the question, 'What is the participant doing in this turn?'

The next step is identifying the actions that are undertaken by the each of the participants. Lines 20–28 show the candidate providing an account for why the oral skills course is needed. He went to a retreat, had to give a speech, and felt nervous because he didn't know how to express himself. At the same time, lines 27–28 are shown to be heard as a form of self-deprecation of language ability by the IN's compliment response in line 31. The compliment 'rejects' the self-deprecation. Upon hearing the compliment (formed as a rejection of the CA's self-deprecation), the candidate himself rejects the compliment. Here is this analysis shown schematically:

```
(12) RA (3:43-4:32)   IN=Interviewer CA=Candidate

20 CA: and (.5) I (d a big want) I had experience very (1.0)ACCOUNT FOR
21     esc(hh)ary [hhh! when I went to one of those retrea:ts (.)NEEDING
22 IN:            [y(hh)ea:h hhh                                    AN
23 CA: [they ask me to give a speech regarding our group and I  ESL COURSE
24 IN: [uh huh
25 CA: was (.8) feel- (.5) very: (.2) .hhh [(mezzed up)]
26 IN:                                     [ne:rvouz:  ] I spose
27 CA: I was really very nervous because I didn't know how to:    SELF-
28     .hhh (.) express myself                               DEPRECATION
29     (1.2)
30 CA: [when
31 IN: [you sound pretty goo:d though             REJECT DEPRECATION/
32     (.2)                                                COMPLIMENT
33 IN: huh? huh hah! [ .hhh ! huh!  huh! .huh!  ]
34 CA:              [I try(ed) my best (I mean)] I did (.)
35 CA: I did (.) I gave them (in) the speech but (.8) I didn't   REJECT
36     it wasn't good as u- (.5) as I wanted.              COMPLIMENT
```

3. *Consider how the packaging of actions, that is, how they are formed and delivered, provides for certain understandings.*

4. *Consider how timing and turntaking provide for certain understandings as well.*

In constructing the compliment in line 31, the IN retrieves the CA's talk from lines 27–28 and judges his ability in terms of sounding 'pretty good', contrasting it with the candidate's self-assessment by the use of 'though'. The candidate shows his orientation to line 31 <u>as</u> a compliment by first apologizing or excusing himself and then qualifying his self-assessment: despite his best efforts, the speech he reports giving didn't live up to his expectations (the standard, in this case, against which the deprecation may be judged).

5. *Consider how the ways the actions were accomplished suggest certain identities, roles, and/or relationships for the interactants.*

What do we make of this sequence? Why does the IN reject the self-deprecation via a compliment? And why does the candidate then reject the compliment? The essential problem for the candidate is this: he must make a case for needing the ESL course, either by showing (via his language ability) or telling the interviewer why. The compliment by the IN, the 'gatekeeper' in this situation, cannot be accepted by the candidate if this amounts to admitting that he does not need the class. If the candidate reads the compliment as a possible tip-off that denial of admission into the courses is likely, he must reject it. So, rejecting the compliment is entirely consistent with the goal of gaining admission into a class. Therefore, his behaviour is consistent with what prospective 'clients' do to gain access to some resource. The interviewer, on the other hand, is responsible for maintaining his objectivity in the encounters by not making judgments about who gets in the courses during the assessments. However, compliments like this one can be seen as a way to 'project' potential 'bad news', and as such, are strategic in this context.

2. This student's discourse more resembles a description than a narrative, a phenomenon that Hatch (1992) mentions: when asked to describe, ESL students may narrate instead. When asked to narrate, they describe: 'the focus is not on a hero who wishes to reach a goal and therefore goes through a series of actions to reach a goal. The focus is more a description of a scene in which an action happens' (pp. 177–178). Evidence of the learner's focus on description can be found in her use of 'on the first picture you can see ...' on through the fourth picture. Although the 'characters' are noted, they do not seem to be part of a story – no feelings or attitudes are attributed to them. Also, there is no complicating event or goal stated for the actions that are described. Note also how the description is never tied to the picture set title, A Clever Dog. Therefore, this response cannot really be said to achieve the task of 'telling the story' as the directions for the task require. It is a nice contrast with segment (3a), where the student includes nearly all the features of a narrative that were expected.

We found both benefits and drawbacks of this test method. On the positive side, for example, all test takers had the same stimulus materials; thus, the discourse produced could be compared across learners at different levels. Additional support for using this approach can be seen in the revised Test of Spoken English, which is also a tape-mediated assessment that uses a printed picture sequence that elicits a story of sorts. Just two of the shortcomings we noted were that the planning and/or production time we allotted may have been inappropriately short or long, and that learners could not draw on their personal experiences to tell this story, since it happened to characters on a sheet of paper. Another method that might produce more authentic data would be to have students tell a story about their own experiences – a near death experience, their first day in the U.S., etc. – in a specified time frame.

3. Candidate 59's CASE movie description discourse is marked below with the features discussed in the chapter. Actually, the only real difference with (4) is that the plot is missing, and notably so: the interlocutor asks for more information in line 9. Unfortunately, the candidate's language skills were so weak that she couldn't explain the plot, she could only name the main character, Clarise.

```
(14) CASE — Candidate 59 (1:28-47) Examiner O Stage 2:
     Presentation
 1     CA: %mmm% (.) eh::: the film's name is soo- Silence of the
                           (title)
 2         Lambs. (.) of- Silence of the Lambs. (.) and (.) this film
 3         was uh (.) (give many:::) (.) prize? (.) prize? of academy?
                                  (awards)
 4         (.) and .hhh (.) mm this film was (.) about psychological
                                           (genre)
 5         thriller. movie? and (.) and uh (.) mm (.) why I I enjoyed
 6         it because .hhh mmm (.) it is (.) so thrilling and uh:: .hhh
           (reason for enjoyment)
 7         (.) and uh:: quite hard for me but (.) ( . ) .hhh and
 8         (8.8)
 9     IN: can you tell us anything else about the movie?
10     CA: yeah. .hhh it (.) this film (.) is mmm (.) it happened that
11         .hhh one (.) mother (.) and uh .hhh (.) mmm (.) uh- (.)
12         one woman who FBI? (.) FBI police police uh called (.)
13                                  (character)
14         Clarise .hhh (.) an::d
15     IN: okay. (.5) we'll stop you there...
```

4. This FCE monologue is marked to show the speech functions that Lazaraton and Frantz (1997) found in the discourse. They considered this an excellent example of comparison–contrast discourse that shows quite a diversity of speech functions.

(15) FCE — Candidate 77 (6:305-325) Examiner 377, Part 2

(Task: Summer and Winter: I'd like you to compare and contrast these
pictures saying when you think it would be more pleasant to spend
time there)

CA: OK they are: the same: place but (.) one is in w- (.) winter and
    (comparison)
the other one is s- spring .hhh so I think I would like to go
        (preference)
there on spring because I I'm from I am from a very (.) warm
   place
      (justification)
and I don't like .hhh snow and heh an this kind of things .hhh
and

it's good for skyi- (.) the: (.2) for skiing the: first (.2) the

first photograph .hhh but I I'm not very fond of skiing because I
      (likes and dislikes)
haven't done it (.2) in my life .hhh so I I think I I won't be
      (speculation)
very good at doing it (.2) but it's good to: to try (.) once in
     (opinion)
your life perhaps .hhh so I will go there (.5) to: (.) in spring

(.) it's more hotter the: flowers very: (.) colorful .hhh and
it's
   (comparison, justification)
more: (.2) interesting to:: (.) the views are very: (.8) very

beautiful .hhh and you can climb (.) with this weather but not

with (.) with snow it's (.) too cold for going out for a walk
(contrast)
.hhh and (.2) this m- I like <u>flowers</u> very much and gardering
     (likes and dislikes)
.hhh and (.) it would be a quite (.2) eh: <u>quiet place</u> in:
    (speculation)
<u>spring</u> (.2) there are small houses not very high buildings
    (description)
.hhh and it's (.) eh: (.) in a <u>valley</u> (.5) and it's I think

it's (.) I prefer (.) the second one (.) going there in s-
   (preference)
(.) in spring=

Of course, the researchers had guidance for this task: the results from
earlier studies by Wagner (1994b) and Lazaraton (1997b) as well as
UCLES' list of hypothesized speech functions. But our analysis would not
have differed substantially without this information: we would have gone
through the transcripts, noting and comparing our impressions, ultimately
generating a list of functions used that we suspect would be much like the
lists with which we started.

5. The first logical step would be to operationally define 'communication strategies' or to consult the test materials for guidance on what exactly to look for in the discourse. In analyzing the entire dataset of 20 candidates, I chose to focus only on instances of 'repair'. The results showed that repair initiations on and repetitions of examiner talk become less frequent towards the upper bands, while self-correction remains fairly constant. For example, the Band 4 candidate in the first segment is able to self-correct:

```
(16) IELTS — Candidate 19 (3:56) Band 4

    C: so but when it was raining and and I don't have I didn't
       have any umbrella...
```

In the second, he demonstrates his ability to initiate repair on something problematic in the examiner's question, but he does not target the specific trouble source:

```
(17) IELTS — Candidate 19 (1:11-14) Band 4

    E: and have you been able to see much of Australia whilst
       you've been here?
    C: ah un a pardon?
    E: have you been able to visit many places?
    C: yeah sure many place just beachies...
```

By Band 5, the candidates exhibit ability to target problematic items in the discourse more precisely in their repair initiations:

```
(18) IELTS — Candidate 15  (6:173-174) Band 5

    E: what type of education are you interested in? what level?
    C: um um da rebel what ah what does it mean?
```

And at Band 6, circumlocution is used as a communication strategy:

```
(19) IELTS — Candidate 17 (2:41-46) Band 6

    E: what does it look like? Is it a very old city?
    C: yes. it is old city becau because it had ah a long long
       history. it is ah we have I don't know how to use da word ah
       bicentenary...
```

Author index

A

ACTFL (see American Council on the Teaching of Foreign Languages)
Alderson, J. C.   3, 50, 114
American Council on the Teaching of Foreign Languages (ACTFL)   5, 24
Anderson, T.   58, 72
Atkinson, J. M.   xii, 34, 38, 39, 42, 45, 56, 60, 69, 202
Atkinson, P.   54–56, 103
Austin, J. L.   28

B

Bachman, L. F.   xiv, 1–3, 5, 6, 9, 10, 13, 23, 113–115, 121
Banerjee, J.   174, 175
Bardsley, W. N.   5, 10
Bargfrede, A.   xv, 34, 170
Barnwell, D.   5, 9
Bennett, A.   3
Benson, D.   81
Berentz, N.   32
Berwick, R.   18, 19, 34, 124, 126, 169
Birdwhistell, R. L.   36
Briggs, C. L.   38
Brown, A.   5, 10, 21, 161
Brown, G.   36, 161
Brown, J. D.   2
Button, G.   34, 38, 39, 43
Byrnes, J.   6, 7

C

Campbell, C.   78
Canale, M.   8
Cascallar, E.   6, 7
Casey, N.   34
Celce-Murcia, M.   14
Chalhoub-Deville, M.   6, 12
Chervenak, C. E.   xv, 56, 59, 97, 170
Clapham, C.   3, 50, 114

Subject index

A

access: test   11, 17, 20, 23, 175
accommodation   14, 18, 19
ACTFL (American Council on the Teaching of Foreign Languages)
1, 4–9, 13, 24, 171
actions   xiv, 27, 29, 31, 32, 34, 44, 77, 79, 83, 86, 88, 90–95, 128, 172,
200, 205–207
adjacency pair   xii, xiii, 33, 34, 36, 77, 79, 199, 200, 201
ALTE (Association of Language Testers in Europe)   x, 117, 126, 139, 144,
153
American Council on the Teaching of Foreign Languages (see ACTFL)
analytic induction   79
argument from example   xiv, 95, 101, 173
Association of Language Testers in Europe (see ALTE)
audiotapes   10, 48, 50–52
audiotaped data (see audiotapes)
authenticity   23, 75, 114

B

bias   10, 54, 82, 102

C

CA (see conversation analysis)
CAE (Certificate in Advanced English)   x, xiv, 59, 112, 117, 119, 120,
123, 139–152, 173
Cambridge (see also University of Cambridge Local Examinations
Syndicate)   xiv, 20, 24, 97, 107, 112, 116–124, 126, 130, 138, 148
152–154, 160, 161, 169, 173
Cambridge Assessment of Spoken English (see CASE)
candidate behaviour   xiv, 17, 18, 20, 21, 112, 152–168, 173
CASE (Cambridge Assessment of Spoken English)   ix, x, xiv, 24, 97, 98,
109, 112, 124–139, 141, 143–147, 151, 152, 169, 173, 208
Certificate in Advanced English (see CAE)
Certificate of Proficiency in English (see CPE)
certification   125
CLA (see Communicative Language Ability)
closings   15, 34, 200

M

marginal case (see fringe case)
Minimum Professional Requirements (MPRs)   123, 124
monologue data   xiv, 68, 74, 95–97, 101, 109, 110, 120, 140, 152, 208

N

narration   xiv, 12, 23, 27, 96, 97, 156, 161, 168, 207
next turn repair initiation (NTRI)   93, 94, 200
nonverbal behaviour   xiii, 20, 26, 35, 36, 47, 52, 54, 70–72, 172
NTRI (see next turn repair initiation)

O

observer's paradox   49
openings   34, 200
OPI (see Oral Proficiency Interview)
Oral Proficiency Interview (OPI)   1, 4–9, 12, 13, 17–19, 21–24, 171
overlap   32, 39, 64, 66, 67, 91, 104, 203

P

packaging   xiv, 90–95, 172, 200, 205
paired format   119, 153
paradigm case   102
pause   32, 56, 61–63, 78, 89, 200, 201, 203
PET (Preliminary English Test)   117, 119, 120, 123
practicality   8, 115
pragmatics   6, 8, 9, 13, 28, 32, 62, 77, 79, 200
preclosing   15, 34, 201, 205
preference   x, xi, 8, 15, 16, 33, 34, 172, 201
Preliminary English Test (see PET) presenting data   103–106
presequence   33, 201
psychometrics   1, 25, 44, 113, 116

Q

qualitative research   xii–xiv, 2–4, 25, 72, 74, 102, 115, 138, 169, 171,
  173–175
quantification   xiii, xv, 75, 82–87, 107
questions   11, 15, 16, 18–21, 33, 38–45, 66, 77, 83, 84, 89, 90, 94, 120,
  125, 128, 129, 131, 132, 140, 141, 143, 145–147, 149, 150, 153, 154, 156,
  157, 160, 166

Lightning Source UK Ltd.
Milton Keynes UK
23 January 2010

148983UK00001B/82/P

9 780521 00267